THE MODAL SYSTEM OF OLD BABYLONIAN

HARVARD SEMITIC MUSEUM PUBLICATIONS

Lawrence E. Stager, General Editor
Michael D. Coogan, Director of Publications

HARVARD SEMITIC STUDIES

Jo Ann Hackett and John Huehnergard, editors

Syriac Manuscripts: A Catalogue	Moshe H. Goshen-Gottstein
Introduction to Classical Ethiopic	Thomas O. Lambdin
The Poet and the Historian: Essays in Literary and Historical Biblical Criticism	Richard Elliott Friedman, Editor
The Songs of the Sabbath Sacrifice	Carol Newsom
Non-Canonical Psalms from Qumran: A Pseudepigraphic Collection	Eileen M. Schuller
An Exodus Scroll from Qumran	Judith E. Sanderson
You Shall Have No Other Gods	Jeffrey H. Tigay
Ugaritic Vocabulary in Syllabic Transcription	John Huehnergard
The Scholarship of William Foxwell Albright	Gus Van Beek
Features of the Eschatology of IV Ezra	Michael E. Stone
Studies in Neo-Aramaic	Wolfhart Heinrichs, Editor
Lingering over Words: Studies in Ancient Near Eastern Literature in Honor of William L. Moran	Tzvi Abusch, John Huehnergard, Piotr Steinkeller, Editors
A Grammar of the Palestinian Targum Fragments from the Cairo Genizah	Steven E. Fassberg
The Origins and Development of the Waw-Consecutive: Northwest Semitic Evidence from Ugaritic to Qumran	Mark S. Smith
Amurru Akkadian: A Linguistic Study, Volume I	Shlomo Izre'el
Amurru Akkadian: A Linguistic Study, Volume II	Shlomo Izre'el
The Installation of Baal's High Priestess at Emar	Daniel E. Fleming
The Development of the Arabic Scripts	Beatrice Gruendler
The Archaeology of Israelite Samaria: Early Iron Age through the Ninth Century BCE	Ron Tappy
A Grammar of Akkadian	John Huehnergard
Key to A Grammar of Akkadian	John Huehnergard
Akkadian Loanwords in Biblical Hebrew	Paul V. Mankowski
Adam in Myth and History: Ancient Israelite Perspectives on the Primal Human	Dexter E. Callender Jr.
West Semitic Vocabulary in the Akkadian Texts from Emar	Eugen J. Pentiuc
The Archaeology of Israelite Samaria, vol. II: The Eighth Century BCE	Ron E. Tappy
Leaves from an Epigrapher's Notebook: Collected Papers in Hebrew and West Semitic Palaeography and Epigraphy	Frank Moore Cross
Semitic Noun Patterns	Joshua Fox
Eighth-Century Iraqi Grammar: A Critical Exploration of pre-Ḫalīlian Arabic Linguistics	Rafael Talmon
Amarna Studies: Collected Essays	William L. Moran
Narrative Structure and Discourse Constellations: An Analysis of Clause Function in Biblical Hebrew Prose	Roy L. Heller

THE MODAL SYSTEM OF OLD BABYLONIAN

by

Eran Cohen

EISENBRAUNS
Winona Lake, Indiana
2005

THE MODAL SYSTEM OF OLD BABYLONIAN
by
Eran Cohen

Copyright © 2005
The President and Fellows of Harvard College

Printed in the United States of America

Library of Congress Cataloging-in-Publication Data

Cohen, Eran, 1967–
The modal system of Old Babylonian / by Eran Cohen.
p. cm. — (Harvard Semitic studies ; no. 56)
Includes bibliographical references and index.
ISBN 1-57506-921-0 (hardback : alk. paper)
1. Akkadian language—Modality. I. Title. II. Series.
PJ3291.C64 2005
492′.156—dc22

2004020546

The paper used in this publication meets the minimum requirements of the American National Standard for Information Sciences—Permanence of Paper for Printed Library Materials, ANSI Z39.48-1984.⊗™

For my wife and kids,

my best source of inspiration

Table of Contents

Preface xi
Abbreviations xiii
1 General Introduction 1
1.1 Methodological principles 1
1.2 Corpus definition 6
1.3 Modality 9
1.3.1 Modality in general 9
1.3.2 Modality in OB 12
1.4 Scope of this study 14
1.5 General practices 15
2 The Asseverative Paradigm 17
2.0 Introduction 17
2.0.1 The link to modality 17
2.0.2 *lū* — an independent adverb or part of verbal morphology? 18
2.1 Literature review 20
2.2 Asseverative forms 23
2.2.1 Form inventory 23
2.2.2 The paradigm 25
2.3 The traditional values of the asseverative 26
2.3.1 Asseverative 27
2.3.2 Oath 27
2.3.3 Concession 28
2.4 Syntax 29
2.4.1 Focus 29
2.4.2 Nexus focussing 38
2.4.3 Nexus focussing in OB 45
2.5 Values of the asseverative in view of nexus focussing 56
2.5.1 Oath 56
2.5.2 Concession 59
2.6 Nexus focussing and modality 65

2.7 Conclusions ... 67
3 *lū* Forms in Royal Inscriptions ... 69
3.1 The syntactic behavior of *lū* forms in royal inscriptions ... 69
3.2 *lū* forms in royal inscriptions compared with asseverative forms ... 71
3.3 Conclusions ... 72
4 The Precative Paradigms ... 73
4.0 Introduction and literature review ... 73
4.0.1 GAG ... 73
4.0.2 Edzard 1973 ... 74
4.0.3 Leong 1994 ... 75
4.0.4 Buccellati 1996 ... 76
4.0.5 Huehnergard 1997 ... 77
4.1 Precative forms ... 78
4.2 Paradigmatics and syntagmatics ... 79
4.2.1 Paradigmatics ... 79
4.2.2 Syntagmatics ... 83
4.2.3 Results: different sub-paradigms ... 87
4.3 Functions and values of the different (sub-)paradigms ... 87
4.3.1 The directive sub-paradigm ... 89
4.3.2 The wish paradigm ... 101
4.3.3 The interrogative sub-paradigm ... 105
4.4 Sequenced precatives ... 112
4.4.1 General characteristics of sequenced precatives — literature review ... 113
4.4.2 The syntactic nature of sequenced precatives ... 114
4.4.3 Connectives and their relationship with the sequenced precative ... 118
4.4.4 Modal congruence — significance and implications ... 123
4.5 Infinitive constructions ... 137
4.5.1 *parāsam* ... 138
4.5.2 *ana parāsim* ... 139
4.5.3 *aššum parāsim* ... 142
4.5.4 Concluding remarks ... 142
4.6 Conclusions — the precative paradigms ... 142
5 The Concessive-conditional Precative ... 144
5.0 Introduction ... 144
5.0.1 The notion of concessivity ... 145
5.0.2 Concessivity in Akkadian ... 146
5.1 Concessive, concessive-conditional or conditional? ... 147
5.1.1 Conditional clauses ... 147
5.1.2 Concessive and concessive-conditional ... 149

5.1.3 Conditional and concessive-conditional 150
5.2 The syntactic and semantic nature of the concessive-conditional precative 152
5.3 The limits of the concessive-conditional precative 154
5.4 Conclusions 157
6 The *-ma* Conditional Pattern 161
6.0 Introduction 161
6.1 Connected conditionals in general, and literature review 162
6.2 The basic structure of -ma conditionals in the corpus 164
6.3 Structural and semantic means to define the *-ma* conditionals 169
6.3.1 Polar lexical resumption 169
6.3.2 Verbal lexemes with opposite polarity to what is normal 171
6.3.3 Polar lexical resumption: nexus focussing vs. *-ma* conditionals 172
6.3.4 The syntagmatic interrelationship with the precative paradigm 173
6.3.5 *arḫiš* as structural device 177
6.4 Conclusions 179
7 The Nominalization of the Precative 180
7.0 Preliminaria 180
7.1 Literature review, problematic issues and objectives 181
7.2 The syntactic role of *ša parāsim* 183
7.2.1 *ša parāsim* as rheme 184
7.2.2 *ša parāsim* as part of the sentence 190
7.3 Conclusions 198
7.3.1 Results 198
7.3.2 The place of *ša parāsim* in the modal system of OB 199
8 General Conclusions 201
Bibliography 208
Subject Index 218
Index of Texts 221

Preface

Describing modality in any language is a delicate issue. Any semantic domain, including modality, is extremely difficult to delimit, and therefore, in many semantically-oriented works, one feels that there is no end to the number of semantic distinctions and minute details to be found in a language.

To avoid this trap, modality is here described according to the structuralist method, which is syntactically oriented; the underlying, most basic principle is that semantic value must be paired with a consistent signal. This signal often turns out to be complex: a morphological unit together with its syntactic environment. Any meaning not corresponding to a consistent signal is thus left out of the description. The immediate advantage is that one does not need to rely upon the *Sprachgefühl* for a long-dead language; linguistic information is arrived at in a relatively objective fashion. The structuralist method, being a sophisticated research tool, enables us to expose many details which remain unnoticed to common sense alone. This tool is also indispensable in highlighting the interrelationships between the various groups inside a language, eventually reaching a systemic understanding and consequently description.

This study is an adaptation of my Ph.D. dissertation. It has been written with the deeply rooted conviction that Akkadian, the most ancient Semitic language, can and should receive more linguistic attention; despite its antiquity, this language, and especially the Old Babylonian dialect, is attested in numerous texts of various genres. This rich documentation can serve as the basis of a deeper, more finely nuanced understanding of this ancient language.

I would like, on this occasion, to thank Gideon Goldenberg, the most important figure in Semitic linguistics today, who taught me Semitic languages, general linguistics, and most of all, critical thinking, indispensable for the profession; Shlomo Izre'el, an expert in both Akkadian and Semitic linguistics, whose knowledge and keen eye for potential pitfalls have often saved me; Ariel Shisha-Halevy, a linguist of Egyptian and Celtic languages, my guide in linguistic theory; Max Taube, an expert in Slavic languages and Yiddish; Lea Sawicki, an expert in Slavic and Baltic languages; and finally Eitan Grossman, an expert in Egyptian and general linguistics.

Thanks are due to John Huehnergard and Michael Coogan, who were kind enough to accept this book for publication in Harvard Semitic Studies and have been very patient with me as editors.

Last but not least, I am indebted to my wife Ruth and my kids, Yonatan, Noga and Omri, who have been a constant source of energy and inspiration for me.

Jerusalem, December 2004

Abbreviations

AbB	*Altbabylonische Briefe in Umschrift und Übersetzung.* Leiden: Brill 1964- (designated by number of volume only)
1	Kraus 1964
2	Frankena 1966
3	Frankena 1968
4	Kraus 1970
5	Kraus 1972
6	Frankena 1974
7	Kraus 1977
8	Cagni 1980
9	Stol 1981
10	Kraus 1985
11	Stol 1986
12	Soldt 1990
13	Soldt 1994
AHw	Soden 1965–81
ARM	*Archives royales de Mari.* Paris 1946-
ARM 1	Dossin 1946
ARM 2	Jean 1950
ARM 3	Kupper 1950
ARM 4	Dossin 1951
ARM 5	Dossin 1952
ARM 6	Kupper 1954
ARM 8	Boyer 1958
ARM 15	Bottéro and Finet 1954
ARM 26	(part 1: nos. 1–283) Durand 1988
ARM 26	(part 2: nos. 284–550) Charpin 1988
ARM 27	Birot 1993
ARM 28	Kupper 1998
Brooklyn	Smith 1985
CAD	*The Assyrian Dictionary of the Oriental Institute of the University of Chicago.* 1956-
Catch	Heller 1965
CH	Codex Ḫammurabi

GAG	Soden 1995
Garp	Irving 1979
Gilg Ishchali	George 2003:259–66
LAPO 16–18	Durand 1997–2000
LE	Yaron 1988
MEG	Jespersen 1961
RIMA 1	Grayson 1987
RIME 4	Frayne 1990
SLB 4	Frankena 1978
TIM	Texts in the Iraq Museum (Baghdad)
VAB 5	Schorr 1913
VAB 6	Ungnad 1914

1

General Introduction

This study is a description of modality in the Old Babylonian variety of Akkadian (henceforth OB). The method followed here is empiric, based on a defined corpus. The data are consequently verifiable, the procedure is repeatable and its results refutable. The results of the analysis are system-oriented rather than describing isolated features. More specifically, the description refers to formal features, whether morphological or syntactic, which correspond to modal values. No description is provided for lexical modality (auxiliaries, particles, expressions, etc.). The following sections of the introduction contain: 1. A synopsis of the basics of the linguistic method used throughout the book; 2. Definition of the corpus used as primary data; 3. A short survey of the linguistic issue of modality; 4. Scope of this study; and 5. General practices.

1.1 Methodological principles

This study is a structural analysis, whose principles are presented, *inter alia,* in the courses of F. de Saussure (published as *Cours de linguistique générale* [=de Saussure 1972]) and continued in a sense in the work of the linguistic circle of Copenhagen (as represented here by Hjelmslev 1961) and various other schools of linguistics such as the Prague School and the Geneva School. These principles are of a theoretical nature and are further developed and applied somewhat differently by each linguistic school.

The synopsis which follows describes succinctly a few principles, some of which are quite old in linguistic thinking, while occasionally referring the reader to those loci where these concepts are explained as part of a whole in a more elaborate way. There is no pretension to give an exhaustive historical account of the structural linguistic analysis, nor a full synchronic account thereof. The aim of this synopsis is but to constitute a working definition of the tools and distinctions which are actually used throughout this book.

The first dichotomy is between the **diachronic** and the **synchronic** perspectives (e.g., de Saussure 1972:114–40). The first is a description of linguistic change across time between two or more consecutive language states. The second is a description of a particular language state at a given time. The present description of the modal system in OB is a synchronic study.

Another basic dichotomy is between **langue** and **parole** (ibid. 23–39). The first stands for the social and abstract aspect of language, viz., the language system common to all native speakers of a given language state. The second is a linear function, viz., the idiosyncratic physical actualization of the langue.

The **langue** is viewed as a system of signs. The linguistic **sign** is defined (e.g., de Saussure 1972:97–103, 166–69) as a relationship between two aspects: The **signifiant** (Hjelmslev's **expression**) and a **signifié** (Hjelmslev's **content**). The first corresponds to any formal (i.e., having to do with form) features (of whatever order — morphological, syntactic or other) whereas the second represents **value**, meaning or function. Hence any change, either in the signifiant or in the signifié, brings about a change in the relationship between them and consequently a change in the sign. Being a **system** of signs means that in the langue there are only relationships or oppositions between the signs themselves and between groups of signs.

This system of interrelationships between signs is not directly accessible, and hence analysis starts with the **parole**, represented by the text. Starting from the text is necessarily the "modèle de récepteur", the decoder's, or listener's role (Shisha-Halevy 1998:10). This implies that the task is to treat anything found in the text as long as it is **pertinent**, viz., having function in the langue (Martinet 1960:37–39). Such pertinence exists with regard to an entity as long as it is in opposition with at least another entity.

Since the **parole** is not a system but only a local actualization thereof, an analysis should be performed using the **syntagmatic** and **paradigmatic** dimensions (de Saussure 1972:170–75), in order to expose the system behind the parole.

The **syntagmatic** dimension is the one present in the text — the linear, or sequential, relationships between the entities in terms of (in)compatibility. The **paradigmatic** dimension is the relationship between all the entities which may figure at the same syntactic location *in absentia* (i.e., not in the text itself, but by bringing together similar text segments between which the only variant would be representative in the syntactic location in question), without changing the syntactic structure of the segment. This kind of relationship is categorial — all linguistic entities, of whatever order or size, which may be found in a fixed syntactic slot, belong in and constitute the same functional category, or the same **paradigm** (Hjelmslev 1961:74ff). Thus it is possible to determine and define at each stage of the analysis the exact interrelationships existing between different paradigms as well as the relationships between the entities within a paradigm. Moreover, the **commutation** (interchangeability) test teaches us important details about the syntagmatic dimension of entities — for example their boundaries, i.e., where entities begin or end.[1]

The **value** of entities (de Saussure 1972:153–69; Hjelmslev 1961:52–54) is defined as the meaning, or function of the entity, which is, however, definable only in **opposition** to the other members of the paradigm and in comparison between paradigms (which in turn have their own value — the **category**). This may well be the most important principle of structural linguistics, viz., that value is directly determined by paradigmatic oppositions and syntagmatic contrast to other entities (Frei 1968:44–45; Shisha-Halevy 1986:6–7).[2] It follows that in the absence of opposition between entities no value can be ascribed to a form (e.g., what is called by Marouzeau [1951:147] *mode grammatical*, where a certain mood is obligatorily marked, but it is not pertinent). However, in describing modality it seems worthwhile to go one step further and acknowledge, in a few cases, important **notions**, i.e., meaning which does not have a definable corresponding formal distinction (e.g., in case of value **neutralization**, see for example §§**4.2.2.2** and **4.4.4.1** below).

Opposition is found between entities in the same paradigm while **contrast** is used to denote differences between entities in the syntagmatic dimention (Martinet 1960:33).

Once the number or type of entities in a paradigm (in other words, the **paradigmatic constitution**) changes, their respective value (being defined only in opposition to other existing entities) is bound to change as well, and so would the paradigm itself and its value, i.e., the category.

The form *aprusu* is a case in point to exemplify these terms. We encounter this form in the **parole** which is in this case a letter — a local, personal (namely, the sender's) actualization of the linguistic system common to all native speakers (or, more precisely, users) of this variety of language,[3] the **langue**. The **form** *aprusu* is found in the text, representing

1. This may look trivial at first sight; however, when analysing syntactic entities such as a clause it may get quite complicated.

2. Actually, the use of **paradigm** by definition presupposes a certain slot on the syntagmatic axis and hence certain syntagmatic conditions.

3. This is not the whole truth about the letters; it is impossible to state the exact relationship between the epistolary language and the spoken language, which, at Mari for example, might have been another language altogether. See **§1.2**

a **signifiant**, which, being merely part of the **sign**, actually does not exist by itself except by abstraction (Hjelmslev 1961:49). GAG tells us that this form is a *modus relativus* (§83) but it is an asseverative form as well (Edzard 1973:129). A serious discussion takes place on whether the ending *-u* in both these uses might be considered the same form (von Soden 1961:52–53; Eilers 1966). This issue may be examined according to criteria of structural analysis: The different coordinates, or the different intersecting point of the two axes (Shisha-Halevy 1986:6–7), or in other words, the point where the **syntagmatic** properties of the form meet the **paradigmatic** properties, shows that these are two perfectly distinct entities despite their identical shape.

The first step is devised in order to see in what syntagmatic context, or **co-text**, these forms are to be found. It is clearly visible that each form is found in a basically distinct co-text (for a detailed, in-depth probing into the co-text of asseverative forms in general, see **§2.4.3.1**). The following illustration shows the **syntagmatic** conditions, i.e., linear compatibilities, for the subjunctive morpheme (GAG's *modus relativus*):

1	*awāt*	
	ša	***aprusu***
	ištu	
	ūm	

This form is necessarily preceded by forms whose common denominator is that they are all in the construct state, i.e., bound forms which never occur without some kind of attribute (in this case the *aprusu* form). The asseverative form, on the other hand, never follows such bound forms, and occurs exclusively in non-subordinate clauses.

The second step is meant to show the **paradigmatic constitution** for the two entities represented by the form *aprusu*. Each of these forms is examined for its commutability with other forms in the same syntagmatic slot. The result is the (partial) **paradigm** of each entity:

2a		*aparrasu*	**2b**		*aparrasu*
	ša	***aprusu***		**ø**	***aprusu***
		lā aprusu			*lū aprus*
		parāsim			*lā aprusu*
		bītim etc.			

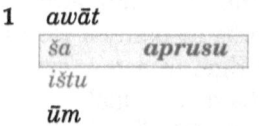

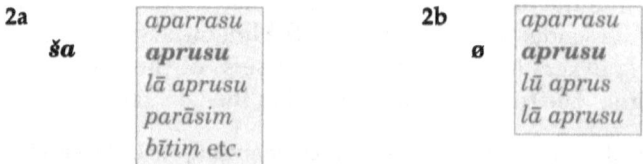

Despite the existence of additional entities which display identical shapes (*lā aprusu, aparrasu*), the makeup of each paradigm is unmistakably distinct, which is reason enough to conclude that the two *aprusu* forms belong each to a different **paradigm** and **category**. The forms in the first **paradigm** (**2a**) include nominals in the genitive as well, and the category may be named after its syntactic function, i.e., **genitive attribute**[4] (von Soden, GAG §83a, is correct in describing the subjunctive as "... eine Art Genitivendung des Verbum finitum ..."). The second **paradigm** (**2b**) contains asseverative forms, all of them constituting independent clauses, hence the asseverative **category**.

The following pair of paradigms is devised to show other important points:

3a		*aparrasu*
	ša	*aprusu*

3b		*aparras*
	ø	*aprus*
		luprus
		aprusu

It is usual to compare *aparras* with its subordinative counterpart *aparrasu*, although under the present approach they actually never meet each other, for they never co-occur in the same syntagmatic conditions. For this reason their respective **values** are completely different. In the first paradigm (**3a**) there are two forms whose values are arrived at by opposing them to each other. The formal **opposition** between them turns out to reflect temporal value in the corpus. As to modality, *aparrasu* has neither indicative nor modal **value** since it is not opposed to any form exhibiting modal value (although various modal **notions**, i.e., without a corresponding formal opposition,[5] do occur), contrary to what happens in **3b**, where such opposition, namely, between *aparras* and *luprus*, is found to exist. In **3b** *aparras* does have indicative value determined in opposition with *luprus*.

The ending *-u* was not discussed separately, and for a reason: There is an opposition between *-u* and ø only in paradigm **3b**, i.e., when *aprusu* is asseverative and is opposed to the indicative *aprus*. In **3a** *-u* is obligatory and is not opposed with anything and is therefore not **pertinent**.[6]

The last point is the number of entities in a paradigm. Once the number of entities varies between two related paradigms, even when the majority of forms have an identical shape, the paradigms are nevertheless distinct. This is because a different number of entities implies different values ascribed to each entity. A case in point is comparing precative

4. By **genitive attribute** (or **genitive equivalent**) is meant here a specific syntactic position, i.e., that of the slot following the construct state, which is termed *sōmeḵ* in Hebrew and *ʾalmuḍāfu ʾilayhi* in Arabic.

5. This issue is developed in detail when discussing modal neutralization (for example, §4.2.2.2)

6. This does not mean it is not important in interpretation, for example, when the nucleus preceding it is not marked, due to various reasons, as *status constructus*.

forms occuring in pronominal questions (for the full paradigm see §**4.3.3.1**) to the sequenced precative paradigm (§**4.4**):

4a	*ammīnim*	*luprus* ~~*purus*~~ *liprus*	**4b** *purus–ma*	*luprus* *purus* *liprus*

These are distinct paradigms since they show a dissimilar number of entities (despite the fact that the rest of the entities exhibit an identical shape), and this stems from the different syntagmatic conditions for each of the paradigms. Precative forms in pronominal questions therefore have a distinct value.

1.2 Corpus definition

The main corpus used in this study is the AbB corpus. In addition, parts of the ARM corpus are used whenever deemed necessary, mainly to help complete the description of various points whose representation in the AbB is not satisfactory (either for reasons of exiguous attestation of certain phenomena or, no less important, for absence of a context extensive enough to enable analysis). Other than that but a few examples were extracted from other corpora — legal documents (VAB 5) and law codices (LE and CH). Since the first aim of this study is to describe modality in OB rather than any dialect or genre in its entirety, the choice of an extensive and somewhat varied corpus is justified in serving this purpose. The combination of corpora is in effect of utmost importance in elucidating and mapping the more elusive features of the modal system of OB. It should be added, however, that the various modal phenomena described herein are all part of the modal system of the AbB corpus, and that the statement as a whole refers to this corpus.

The AbB corpus is composed of around 2500 letters and fragments, contained in 13 volumes (F. R. Kraus et al. *Altbabylonische Briefe in Umschrift und Übersetzung*), which mostly stem from irregular excavations. The letters whose place of origin is known (mainly from textual information) come from various cities of Mesopotamia proper (that is, the alluvial plain of the Euphrates and the Tigris, including the Diāla region in the northeast of this plain): Babylon, Isin, Kiš, Larsa, Nippur, Sippar, etc. The corpus represents the most important and largest medium for everyday language of Mesopotamian OB.[7] It is an extensive corpus which promises the widest portrayal of a linguistic state. Moreover, this corpus is more often cited in grammar-related research than any other

7. I adopt Sallaberger's approach according to which everyday language does not imply spoken language (idem 1999:2, n. 2). See further below.

similar corpus, and used as a corpus by linguists and Assyriologists alike (Patterson 1971, Maloney 1981, Illingsworth 1990, Leong 1994, Sallaberger 1999, and Deutscher 2000 in addition to various articles using the AbB as data corpus). This fact facilitates research since some linguistic issues pertaining to the AbB corpus have already been referred to and may thus serve as basis, or at least a point of reference, for further research.

The AbB corpus has nevertheless a few acknowledged flaws as far as the homogeneity of the texts is concerned. Both the long period of time during which these letters were written and the extended territory over which they were excavated legitimately raise the question whether the AbB is homogeneous enough to qualify as a linguistic corpus.

The time period to which the letters in the series belong is, linguistically speaking, a very long one — the first four centuries of the second millennium (one may compare the English written by Shakespeare with contemporary English, the temporal difference between both varieties is approximately four hundred years). However, most of the letters seem to stem from the later period, viz., the 18th-17th centuries (Sallaberger 1999:4). Dating the letters on the basis of external criteria is usually impossible (for most of the letters do not originate in regular excavation, so the archeological context is usually missing). Internal criteria are no less problematic; there is hardly any paleographic research of the OB period,[8] so dating (apart from acute cases) cannot be achieved on the basis of writing (Sallaberger 1999:5). Dating the letters basing upon internal criteria may be achieved for but a relatively small number of them (Pientka 1998, dating various documents and letters from the late OB period, is based upon internal information). Letters written on the verge of the MB period are many times discernible on morphophonological grounds. On the whole, despite the margins (i.e., very early or very late letters) being somewhat different, the body of text for the most part is quite homogeneous, and the putative reasons for this relative homogeneity are discussed further below.

The geographical area from which the letters had been excavated would naturally be considered a vast linguistic territory (ca. 300x200 kilometers), which probably comprised quite a few dialects (compare the territory of modern Iraq, which exhibits a rich dialectal situation). In view of this, one would expect a much greater linguistic variety even within the same time period. The situation is different, however. The language of the letters in the corpus is quite uniform and attempts to distinguish different dialects within Mesopotamian OB on the basis of

8. Goetze 1958, for example, refers to the geographical dimension, rather than to periods of time (at least within OB); Janssen 1991 is a case study of four copies of the same letter.

textual information have not been successful. The provenance of most of the letters has not been determined, and even when it is known, the most important detail, viz., **where they were originally written**, is mostly unknown. As a matter of fact, Kraus (1973a:33) reasons that the differences between the so-called northern and southern OB are nothing but a few orthographic peculiarities (Goetze 1958) and only one isogloss — *ṭuppum* vs. *unnedukkum*. In view of these data Kraus states that dialects (setting aside Mari and Susa) cannot be duly distinguished. He concludes, therefore, that the present situation only allows us to view Mesopotamian OB as one linguistic entity and he recommends refraining from attempts at any further sub-division.

Kraus's conclusions are accepted here. This relative linguistic uniformity leads to another important conclusion, namely, that the language is an everyday language but, being very conservative and of a formulaic nature, it is by no means a spoken language. This is worth mentioning mainly because a close affinity of this language with the spoken language has been quite often suggested (Maloney 1981:2, Leong 1994:2, Buccellati 1996 §0.3, Huehnergard 1997:260). How close it might have been to the spoken language we cannot tell, for the spoken language remains obscure for obvious reasons (Sallaberger 1999:11).

The secondary corpus comprises letters found in the royal archives of Mari, the modern site of Tell Ḥarīrī (*Archives royales de Mari*). The entire corpus contains around 5000 letters, only a part of which has been published. The volumes used here as secondary corpus are mainly volumes 26-28 (being the most recent, extensively commentated volumes of the series), containing around 800 letters and fragments. Occasionally examples are drawn from earlier volumes of the series as well (mainly volumes 1-6). The various letters, although by and large written within a period of ca. 50 years during the 18th century, still originate at various places (Lambert 1967:29–30). The letters here tend to be longer than in the AbB series, and their extralinguistic context is better known.

The ARM corpus has its own early grammatical description (Finet 1956) and its own syllabary and glossary (ARM 15). The series (containing 28 volumes, only some of which are letters) is fully commentated by now: The later volumes are edited accompanied by extensive remarks regarding practically every aspect of the texts; the earlier volumes (up to ARM 18), which had not originally been annotated in this way, are now given new interpretation and occasionally new readings and are arranged thematically in LAPO 16–18. This peripheral information regarding the texts is occasionally of critical importance in the linguistic interpretation of texts.

1.3 Modality

Modality is a semantic category, which is much more difficult to define as a general category than tense. The most precise description of modality may be achieved by the analysis of one language only, with respect to the other sub-systems in that very language. This cannot be performed via a bird's eye view but is rather the result of a profound acquaintance with the whole linguistic system in question, taking account by this very analysis of the interrelationships between paradigms and between entities in each paradigm. This way the finest possible demarcation of classes in any system may be carried through. The following sections attempt to serve as preamble to the subject of modality — first from a typological, second from an OB point of view. The scope of the present study is revealed at the end of this preliminary review of modality.

1.3.1 Modality in general

Modality is examined from a few points of view:
1. Philosophically, within modal logic (part of Kiefer 1987);
2. Semantically, always having an interface with the former (Lyons 1977; Kiefer 1987; Wierzbicka 1987; Sweetster 1990);
3. From the point of view of grammaticalization (Bybee 1985; Bybee et al. 1994; Givón 1994);
4. From a formal, synchronic typological point of view (Palmer 1986 and partially Givón 1994); and
5. The traditional point of view, which is by and large a language-specific treatment of modality, i.e., within one system. This point of view is not uniform and depends upon the general framework chosen by the author.

The purely philosophical treatment of modality is of little applicability within a natural language (Sweetster 1990:58–59; Palmer 1986:11–12; and above all Kiefer 1987, which is an attempt to reconcile both approaches). It is hence excluded from the present discussion. The semantic approach (e.g., Lyons 1977:745–59) seems to suffer from similar symptoms: It tends to be Eurocentric, or in other words, treats modality along the lines of the better known western European languages[9] and therefore has little applicability to other languages (this is one of the great difficulties encountered in many traditional accounts as well, see below). Another symptom is that the discussion is too general, few examples (if any) are adduced and these are usually invented rather than taken from a corpus (a noteworthy exception to this is Sweetster 1990).

9. The focus is on verbal morphology (as is common in the old IE languages), modal verbs (typical of modern Germanic languages) and modal particles (German, Dutch).

Grammaticalization is concerned with the allegedly predictable ties between various modal values and forms, and tendencies in their development. The comparison is cross-linguistic and is very useful in that it is not confined to the *terra cognita* of Eurocentricity. The main problem with these diachronic tendencies is that one can always find the opposite paths.[10]

The most useful approach for the present purposes seems to be the comparative typological approach adopted by Givón 1994 and Palmer 1986. The former is confined to the more or less binary distinctions in the function of various subjunctives. The latter exposes a large number of important distinctions which are found in various, at times peculiar, language systems. As a matter of fact, Palmer 1986 is the only full monographic volume, to the best of my knowledge, entirely devoted to linguistic modality from a typological, cross-linguistic point of view.[11]

The definition of **modality** is quite vague. Jespersen (1924:313) defines what we refer to today as modality as representing "certain attitudes of the mind of the speaker towards the contents of the sentence". Lyons (1977:452) similarly refers to modality as "opinion or attitude of the speaker". Palmer (1986:4, 16–18, 1994:2536–37) broadens the definition to include **non-factuality** (i.e., sentences which are not used to make statements of facts) and **subjectivity** (involving the speaker). In addition he reservedly mentions two notions, viz., **possibility** and **necessity**[12] as central to modality, at least in European languages. Another strategy is an attempt to enumerate the whole range of notions involved in modality. Steele et al. 1981:21, referring to modality from the cross-linguistic perspective of auxiliaries, mention three pairs: possibility or permission, probability or obligation and certainty or requirement, where modality will contain any of these. One thing should be emphasized: Some expressions do not comply with any of the notions enumerated above, and yet would (or should) be considered modal, for their **systemic** interrelationship with other expressions which are clearly modal. One notable example is the auxiliary *can* in English which is considered in most frameworks to be modal mainly

10. For instance, stating that future tenses are closer to modality than other forms (Lyons 1977:816, Bybee et al. 1994:210–12) may be exemplified by the morphological relationship between *iparras* and *lā iparras*, reasoning that it is a natural path for a form used for futurity to give rise to a directive. However, one could argue that the pair *iprus* and *liprus* (or Arabic *faʿala*, used both as preterite and optative) show another natural path just as well, i.e., a form which is used as aorist, or narrative tense, giving rise to a directive.

11. Palmer 2001, being the second edition thereof, is radically revised, and may be considered another book.

12. These two notions are central mainly to modal logic (Palmer 1994:2537).

due to its paradigmatic association with the other modal auxiliaries, rather than its value which is many times both objective and factual.

Distinguishing the terms **mood** and **modality** reveals a serious gap in terminological coverage of the modal domain: **Mood** is traditionally the exponent of the semantic categories of modality which is expressed by verbal morphology.[13] (The term is therefore useful for the ancient IE languages and for Arabic where one does indeed finds **mood** in this narrow sense.[14] This, however, is clearly not universal.) Modality is equally signaled by modal verbs, by particles and by various syntactic devices.[15] This puts mood (the formal expression of modality by verbal inflection only) in the same hierarchy level with other signals of modality, leaving us with no term designated for the entire group of formal features which mark modality. In other words, **modality** is the *signifié*, whereas mood is only a part of the *signifiant*. Yet, despite this terminological (and possibly conceptual) inadequacy, the aim of the present study is to describe modality in OB as well as its exponents, of whatever order they may be, as long as they are regular formal features (for more specific details see further below).

Jespersen (1924:320–21) divides modality according to whether it contains an element of will or not. This distinction is further continued and elaborated to the point that the dichotomy of modality into **epistemic** and **deontic** modality seems to be widely in use (Lyons 1977; Kiefer 1987, 1994; Palmer 1986, 1994; as well as others). The former has to do with the notions of belief, knowledge and truth towards the proposition, whereas the latter involves volition and obligation. **Epistemic modality** includes, according to Palmer 1986:20–21, **evidentials** (i.e., the commitment of the speaker to the truth of what he is saying in terms of the type of evidence he has), and **judgements** (which express doubt towards a proposition with no evidence, ibid. 53). **Deontic modality** includes (ibid. 97) **directives** (initiating action) and **commissives** (where one commits himself to do something), both with the intention of changing the future. Yet, this dichotomy is not always helpful in that it does not easily allow for the

13. In OB the exponents of modality are predicational, rather than verbal, consisting occasionally of non-verbal, as well as verbal, clauses.

14. That is, the tendency to consider only suffixation — the characteristic exponents of modality in the IE languages — leading, in the research of Akkadian, to consider the subjunctive and the ventive as modi and, on the other hand, to count out the precative.

15. Via a distinctive order of elements, or a distinctive pattern (see below, mainly **chapters 5** and **6**). This type of formal features is hardly ever mentioned in discussions about modality. As a matter of fact, employing structural criteria (i.e., the syntagmatic and paradigmatic axes, see above **§1.1**) actually yields syntactic results.

semantic classification of some types of modality encountered in OB: For example, **conditional** protases are concerned with possible action, which is related by Palmer (1986:97) to **deontic**, rather than epistemic modality. Based on this, one could claim that in OB both precative conditionals (**chapter 5**) and *-ma* conditionals (**chapter 6**) are associated more with deontic, than with epistemic modality. There is a problem, however. *šumma* conditionals are closely associated (not only semantically but formally as well) with such modal particles as *pīqat* or *midde*, which are clearly epistemic. In addition, both types of conditional treated hereunder are very close in nature to *šumma* conditionals. These facts strongly suggest including conditionals, *pace* Palmer, in the epistemic group. Another example for the difficulties inherent to this classification are **emphatic affirmations**, or **counterpresuppositional assertions**, which are close in nature to the **asseverative** paradigm (treated in **chapter 2**). They are suggested to have a tight link with **epistemic** modality (Palmer 1986:91–95), despite the fact that in OB, especially when involved in a promissory oath, they resemble Palmer's **commissives**, which are rather classified under **deontic** modality. This dichotomy is therefore used sparingly, since the internal relationships between different modal paradigms in a language do not necessarily comply with it.

1.3.2 Modality in OB

Edzard 1973 is the fullest description of modi in Akkadian and the only study entirely devoted to this issue. It is therefore viewed as central and used as a point of departure. A few works that discuss mood in Akkadian are reviewed at the beginning thereof (ibid. 121–22) and the inevitable conclusion is reached, that in view of so many different opinions a new analysis is needed as to what is mood in Akkadian. Edzard spots the problem: Mood is viewed as an inflection (as it is viewed in traditional grammar, see above), and this somehow leads to an erroneous perception of the function of mood, which is to signal modality. This may explain, at least partially, why in GAG only the imperative is explicitly considered a mood (§74b) whereas the other forms which are tightly related to it (§81) are not termed modal (though they are grouped that way). The term **modal** is used in GAG with regard to the modal particles (§§121, 152). Gelb 1961:169–74 expands mood to include the indicative, the ventive (his "allative"), the subjunctive, the imperative, the precative and the vetitive (which he terms "prohibitive"). Reiner 1966:71 similarly considers the suffixed forms as modi, but adds (somewhat carefully) that it is possible to consider other forms (the precative, the imperative, the vetitive, etc.) as moods. Counting the subjunctive, or the ventive, as moods and paying no attention to their value is criticized by Edzard, who considers the form only as part of the whole picture.

Edzard's point of departure is the verbal paradigms[16] — *iprus, iparras, iprusu, iparrasu,* etc. However, since negative forms stand apart from positive forms, and past forms apart from present forms, one may get the impression that they have nothing to do with each other. This, however, is corrected in the course of the remarks that follow these paradigms. The morphologically based partition analytic vs. synthetic serves little purpose, and negation particles are considered part of the form, implicitly deemed inseparable. Form and content intersect each other and Edzard indeed shows that two identical forms could function differently, which is one very basic feature of the modal system (and indeed of other systems as well).

The ventive is discussed briefly as a response to Kienast 1960, who assumed the ventive to have been an original mood. Edzard refutes this idea based on two points — the conceptual incompatibility of two modi in the same form and the value of the ventive — which is directional (or something else whose value is not fully understood) — and therefore has nothing to do with modality. Note, however, that Kienast's perspective is diachronic while Edzard's is synchronic. Synchronically, since the ventive is still a puzzle it cannot be counted as modal. For anything to be considered as modal we need both a formal distinction and modal value.

The modi Edzard puts forth for discussion are the indicative, the positive affirmative (our asseverative), the precative, the plural cohortative, the imperative, the prohibitive, the vetitive and the negative affirmative (an oxymoronic term in itself). Left out are the ventive and the so-called ***-a*** and ***-i*** modi. The subjunctive is simply considered indicative in subordination. When evaluated in structural tools, the **subjunctive** marked form does not have the same value as does the unbound indicative. The indicative, unlike the subjunctive, is opposed to various modals in the same paradigm and thus has a non-modal value. The subjunctive, however, is here characterized as **amodal**, or **modally neutralized**. Modal distinction between *liprus* and *iparras* is absent in subordination (among other syntagmatic conditions, such as in *šumma* clauses) in OB.

Buccellati 1996 (chapters 28–29) is the second largest treatment of modality, or rather mood, in Babylonian. Buccellati indeed deals with formal categories, but his use of the term "formal" refers to forms (i.e., morphology) rather than to any concrete expressions in the language, such as structure, or more specifically, the paradigmatic and syntagmatic dimensions (despite the fact that he does mention these terms in his introduction). His first division is made according to type of inflection — internal inflection ("primary moods": indicative and imperative), external

16. In compliance with the traditional, rather than the structural term.

inflection ("secondary moods": desiderative, subjunctive and ventive moods) and periphrastic moods (by adverbial particles: asseverative and prohibitive). Later on (ibid. §29.1), he admits that notional categories (=meaning) cut through morphological categories. Arranging the forms according to their type of derivation is secondary with respect to the synchronic view of a language as a system (which is supposedly Buccellati's perspective).

Another problem is treating the particles *lū* and *lā* as adverbs which add semantic nuance (Buccellati 1996 §28.6). *lū* is discussed below (§**2.0.2**). *lā* appears not only in the prohibitive but in subordination, in negative asseveratives, in pronominal questions and in *šumma* conditional protases as well — so there is nothing fixed about the meaning *lā* adds (except, of course, that it negates what follows). It is rather a part of the syntagm which constitutes the form — it shows the same close association with the verbal form as does *lū*, which has no fixed value in itself, for value is actually ascribed to the entire syntagm of which it is a part, be it asseverative or directive.

On a few occasions other modi have been discussed, viz., the *-a* and the *-i* modi. In Jacobsen 1960 one finds an attempt to account for these so called modi (mainly in the substantial n. 12, ibid. 110–11). Jacobsen's designation of these modi and his explanations of their functions do not reflect any existing synchronic situation of Akkadian, to the best of my knowledge. Moreover, his derivation of the *-a* modus via breaking down of the ventive morpheme into two elements looks suspicious synchronically and does not comply with the linguistic method with which he does seem to be acquainted. Edzard 1973:127 says that the ***-a* modus** has not enough occurrences to enable analysis. The *-a* morpheme described by Gelb (1961:170) is proved to be an additional subordination marker in Old Akkadian. Regarding the ***-i* modus**, Kraus 1973b:257 remarks that this phenomenon of -(*C*)*i* has nothing to do with a mood (having no modal value). Edzard 1973:127–28 notes two important points: It is not only *-i* but *-Ci* (that is, it involves a reduplication of the last consonant) and, more importantly, it appears on non-verbal elements of a verbal sentence as well.

1.4 Scope of this study

The present description is concerned with modality which is expressed by formal features of (mainly) predicational syntagms, i.e., the verbal system and anything that is in paradigmatic relationship with verbal forms[17] (non-verbal clauses for example). A structural scrutiny of verbal

17. For instance: ***kīdam–ma*** *īpulūninni–ma* "They answered me: '**Out!**' ..." (ARM 26, 145:6). *kīdam-ma*, despite its being morphologically marked as an

forms (i.e., examining each form for its special syntagmatic and paradigmatic conditions) yields results which enable us to map the paradigms and sub-paradigms of the modal system and establish the relationship between those paradigms.

-(C)i, *-a* and the ventive are not discussed for reasons discussed above.

-u is not regarded as mood either, but it is nevertheless discussed because when appended to *iparras* it is associated not with indicative, but rather with a neutralization of modality, being neither modal nor indicative.

The signals of epistemic modality in OB, viz., modal particles and *šumma* conditionals, are not in the scope of this work, for each of these substantial issues must be discussed separately.[18]

Lexically expressed modality, such as the auxiliaries *leʾûm* (=be able), *nadānum*[19] (=permit, allow), *lemûm*[20] (=refuse) *and libb-*[21] (=want), is not treated either.

1.5 General practices

1. The **transcription** here follows Huehnergard 1997, save for a few differences: An underlined vowel (a̲) means that it is originally marked as long (*a-a*) and that it is deemed distinctive, i.e., denoting a question or some FSP (functional sentence perspective, see **§2.4.1.1**) related information.

A mere stress-related length is not indicated, despite the fact that there are morphophonological reasons to indicate it. This is because it is deemed obligatory and therefore it is generally impertinent syntactically, interfering with distinctions which are syntactically pertinent such as number (*bēl**i**šu* vs. *bēl**ī**šu*). Such length **is indicated** when it is not merely stress-related, as in the case of III–weak finite verbal forms when they are followed by pronouns, or by the connective particle *-ma*.

2. The classification problem of the (deverbal) **permansive** has been debated for several decades now, the discussion started by Buccellati 1968, continued by Kraus 1984 and Huehnergard 1987 and resumed by Kouwenberg 2000, concerning the permansive's (non-)verbal nature. Diachronically it is no doubt a non-verbal clause. What it is synchronically depends upon

adverb, may formally commute with an imperative and has precisely the same function.

18. For OB modal particles see Wasserman 1994 as well as Krebernik and Streck 2001.

19. *ana er[ēb]im ul* ***iddinūninni*** "They did not let me e[nt]er" (6, 181:13').

20. *alākam–ma* ***lemiāt*** "(It is) *to go* (which) you refuse" (1, 30:18-19).

21. *šumma dabābam* ***libbaka*** "If you wish to speak ..." (10, 198:17).

what point of view is taken. From the structural view, which considers any linguistic entity syntagmatically and paradigmatically, the deverbal permansive belongs with verbal forms in the corpus. The reason for this is that it occurs exactly in the same slot as verbal forms (as opposed to a non-verbal nexus which may occur anywhere in the clause), and has the same syntagmatic compatibility, e.g., with regard to juncture (a non-verbal clause does not connect forward with *-ma,* for instance).

3. The distinction of the term **verbal lexeme** from **verbal root** is made here in order to zoom in on the exact value, e.g., the difference between *alākum* and *atlukum,* which share the same root, but are distinct in their respective values.

4. As to the translation of the examples, I do not generally deviate from the one offered in the edition, save, occasionally, for the point whose clarification is intended. When deviations do occur, they are mostly self-explanatory in view of the array of issues discussed throughout this book (e.g., the issue of focus is discussed in **chapter 2**, but the insights arrived at are implemented in translation everywhere). The translation itself is viewed as a way to reflect, as precisely as possible, the **linguistic interpretation** of the original text. Contrary to the philological point of view of often trying to understand a point from within a single location, a wider point of view is taken here, wherein insights are gradually deduced from a multitude of cases which display a similar structure.

2

The Asseverative Paradigm

2.0 Introduction

The present chapter is the description of those forms called **asseverative**[1] forms (Beteuerungsformen) or forms of oath (Eidsformen). The unity of these two terms or rather, whether the forms belong together in the same category, is not self-evident. The forms are briefly described in almost any Akkadian grammar and in Edzard 1973. There are, however, certain features peculiar to all these forms which have not been discussed. These features and their underlying function make it possible to provide an explanation of how the same forms can denote insistence, be used in oaths, and occur as concessive clauses. All these uses are accounted for under one syntactic function, namely, **nexus focussing**. This function is developed, explained and exemplified both inside and outside of OB. The connection of this syntactic function to modality in OB is discussed as well.

2.0.1 The link to modality

It is important to mention that the link between the asseverative forms and modality does not have any necessary relationship with the syntactic phenomenon of nexus focussing which is elaborated below (see **§§2.4.2** and **2.4.3**). It is enough to acknowledge the existence of certain forms (*signifiants* in Saussurean terminology) and the general value attributed to them (*signifiés*). The value of these forms is a basis for a discussion about the link to modality. (Other points, which have to do with a better and more refined understanding of the mechanism in question, are discussed under **§2.6** below.)

1. Asseveration: "... Solemn affirmation, emphatic assertion, avouchment..." (*Oxford Dictionary* ²1989 1:711a). The term in the present connection is used in Huehnergard 1983:569: "By 'asseverative particle' we mean one which accentuates the words or clause ... affirming the truth or certainty of a statement ...".

In GAG §81 von Soden treats various forms, i.e., imperative, precative, asseverative, prohibitive, vetitive, etc. The motive for such classification is not solely morphological, for *lā iparras* and *liprus* are not similar from this point of view, nor are *lū iprus* and *purus*. Despite the title of this section ("Der Imperativ und die Formen für Wunsch, Beteuerung und Verbot"), which avoids any commitment in circumscribing the semantic common denominator of this group of forms, this group constitutes by and large those forms of Akkadian denoting modality. Another likely explanation is that von Soden felt the interrelations between the forms — both morphological and syntactic — but had difficulties describing them. The paradigmatic (or categorial) relationship between *lā taparras* and *purus* (overlooking the morphological dissimilarity) and the morphological identity of *lū paris* used either as a directive (see **§4.1**) or as an asseverative (despite the fact that these uses reflect two different paradigms) are not simple to settle.

Edzard 1973:129–30 describes the function of the asseverative forms as an emphasis of an utterance either as reaction to a doubt (whether real or imaginary) emanating from the addressee or in order to swear about this utterance. Even if these forms occur in different environments, they are modal as long as they have to do with reacting to doubt. Moreover, it cannot be said about these reactions to doubt that they reflect factuality — they do not, much like the other forms described in GAG §81. The same holds for the English *I díd do it* (whose relevance to the OB asseverative is discussed further below, **§2.4.2.2**) — for it reflects non-factuality as well.

Such asseveratives are hardly given any space within descriptions of modal systems, although semantically they belong there. An exception to this is Palmer 1986. In a section titled "discourse and modality" (ibid. 91–95) he mentions that the distinction between discourse and modal features is not always easy to draw. A more detailed discussion of this issue is given below only after the syntactic behavior and peculiarities have been described (**§2.6**).

2.0.2 *lū* — an independent adverb or part of verbal morphology?

Special interest in asseverative forms is prompted when it becomes clear that *lū* here is not just another modal particle but rather a bound morpheme, a building block of syntagms which are part of a paradigm. This paradigm consists, in addition, of non-verbal and verbal forms, which have temporal variations, negative syntagms, etc. *lū*, unlike modal adverbs, is tightly bound to the rheme,[2] whether a noun or a verbal form, being directly

2. The rheme is the new information in the clause. See **§2.4.1.1** below.

linked in such a way that nothing can come between them. The same applies to the negative forms of the paradigm with the negative particle *lā*, which exhibits the same tight link with either the nominal rheme or the verbal form and, in the latter case, with the suffix *-u* as well. That negation is a pertinent part of the verbal complex is made evident by the fact that the negative particle is the one which distinguishes between different verbal paradigms — for instance the indicative ***ul iprus*** as opposed to the negative wish ***ayyiprus***.[3] This tight link is observed quite strictly, and when the negative particle is separated from the verbal form the result is a change in functional sentence perspective (see **§2.4.1.3**) where the element next to which the negative particle stands is the rheme or the focal element (see **§2.4.1.1** below). The abstract formula for the asseverative forms is as follows:

affirmative	negative	
lū V[4] (or øV-***u***)	***lā*** V-***u***	(V=verbal forms, including the stative)
lū N	***lā*** N	(N=nominal rheme)

Despite the morphological transparency of these syntagms it is impossible to reduce them any further or attribute specific value to each formative component. Only the whole syntagm belongs in the paradigm. Any further reduction may lead to misconception of the various paradigms in the system. The verbal system in OB is characterized by a relatively small inventory of elementary forms but by a considerably larger number of distinct paradigms. There are more paradigms than forms due to different combinations of elementary building blocks and also due to their occurrence in various environments. The resulting syntagms are composed of verbal forms with one prefix (ø-, *lū*, *lā*, *ul*, or *ayy-*) and one of two suffixes (*-u* or its absence) in different syntactic environments (such as independent, genitive equivalent, pronominal question, *šumma* protasis and so on). So ***lā*** **V** may appear in a pronominal question and in a *šumma* protasis whereas **øV-*u*** occurs either in genitive equivalent status or as a by-form of the *iprus* asseverative.

Another point which is indicative of the close link between *lū* and the rheme becomes evident once we compare it to the conditional particle

3. The negative particle, however, is **not** in itself a signal of modality (although it may look that way in case of *ayyiprus* or *ul iprus*). The signal of modality is a complex one involving, in addition to the negative particle, the syntagm itself and occasionally even the whole pattern. An example for this would be *ul iprus* in the *-ma* conditional protasis paradigm (**§6.2**, examples **[6.14]–[6.16]**), which is definitely not indicative, but rather conditional.

4. Ø is not marked here because *-u* does not occur in this syntagm (that is, **lū aprusu* is not attested in OB).

šumma. The latter, although certainly having influence over the clause which follows it, shows a looser juncture: Besides the possible physical distance between *šumma* and the verbal form, when negation is effected the negative particle is just added whereas in the asseverative paradigm one syntagm is exchanged for another, forming a paradigm.

The asseverative paradigm as a whole is unique with regard to the syntactic function it fulfills (namely, nexus focussing) and the relationship of this function with notional categories such as the oath or concession.

2.1 Literature review

The basic value of the asseverative *lū* was understood as early as 1889:

> *lu*(-*u*) 'fürwahr'; der 3m. (sic) und 1c. sing. und plur. praet. vorgesetzt, hebt es das vom Verbum Ausgesagte als wirklich geschehen hervor... (*lu*(-*u*) 'truly', which is prefixed to the 3rd pers. masculine (singular) and the 1st pers. common singular and plural of the preterite, emphasizes that which is expressed by the verb as (if it) really happened...) (Delitzsch 1889:211)

The occurrences of the asseverative *lū* are not all treated in GAG under one heading. The relevant forms are classified according to two different criteria, morphological and semantic.

Under GAG §81f it is mentioned that these *lū* forms rarely occur except in the corpus of Royal Inscriptions (for which see **chapter 3**). In addition, it is said (GAG §152b) that in contrast to the oath, where all forms may occur, asseverative forms occur only with *iprus*. No negative forms are discussed in these sections. GAG §158c discusses *lū* forms together with the precative regarding concessive clauses and finally, under GAG §185 ("Die Ausdrucksmittel für den Eid"), comes the fullest survey of the forms, including their classification into assertory and promissory oath (roughly corresponding, respectively, to past and future). Although the oath is not a linguistic, but rather a social term, only there do we find the fullest inventory of asseverative forms.

The suffix -*u* on the asseverative form ***aprusu*** (termed by von Soden, in this context too, "subjunctive", GAG §185b) is quite rare in OB. *lū* V is attested more often (a fuller syntagm, combining both possibilities, viz., ***lū aprusu*** occurs in both OA and OAkk, and is probably identical to the original form which diachronically gave rise to the OB ***lū** aprus*). In GAG §185c it is mentioned that negative forms in OB are always *lā* ... -*u* (as is stated above) and that there are ***aparrasu*** forms in promissory oath. Mari OB is quite similar to Mesopotamian OB in this respect. The issue of the so-called subjunctive morpheme (habitually named after its principal role) is repeated in von Soden 1961:52–53, where he comments that it is not clear how to explain the use of the *modus relativus* in oaths. This morpheme is indeed identical to the subordination marker in OB and there may well be a diachronic link between them. Yet, synchronically, it is not the same morpheme — for a morpheme has, besides its shape, both content and (syntactic) context. These are not the same: First, the subjunctive *-u* appears only when it is appended to a nucleus in the construct state (i.e., it is a genitive equivalent) while the asseverative *-u* always occurs in a clause not depending on a nucleus (see Huehnergard 1997 §36.3 "the absence of *ša* or any other conjunction governing the verb marks this construction unambiguously as an oath."). Second, besides the affirmative *-u* forms there are other forms (*lū aprus*) which belong in the same paradigm but neither resemble the subjunctive nor occur in the same syntactic environment. Third, whereas the subjunctive carries very little semantic value, the asseverative forms certainly have a clear (and distinct) value.

Finet 1956 §91f mentions and explains the "subjonctif d'insistence":

> Bien qu'il ne soit pas fait allusion à un serment, le subjonctif indique peut-être que celui qui parle prend implicitement la divinité à témoin de la véracité ou de l'irrévocabilité de sa décision. (Although an oath is not alluded to, the subjunctive may indicate that the speaker implicitly takes the divinity as a witness to the verity or irrevocability of his decisiveness.)

Finet does not mention *lū* forms in that very function, although they do occur in the Mari texts (see for instance example **[2.41]** further below).

Hecker 1968 §131–32 tells us that the "subjunctive" is part of almost any form used for an oath in OA (a detail which might have diachronic implications, for OA morphology is of a more archaic nature). Another important detail is that the **stative** is used for an assertory oath.

Buccellati 1996 §28.6 describes the asseverative as a periphrastic construction which is sometimes regarded as mood, but cannot be considered as inflection and hence it is not mood in the morphological sense. He treats *lū* as an independent adverbial particle which adds a semantic nuance of emphatic affirmation to the verbal form. *lū* according to him means *indeed* or *certainly*. This adherence to types of inflection to the point that it becomes the most important instrument for classification of items in the verbal system is, at best, misleading. One result is that the negative asseverative is not at all discussed. Another, graver one, is that the ventive is counted as a mood. Mood is defined as marking of modality by **formal features** (Palmer 1986:21). The latter traditionally is, but need not be, limited to morphology, let alone inflectional morphology. In the older stratum of Northwest Semitic languages (and in Arabic) modi indeed happen to correspond inflectional morphology, namely, *-u*, *-a*, *-ø*. That in

Akkadian this is not so does not mean that the only moods are imperative, indicative, and subjunctive.

Buccellati 1996 §29.5 compares *lū iṣbat* to *ina kīnātim iṣbat,* claiming that *lū* is no different than any other adverb and hence should not be considered as a mood (mood, however, pertains to formal features, rather than to semantic features). The asseverative according to Buccellati "... is included in this chapter only because it is considered as a mood in traditional grammar" (ibid. §29.5 at the end). Even if the asseverative *lū* is to be classified with adverbs, it would probably be the group of modal adverbs (GAG §121) rather than any other group.

Huehnergard 1997 §29.3 describes *lū* as an asseverative particle meaning *indeed, certainly* or *verily.* This particle joins all tenses in oaths, otherwise it joins the preterite only, which rarely happens outside royal inscriptions. In §36.3 two types of oath are mentioned — assertory (which pertain to the past and the present) and promissory (pertaining to the future). The means to express the oath are *-u*, *lā* ...*-u*, and *lū* ....

Edzard 1973 does not discuss *lū paris* forms, which may formally belong to either the asseverative paradigm or the precative paradigm. As is mentioned above (**§2.0.1**) the function of the asseverative is explained as an **emphasis of an utterance either as reaction to a doubt (whether real or imaginary) emanating from the addressee** or in order to swear about this utterance. This is the most advanced observation made regarding the function of these forms. Edzard attempts to include all the occurrences of the asseverative under one explanation, including the function of this form in royal inscriptions. It seems, however, that in that corpus *lū iprus* is another paradigm altogether, containing different items and functioning differently (see **chapter 3**).

The question whether the morpheme *-u* (when appended to the forms denoting oath) is the same as the subjunctive *-u* (i.e., an elliptic structure where the main verb is missing, as suggested by Buccellati 1996 §89.8) comes up here again. Edzard thinks that the formal identity of these two *-u* did not exist in the linguistic reality of Akkadian, and that it is probable, in view of an oath protocol in *TIM* 4, 36 containing such forms as *la ad-di-i-nu* (l. 14; to be analyzed as */lā addínu/*?), that there was a difference of stress between the two forms. As to the possibility of ellipsis of the verb expressing oath, if this were true we would expect not only the verbal form marked by *-u*, but also a conjunction. A verbal form, when marked as subordinate, is never independent in Akkadian and needs some kind of nucleus (as does a substantive marked as genitive).

2.2 Asseverative forms

Delimiting the forms which belong to the asseverative paradigm can be achieved only for some of the forms based on morphological criteria alone. For other forms, only syntactic and contextual criteria, which are developed below (and constitute the greater part of the present chapter), can account for their true identity. The first group consists of syntagms containing *lū* and verbal forms (prefix conjugation), namely, *lū iparras*, *lū iptaras* and *lū iprus*. The first two syntagms are not contested by any other similar syntagms. *lū iprus* is similar to *liprus*, but a vowel break (*lu-iC*, *lu-aC*, etc.), or the common representation of the particle *lū* as *lu-ú* are many times sufficient signals to enable distinction. However, in the D and Š stems and in I-*w* verbal roots, all characterized by a base of inflection *u-* (*-uparris*, *-ušapris*, *-ubil*), there are difficulties. For example, the graphic segment *lu-ub-ta-az-zi-iʾ* (√bzʾ) may be interpreted either as asseverative (*lū ubtazziʾ*) or as precative (*lubtazziʾ*).

The syntagms *lū paris* and *lū* with a nominal may be interpreted either as asseverative or as precative. Distinction is possible only based upon syntactic and contextual criteria. The ubiquitous expression *bēlī lū īde* is an example for this group — morphologically it is either precative (let my lord know) or asseverative (my lord does know).

The negative forms (*lā* V-*u* or *lā paris*/*parsu*) may occur both as asseverative forms or in subordination. The difference here would be syntactic — asseverative forms do not follow a nucleus (namely, any entity in construct state).

Another such neutralization is to be found with *lā iparras**am*** and *lā paris*, both of which could stand for negative directives as well as for asseveratives. An example of such a neutralization is *lā tadukkannêti* (ARM 26, 409:28) which is interpreted as asseverative only on account of the overt reference to an oath.

This considerable amount of possible neutralizations is a case in point: Morphology is but a part of what is referred to as formal features. The rest should be sought after in other features of structure and consistent contextual characteristics.

2.2.1 Form inventory

The total number of various forms belonging to the asseverative paradigm is small in Akkadian in general and in the AbB corpus in particular. This small number of examples in the AbB corpus by itself is not sufficient, beyond any doubt, for the analysis and description of this phenomenon. It was therefore decided, rather than to adhere to one corpus, to analyse these forms in the various corpora in which they occur. An attempt to use royal inscriptions of the OB period (RIME 4) for the same purpose resulted in the conclusion that in that corpus the picture is radically different and that the allegedly identical forms are not asseverative but function differently (see **chapter 3**). The asseverative occurrences collected from the rest of the corpora were consistent enough functionally to enable a description of this modal subsystem which is necessary for a complete description of the OB modal system, for a syntactic description of nexus focussing and for its general linguistic implications. The additional OB corpora used for this scrutiny are mainly OB letters (ARM, Falkenstein 1963), OB legal documents (VAB 5) and a legal code (LE).

The forms found are arranged in the following table according to their morphological features:

	lū iprus	*lā iprusu*	*lū iparras*	*lā iparrasu*	*lū paris*	*lā paris*	*lū* N	*lū iptaras*
1csg.	**AbB**	**AbB**	**AbB**/(-***u***)	VAB 5	**AbB**		**AbB**	
2msg.	**AbB**	**AbB**	ARM/(-***u***)	ARM		LE		
3csg.	**AbB**/(-***u***)	**AbB**	ARM	VAB 5	ARM			**AbB**
1cpl.	(-***u***)	VAB 5						
2cpl.								**AbB**
3mpl.		ARM			ARM			

The chart shows the textual origin of the various attested forms. The AbB corpus covers the paradigm only partially and no special pattern can be pointed out for this distribution. The exact number of forms is not indicated. What counts for the purpose of analysis is the nature and analysability of the syntactic context (or co-text).

As to the affirmative asseverative forms in *-u*, there are six verified occurences in the AbB corpus (marked by (-***u***) in the table above) which seem to exhibit the same co-textual characteristics as *lū* forms. The same forms occur in other corpora as well. In the ARM corpus there are a few occurrences, mentioned by Finet 1956 §91f, which, however, do not come with sufficient contextual information for them to be analysed.

The following chart contains the forms discussed by Edzard 1973:125–26:

	lū iprus	*lā iprusu*	*lū iparras*	*lā iparrasu*
1 csg.	+	+	+	+
2 msg.	+	+	+	+
2 fsg.	+		+	
3 csg.	+	+		+
1 cpl.	+	+	+	+
2 cpl.	+		+	
3 mpl.	+			
3 fpl.	+			

The differences between Edzard's morphological data and the present data are probably due to different corpora (Edzard's corpus is not defined) and due to differences of analysis (forms whose nature has not been verified are not included here). *lū iptaras* forms are not mentioned by Edzard (and neither are asseveratives such as *lū paris*). The former do occur, possibly due to formal attraction (see **§2.4.3**).

2.2.2 The paradigm

A paradigm is a group of forms which belong together due to their commutability in the same syntagmatic slot. The next three examples illustrate negative and affirmative forms in the same environment:

> [**2.1**] *ina kaspim u kīsim ša tappîm eqlam bītam amtam wardam abī* ***lā išāmu*** *ina ša ramānišu–ma* ***lū išām***
> My father did *not* buy a field, a house, a maid (or) a servant from the partner's silver or (his) purse. He *did* buy only from his own (property).
> VAB 5, 287:18–22

The setting is the same — the father is the referent in both clauses, and the verbal lexeme *šâmum* pertains to the same purchase. This is why it is possible to regard these two forms as belonging to the same paradigm.

The next example is similar, containing 1st pers. forms:

> [**2.2**] *u anāku nīš bēliya atma umma anāku–ma [... an]a ṣibûtiya* ***lā ašpuru*** *ana awāt 1 awīlim warad bēliya* ***lū ašpuršu***
> And I swore by my lord saying: 'I did *not* send [this man fo]r my purposes. I *did* send him concerning a matter of a servant of my lord'.
> ARM 27, 151:94–95

The link between negative and affirmative forms of the asseverative forms is thus established regardless of the morphological disparity.

The third example is taken from a divorce statement containing different forms from the *iparras* formation of the asseverative paradigm:

> [**2.3**] *šaptīya* ***lā inaššiqu****–ma ša zikarim u sinništim* ***lā amaggarušu****–ma ana utūl sūnī liqrianni šībūt ālim u rabiānam* ***lū ušedde***
> He shall *not* kiss my lips and I will *not* consent to sexual relations and should he call me to lie in (my) lap I *will* notify the city elders and the mayor. BM 13912:8–12, Anbar 1975:121

Here two types of links inside the paradigm become apparent: The first is between the 3rd and the 1st pers. forms (*lā* ***i****naššiqu* vs. *lā* ***a****maggarušu*). The second is, once again, between negative and affirmative forms in the same person (***lā*** *amaggar****u*** **:** ***lū*** *ušedde*).

These examples are all found in the context of an oath, but according to the present point of view all the asseverative forms belong in the same paradigm (see **§§2.4.3.1** and **2.5** below for an elaborated justification).

The various forms seem to be compatible with the ventive, dative and accusative suffixation. This may be the reason that by-forms of the type *iprusu* are so rare, remaining undetected, masked by the ventive suffix. The ensuing example illustrates this type of neutralization:

[**2.4**] *aššum ṣuḫāriya šuāti u* PN_1 *museppīšu ana* GN_1 *šūrîm a[šp]ur–ma* PN_2 2 *rēdî* ***iddinam***–*m[a an]a* GN_2 ***nisniqu***–*[ma] ana bīt* PN_1 *muse[ppi] ṣuḫāriya awīlû* GN_2 ... *ana er[ēb]im ul iddinūninni*
As to this servant of mine and PN_1 who abducted him, I w[ro]te to have (them) brought to GN_1 an[d] PN_2 *did* give (or: gave) me two soldiers and we *did* arrive [a]t GN_2, [but] the inhabitants of GN_2 ... did not let me e[nt]er the house of PN_1 who abd[uct]ed my servant. 6, 181:8'–13'

The form *iddinam* may be interpreted either way, namely, as indicative or as asseverative. If it had not been for the clear-cut asseverative form *nisniqu,* it would have been impossible to guess. There might have been some additional mechanism for differentiation in the spoken language (as Edzard 1973:133 in fact suggests) but it is inaccessible via written texts.

Following GAG §185a, Huehnergard 1997 §36.3 discusses the temporal reference of the forms used for oath, the first of which (assertory) pertains to the past and the present and the second (promissory) pertains to the future. This seems to be the case for the whole paradigm, and not only for the oath. This is important because the temporal value of the asseverative paradigm is different from indicative forms. Asseverative forms with *iparras* refer to the future (present-future when indicative), nominal asseverative forms have a non-future reference (atemporal when indicative) and forms with *iprus* pertain to the past. The point of reference is always the moment of the utterance for, as is made clear below, this paradigm belongs in dialogue. Besides having special forms and values, this paradigm occurs in rather definable syntactic conditions; example [**2.4**] is not the rule (for further discussion see **§2.4.3.1** below).

2.3 The traditional values of the asseverative

Asseverative forms have three traditional meanings, or in other words, are used to express three different notions — insistence, oath, and concession. These notions were differentiated on the basis of the respective logical categories represented by the notions which were corroborated by different models for each notion. That is, the asseverative is paralleled semantically by *ina kīnātim* (Buccellati 1996 §29.6), the oath is to be found in other structures as well (such as a conditional clause with no apodosis, GAG §185g) and the concessive is expressed by precative forms as well (GAG §158c). These notional criteria cannot, however, be used for a formal classification of structural units. The notions of oath and concession are elaborated in view of the syntactic mechanism under discussion further below, under **§2.5**.

2.3.1 Asseverative

The asseverative notion is discussed above under **§2.1**. It is best translated into written English by italicizing the auxiliary verb (or using a construction with the verb "do"). In case of the negative, by italicizing the negative element, as the graphic equivalent of nuclear stress in spoken language (see **§2.4.2.2**):

[**2.5**] *aššum ipir* GN *nadānim* ***lū ašpurakkum*** *ana mīnim lā taddin* ...
I *did* write you about giving the ration of GN; why did you not give (it) ... ? 2, 129:4–5

[**2.6**] PN_1 *ṣuḫārī* ... PN_2 *imqut–ma ubtazziʾšu u yâšim magriātim ša ana eṣēnim lā naṭâ idbub ṣuḫārī–ma* ***lū ubtazziʾ*** *yâti ammīnim inazzaranni*
PN_1 my servant ... attacked PN_2 and hurt him but (the latter) has spoken insults which are not fit to smell *against me*. My *servant did* hurt (him), why does he hate *me*? 2, 115:6–16

This example is discussed further below, under **§2.4.3.1**.

2.3.2 Oath

The oath in Akkadian is given special attention by von Soden. An entire section (GAG §185) is devoted to this phenomenon, probably because this is the point where an important social practice meets specialized linguistic means. The oath is linked to the asseverative by von Soden (GAG §81f) and a similar attempt is made by Edzard 1973:129, in view of the identical forms used to express both. The most prominent signal for the oath are certain verbal lexemes such as *zakārum* or *tamûm* and the syntagm *nīš X* representing the entity one swears by:

[**2.7**] *kīam lizkurū dāʾik* PN ***lā īdû*** *anāku* ***lā ušāḫizu*** *u bašītam ša* PN ***lā elqû lā alputu***
Let them swear thus: I do *not* know the the one who killed PN, I did *not* incite (it) and I *neither* took *nor* touched PN's property. VAB 6, 218:12–15

[2.8] *lamassam ša* PN *atma īkam šuāti ē tudannin [b]īt abīka [k]alâšu* ***lū ušmāt***
I swear by the protective spirit of PN, should you not strengthen this ditch I *will* put your entire family to death. 12, 169:20–26

[2.9] *eqlum ša pī kunukkišu liter limṭi* ***lā aturru****–ma* ***lā abaqqaru***
Should the field according to his document be more (or) be less, I will *not* claim (it) again. VAB 5, 156:1'–3'' (side 1–2 and rev. 1–3)

2.3.3 Concession

The concessive relation as a category is discussed in **§2.5.1** and in **chapter 5** below. As is mentioned above, there are a few models for concessives in OB (GAG §158c), and the term *concessive* represents a certain notion of a logical connection between clauses. The first model contains the precative:

[2.10] *u pūḫātim* ***liddinūnikkim*** *ul damiq*
Even if they give you substitutions (for the barley), it is not good. 11, 40:14–16

This kind of concessive is a concessive-conditional, referring to an action which may or may not happen from the point of utterance on. Another, somewhat similar model is a *šumma* conditional preceded by *u* (perhaps confined to the Mari Texts, see the Arabic *walaw*). It may refer to an action which is temporally of a much wider range, namely, before, during or after the point of utterance:

[2.11] ***u šumma*** *atta mīšātanni anāku elīka aḫabbuṣ*[5] *nakrīka ana qātika umalla*
Even if you forsake me I will kill for you (and) hand your enemies over to you. ARM 26, 214:9–14

The third model is the one at issue:

[2.12] ***lū ša ištu ṣeḫḫerēnu–ma ištēniš nirbû*** *ištu ilam taršî matīma ... šumī ul taḫsusī*
Despite the fact that we grew up together practically[6] since we were very young, since you have become lucky you never mentioned my name... 9, 15:7–11

This structure is a part of the asseverative paradigm, namely, *lū* N, when the N slot is taken by an abstract *ša* clause (the fact that...). Von Soden (GAG §158c) discusses the various possibilities to denote concession in Akkadian: *lū* with a nominal sentence (rarely), *lū* with the stative, *lū*

5. ARM 26, 214, n. a.

6. "Practically" is meant to reflect the focus marker on the syntagm *ištu ṣeḫḫerēnu*.

with *iprus* (for expressing the past) and the precative (for expressing the present or the future). The first two possibilities, namely, *lū* N/*lū paris*, may actually belong either in the precative or in the asseverative paradigm. The difference in the temporal frame of the forms is not the only difference. The overall characterization of the two models (precative/asseverative) is different as well (for the concessive precative see **chapter 5**, for the concessive asseverative see **§2.5.2** below).

2.4 Syntax

The present section describes the syntactic mechanism of the asseverative paradigm, which has to do with a special kind of focus. The development of this special focus depends upon existing general explanations of focus phenomena and requires a general description of focus phenomena in OB, which has not been done so far.

2.4.1 Focus

2.4.1.1 Focus — definition

Focus is one function in what is called **Functional Sentence Perspective** (FSP), the analysis of texts with respect to the information they contain. It was developed, among other places, in the Prague Linguistic Circle (a short historical background is found in Hajičova 1994:245–46 and Sgall 1987:176–77). The basic terms involved in FSP are **theme/rheme** and **topic/focus**.

Topic "is the thing which the proposition expressed by the sentence is about" (Lambrecht 1994:118). More explicitly, topic is defined as follows:

> In the ultraclausal textual information unit ('block'): the element(s) or textual segment that, being cotext or context bound, feature the cohesive factor of 'what is being discussed' within the block. (Shisha-Halevy 1998:236)

The latter definition attempts to differentiate between **topic** and **theme** (a debated issue in its own right, e.g., Sgall 1987:179), which is viewed as

> One of the main constituents of the basic information structure of the clause: the information basis segment (given, presupposed or taken for granted) **in the clause extent**... (Shisha-Halevy 1998:236, my emphasis)

Focus is defined as

> The pragmatic function of Focus pertains to the focality dimension of discourse. The focal information in a linguistic expression is that information which is relatively the most important or salient in a given communicative setting. (Dik 1997 I:326)

Or, with the intention of differentiating between **focus** and **rheme**:

> In the ultraclausal textual information unit ('block'): the element(s) or textual segment carrying the center or highlight of an information block. The focus may, in clause extent, coincide with the rheme. (Shisha-Halevy 1995:214)

The **rheme**, on the other hand, is the constituent which carries the information in the clause level.

A somewhat different definition which points, rather than to the highlight of information, to some **contrast** conveyed by the focus is the following:

> Less precisely, we may consider focusing as a sort of 'emphasis' which, as such, **must stand in contrast to something.** (Goldenberg 1985:330, my emphasis)

As such, **focus** differs from the **rheme** exactly by such contrast. The issue of contrast vs. emphasis comes up in Dik et al. 1980:45 where it seems that the answer largely depends upon the nature of distinctions found in a specific language.

2.4.1.2 Types of foci

An example of a language which distinguishes quite a few types of foci is a Bantu language called Aghem, used as a basis for Dik et al. 1980. Aghem seems to distinguish between six types of foci (Dik et al. 1980:48–59):

1. **Unmarked focus**: Focus not formally marked, basic word order.
2. **Assertive focus**: New information with respect to the addressee.
3. **Counter-assertive focus**: Information contrasted with another asserted in a previous utterance.
4. **Exhaustive listing focus**: Information which is unique with respect to a substitution list.
5. **Polar focus**: Assertion of the truth value regarding a proposition.
6. **Counter-assertive polar focus**: Truth value in contradiction to a previous utterance.

These types aid in perception of the possible extent of a focus system.

Dik 1997 I:330–35 uses two parameters to categorize foci, viz., the scope of the focus and the pragmatic reasons for the assignment of focus:

I. Scope of the focus
   1. Tense, mood, aspect, and polarity (yes-no truth value)
   2. Predicate
   3. Arguments

II. Pragmatic reason for the assignment of focus
   1. Information gap
      a. Answer
      b. New information
   2. Contrast
      a. Parallel constituents
      b. Counter-presuppositional (by the addressee), etc.

This partition, suggested for languages of an elaborate focus system, is still related to a specific system. It is nonetheless important in attempting to take everything into consideration when discussing focus. It is one of the few discussions of focus which incorporate occurrences such as *he did NOT solve the problem / he DID solve the problem* in a description of a focus system. Such clause patterns in English are highly related to the asseverative paradigm in that both perform the same syntactic function and have rather similar values.

2.4.1.3 Focus in OB

The focus system in OB has not been given separate attention. The old grammars only touch upon the subject describing individual particles, but never the system as a whole. One study which has achieved considerable advances describing the function of one focus signal (*-ma*) is Rainey 1976. Other studies by the same author (Rainey 1992, 1999), concerning the same subject, pertain, however, to peripheral Akkadian, and are hence of little help in studying OB. Another pertinent study, Huehnergard 1986, although dealing specifically with non-verbal clauses, has nevertheless contributed some important insights to this subject.

The newest typology of emphasis phenomena in OB is offered by Buccellati 1996 §§66.8–66.9. Buccellati habitually separates the description of both sides of the linguistic sign — treating the formal features (the signifier) apart from the notional features (the signified) as if they were not two inseparable sides of the same coin. This distinction is no doubt important but the physical separation of form from substance in description causes the loss of the necessary link between signifier and signified and hence loss of the sign. Moreover, Buccellati says nothing about the basic dichotomy in FSP, that is, the distinction between topic and focus.

Describing the formal features of emphasis, Buccellati 1996 §66.8 offers nine theoretical patterns. These patterns are not exemplified, and some of them may represent more than one signified.[7] A few existing patterns are not given due representation.[8] The notional typology (ibid. §66.9) is characterized by confounding essentially different notions (and exponents) under the same heading.[9]

Focus in OB is signaled by various means — morphologically, syntactically, by particles, or by a combination of these means.

The present description is occupied mainly with verbal clauses. In verbal clauses there are difficulties which are not encountered in non-verbal clauses (excluding the predicative, i.e., the stative, which is like the verb in this respect — being a "built-in sentence"). Whereas the rheme is normally regarded as residing in the verbal form, the focus of the sentence is rather another entity, which is explicitly marked as such. This is usually evident from the context.

Focussing of nominal and adverbial elements in OB is signaled in at least four ways — marking the focus by the particle *-ma;* by preposing the negative particle *ul* (or *lā*) to the focal element; by using different pattern of the order of elements; and finally, using the relative converter *ša* in cleft constructions. These means are occasionally used in combination, which means both that they are not mutually exclusive and that the complete picture may be very complicated.

The first to be discussed is the enclitic particle ***-ma***, which is the most widespread focus signal. This form represents two different particles, which, although both are enclitic and written in the same way, have different functions. The two are mutually exclusive, namely, one does not occur in the same slot as the other, that is, they occur in different syntagmatic conditions. One is the connective *-ma,* which connects series of verbal forms, thereby denoting some kind of logical or temporal relation between them (Huehnergard's "coordinating *-ma*", see **§4.4.3**). As such it is enclitic exclusively to a verbal form, demarcating the clause and representing the connection to the next clause. It belongs with other connectives. The other *-ma* (Huehnergard's "non-coordinating *-ma*") focalizes (in our corpus) what precedes it, marking as focus (the rheme is usually marked, in non-verbal clauses, by the order of elements) pronouns, nominal, and adverbial forms and syntagms. *-ma* is sometimes referred to as copula (at

7. Pattern 5 (ibid. §66.8) *amārum–ma īmur* may represent 1. focussing of the verbal lexeme (see examples **[2.24]**–**[2.25]** below), 2. nexus focussing (**[2.45]**–**[2.47]** below), and even 3. topicalizing of the verbal lexeme. See Cohen 2004.

8. The cleft pattern (containing no *-ma*), exemplified in examples **[2.21]**–**[2.23]** below, and focalizing word order, exemplified in examples **[2.18]**–**[2.20]** below.

9. Examples 9–10 (Buccellati 1996 §66.9) under the heading *contrast* show personal pronouns serving as themes, while example 11 has a focalizing *-ma*.

least in non-verbal clauses; Huehnergard 1986:238, n. 74). It seems better, however, to ascribe a wider function to it, first, because many non-verbal clauses do without it, and second, because it is certainly not a copula in verbal clauses which are our main concern.[10]

The first example exhibits focus for reasons of contrast — *anāku* of the first speaker as opposed to *anāku* of the second:

[2.13] *umma* PN_1–*ma anāku ša elqû appal–ma u umma* PN_2–*ma* ***anāku–ma*** *appal–ma*
PN_1 (said): 'As for me, I will pay for what I took...', but PN_2 (said): '*I*'ll pay.../(it is) *I* (who) will pay...' 1, 10:17–21

The first occurrence of *anāku* represents the theme (or topic), i.e., what is being discussed. The second *anāku* is in contrast to the first, and therefore marked as focus.

The following pair of examples both exhibit an element which is an answer to an explicit question.

[2.14] *um[m]a šū–[m]a pānūki eliš [š]ap[l]iš umma anāku–ma* ***š[a]pli[š]–ma***
S[o] he (said): 'Are you up or do[wn]?' I (said): '[*do*]*wn*'. ARM 26, 232:9–11

The minimal answer, containing only the essential information asked for, is always the rheme. Here it is marked as focus too (possibly **down** as contrasted with up), whereas in the second example it is the rheme only (not being contrasted with anything):

[2.15] [*umm*]*a anāku–ma* [*m*]*annum iddinakki umma šī–ma* PN
[So] I (said): '[W]ho gave (it to) you?' She (said): 'PN'. 1, 133:17–19

The particle *-ma* can focalize any nominal or adverbial element (Finet 1956 §100), be it morphological or syntactic. By "syntactic" is meant either a nominalized clause (by means of *ša* or *kīma*) or an adverbialized phrase or clause:

[2.16] ***inūma ana*** **GN** [***t***]***allaku–ma*** [*š*]*upram–ma*
Write me *only when*[11] [*you*] *go to GN*... 9, 12:6–8

Here, although *-ma* immediately follows a finite verb, it is **not** the connective *-ma*, but rather the **focalizing** *-ma* marking the whole adverbial

10. For instance, when appended to a one-term non-verbal clause it seems to signal existence, rather than to be a copula or a focus marker: *u kīma teštenemme* ***nukurtum–ma*** *mamman bābam ul uṣṣi* "As you keep hearing, (there is) **war**, nobody leaves the gate" (6, 64:15–17).

11. The edition has *as soon as* which could be paraphrased as *right at the moment...*, which could be interpreted as reflecting focus as well.

clause, which is syntactically equivalent to a simple adverb, as focus of the sentence. This possibility is already mentioned in Finet 1956 §100g.

The second focus signal is the **negative particle**. Von Soden, GAG §151a, mentions that the negative particle immediately precedes the predicate. In §151b he adds that separation of the negation from the predicate does not occur in OB (except for negative alternatives, i.e., *neither... nor*). When it does occur (in other dialects), another part of the sentence is to be **emphasized**. Huehnergard 1986:227, n. 38 suggests that it is probable that *ul* marks what follows it as logical predicate, and this suggestion is adopted here. It is accepted that a negated element (except when originally negative and other than the verb) is focus, or rheme, of the clause (Goldenberg 1985:326). Such focalization in OB is generally signaled by *ul*. There are few examples of this mechanism in the AbB series, either due to syntactic rigidness or to the high formularity typical of these letters:

> [2.17] PN ***ul ana tamkarūtim ul ana ṣibût ramānišu*** *illik ašar taqbîšu warki* DN *rā'imiki illik*
> As to PN, (It was) not *for mercantile activity*, nor (was it) *for his own needs* (that) he went. He went after DN who loves you, where you had told him (to go). 9, 51:17–22

The person in question did go (contrary to what could be inferred from the edition: "PN did not go away for any mercantile activity, nor for ..."). The issue is where, and therein lies the focus of the first two clauses. As to the third, *ašar taqbî* is expected as focus too, but it is not marked as such. The next example is easier in that respect for both sides are marked as focus:

> [2.18] 2 *immerī(n)* ... *ša* P[N] *iddin[am]* ***anāku*** *apqid[akkum]* ***ul ṣuḫārī*** *ipqidakkum*
> *I* handed out [to you] two ... sheep which PN gave [me], (it was) not *my servant* (who) handed (them) out to you. 3, 76:4–9

The main issue of the sentence is not about handing out the sheep but rather about who did it. *ul* marks the centre of information in the clause — *ṣuḫārī*, which, in turn, is contrasted to *anāku* in the first clause. *anāku* is focussed as well. However, it is marked as such by another mechanism — a **different pattern of the order of elements**.

Buccellati 1996 §66.8 mentions such a mechanism, but does not adduce examples for it. Such a mechanism is harder to recognize and prove, and at this stage it could be stated only in reference to elements marked as nominative (substantives or nominative pronouns), filling the slot preceding the verbal form. This can be seen in the first clause in **[2.18]**, where 2 *immerī* ... *ša* PN *iddin[am]* ***anāku*** *apqid[akkum]* exhibits these criteria, in addition to being symmetrically contrasted with another substantival agent, *ṣuḫārī*, marked as focus by *ul*. Such double construction of focus is repeated a few times throughout the AbB corpus.

The following example shows the same type of focus marking:

> [2.19] *aššum ina mu[ḫ]ḫi epennim izuzzim ša tašpuram ina muḫḫi epennim šuāti* **PN** *l[i]zziz*
> As to supervising the plough(ing) (about) which you wrote me, let *PN* supervise this plough(ing). 9, 137:9–14

PN is not treated as focus in the edition, yet in the edition of the previous example, in the same position, ***anāku*** is translated as focus. If we devise an imaginary subtraction of the first (topical ***aššum***) clause from the second, we can extract the new informative element. It would be PN, for *šuāti* is an anaphoric pronoun (identifying an element with one already mentioned) and the directive element in *lizziz* is already hinted at in the verbal lexeme *šapārum* "to order in writing".

The following example similarly contains a nominative substantive, which is marked as focus in the same way:

> [2.20] *ša bīt kittum* ***ša ana ka[s]pim šuddunim i[ll]a[k]am–[m]a*** *kaspam š[uāti] lā ušadd[a]n kasap ālim* **r[a]biānu[m]** *lišaddin*
> (It is the man) of the Kittum temple, *the one who c[o]m[e]s to collect the silver,* (who) should not collect t[his] silver; (it is) *the may[or]* (who) should collect the city's silver / let *the may[or]* collect... 13, 109:7–10

The key form is *i-[l]a-[k]am–[m]a*, a restoration suggested in remark c to the translation, where the -*[m]a* is regarded as a mistake. Here it is considered as belonging, being the focalizing *-ma*. ***rabiānum*** is thus contrasted with the entire clause ***ša ana kaspim šuddunim illakam*** which is marked as focus by *-ma*.

In a clause of this type where we have only a nominative element and a verbal form (like ***anāku apqid***) this mechanism is neutralized because it is in conflict with another mechanism where the first slot of the clause is kept for the theme, or the topic, namely, what is being discussed.

The last exponent is the **cleft construction**,[12] whose English and French versions are *it is X who/which/that Y* and *C'est X qui/que/dont Y* respectively. It is a common pattern in many languages, whose function is to mark any element of the the sentence (usually other than the verb) as the **rheme** (*X*) and the rest of the sentence as the thematic clause (*that/que Y*). In the OB cleft constructions, *ša* formally marks anything which is not the rheme as a syntactic, or functional noun and the rest is thus marked by default as a rheme. This mechanism is statistically the

12. The structure is thoroughly surveyed cross-linguistically for the first time in Polotsky 1944:53–68.

least common of all, and therefore it is described last. It frequently occurs with interrogative elements. Interrogatives are naturally rhematic, for they represent, due to their nature, the new information sought after and yet to come. The conceptual apposition of the interrogative in the answer is the rheme too. This too is a case where morphological features are overridden by syntactic data — although interrogatives in verbal clauses appear in various morphological forms (*mīnum*, *mīnam*, *ammīnim*, etc.) they still are the rheme, whether they are marked thus or not. Such clefting of the interrogative is the norm in French, where instead of *que fais tu*? one rather uses ***qu'****est-ce que tu fais*? — literally "*what* is it that you do?":

> [2.21] ***mannum*** *ša ina qāti bēliya ušezzebanni*
> *Who* (is the one) who will save me from my lord? ARM 26, 326:10'–11'

In example **[2.21]** we have a **cleft construction** where the interrogative pronoun is marked as the rheme and the rest, namely, the *ša* clause, is an independent adjective clause[13] functioning as the theme of the clause. Note that interrogatives, when functioning as such (and not as relatives or as indefinites), are not expanded by attributive relative clauses. As for the appositional pronoun or the copula, such as we find in English ***it*** *is*... or French ***c'****est*..., these are not to be found in cleft constructions in OB. The minimum requirement for cleft structure in OB is the nominalization of part(s) of the sentence designed to be the theme while the rest of the sentence is the rheme.

Other elements other than interrogatives rarely occur in clefts:

> [2.22] ***annûm*** *ša unaᵓᵓiduka umma anāku–ma*
> (It is) *this* (about) which I instructed you, saying... 12, 53:4–5

Other examples for clefts are found, rarely, with the negative particle:

> [2.23] ***ul anāku*** *ša ina* [*qabê*] *elamtim art*[*abû*]
> (Is it) not *I* who beca[me im]portant by [the word] of the Elamites? ARM 26, 306:33–34

2.4.1.4 Focus of the various verbal components

As a matter of fact, any element may be focussed. That is, besides various syntactic categories, one finds focus of contrast between elements which are semantic components, such as various tempora, modi, etc.

As is mentioned above, *-ma* may focus only adverb(ial)s or (pro)nominals (substantives or adjectives) both morphological and syntactic (that

13. An example for an independent adjective clause would be found in *ana* ***ša ațrudušu*** *iddin–ma* "He gave (them) to (the one) whom I sent..." (7, 86:30), which, unlike English, does not need to have an additional referential nucleus.

is, substantival, adjectival, and adverbial clauses).

As for the verbal complex, which has not been discussed here thus far, it too may be subject to syntactic analysis and hence to focussing of each of its components. Such analysis of these components by showing each of them to be capable of various syntactic transformations (including focussing) is shown in Goldenberg 1985. The verbal complex is said to be syntactically composed of 1. the person marker; 2. the verbal lexeme; and 3. the predicative link between them — the **nexus** (a term originally used by Jespersen 1924:114–16). Based on this analysis, performed mainly on Biblical Hebrew, it can be shown that in OB all three verbal components may be focussed as well. It is done, much as in Biblical Hebrew, by extraposing these components (or more precisely, their independent representatives) and marking them as focus, whenever possible. Example [**2.13**], already discussed above, illustrates focussing of the person marker:

> [**2.13**] *umma* PN_1*–ma anāku ša elqû appal–ma u umma* PN_2*–ma* ***anāku–ma*** *appal–ma*
> PN_1 (said): 'As for me, I will pay for what I took...', but PN_2 (said): '*I*'ll pay.../(it is) *I* (who) will pay...' 1, 10:17–21

The morphological representation of the 1st person (*a-*) cannot be focussed, so it is the syntactic representation thereof, *anāku*, which is focussed instead.

The second component of the verbal complex, i.e., the verbal lexeme, is focussed via *-ma* in paronomastic infinitive constructions. Such constructions have already been discussed by Finet 1956 §93n ("l'infinitif renforçant un verbe conjugué"), by Aro 1961:111–15 (under "Infinitiv in Lokativ-adverbial auf *-um*"), and by Cohen 2004. In Biblical Hebrew we find similar cases whose structures were explained, along with similar cases in many different languages, by Goldenberg 1971. Goldenberg's type B refers to cases where the infinitive, representing the verbal lexeme, is focussed and hence is the salient information, usually for reasons of contrast. The following example shows how it is done in OB:

> [**2.24**] *mimma atta ana bēliya ul tuḫaṭṭi ... atta ana bēliya* ***dummuqum–ma*** *tudammiq...*
> You absolutely did not mistreat my lord... (on the contrary, it is) *to treat my lord kindly* (that) you did.../ what you did was rather *treat my lord kindly.* ARM 26, 449:25–27

Overlooking the limitations of standard English in rendering a literal translation, the point is that the verbal lexeme (*treating kindly*) is in focus, in contrast to another verbal lexeme carrying the opposite meaning (*to mistreat*). The following is quite similar:

[2.25] *ina pānītim ina aḫītiya ešme* [*ummāmi*] *sukkal* GN *imtūt ana bēliya* [*ašpur*] *inanna marū šipri* GN *ana ṣēr* RN *illikūnim–m*[*a*] *umma šunu–ma* ***marāṣum–ma*** *imraṣ–ma*[14]
Formerly I heard in my entourage [as follows]: 'The minister of GN died'. I [wrote] to my lord. Now, the messengers of GN came to RN saying: 'He is *just sick* (rather than dead)'... (lit. [it is] *to be sick* [that] he is...) ARM 26, 384:3''–6''

The contrast here is between being dead and just being sick, that is, **not** dead.

Paronomastic infinitive constructions are dealt with briefly by Buccellati 1996 §66.9 (examples 1 and 7), but his explanation for such structures is merely semantic rather than syntactic.

The third component of the verbal complex, discussed by Goldenberg 1985:332 and Goldenberg 1971:70–72, is the **nexus. Nexus focussing** is signaled in OB mainly by the asseverative paradigm and occasionally by other means as well.

2.4.2 Nexus focussing

Prior to the description of the nexus focussing function of the asseverative paradigm in OB, nexus focussing in general must be discussed. The reason for this is that linguistic studies seldom recognize nexus focussing for what it is and few works actually refer syntactically to this phenomenon.

2.4.2.1 Linguistic treatment of nexus focussing

Describing the syntactic mechanism of paronomastic infinitive constructions, Goldenberg 1971 establishes three types of such constructions: infinitives in extrapositive topicalization of the verbal lexeme (type A), focussed infinitives (via clefting or other means, thus actually contrasting the verbal lexeme with another one — type B), and nexus focussing (type C), where the infinitive construction is **contrasted with its own negative**. Comparing the different types, Goldenberg states that construction C is an independent phenomenon, whereas types B and A are just special cases of general constructions (viz., focussing and topical extraposition respectively).

The explicit function, viz., nexus focussing, is mentioned in a later study (Goldenberg 1985:332) as one of the tests applied to each of the

14. This *-ma* which is appended to a verbal form but does not connect it to a following verbal form is referred to as "*-ma* d'insistance" (ARM 26, 384, n. r). This *-ma* also figures in some peripheral Akkadian texts. The mechanism underlying this rare occurrence of the particle has not yet been explained.

components of the verbal complex which are mentioned above (**§2.4.1.4**). The example is *yāṣō tēṣē*, the negation of which is *lō tēṣē* in Biblical Hebrew, *kén teṣe* (opposed to *ló teṣe*) in spoken contemporary Hebrew.

Shisha-Halevy 1995 (163–65) describes a Middle Welsh morpheme which signals nexus focussing as having a responsive function inside the dialogue, meaning that this morpheme reacts and relates back to the former co-text by virtue of resumption of the verbal lexeme. The function of this morpheme is described as follows:

> This is in fact no less than a high-order rheme, paraphraseable as: 'predication or assertion of the validity (or cogency) of predicating [RHEME] of [THEME]'... (Shisha-Halevy 1995:163)

The Middle Welsh particle is compared to the particle *sì* in Boccaccio's Italian (ibid. 164–65), which functions as a nexus focussing exponent in dialogue as well. The latter is related to the modern Italian syntagm *sì che* having a similar function, namely, a responsive insistence to a negative context (see example **[2.62]** in **§2.6** below).

A study which is only partly concerned with the subject is Joly and O'Kelly 1987. The authors discuss the auxiliary *do* in English, attempting to show that when *do* is stressed it has a cohesive function in discourse. The particular explanations regarding the syntactic mechanism itself are at the margin of the general discussion:

> Une phrase assertive affirmative avec *do* sert non seulement **à affirmer l'existence du rapport incidentiel du prédicat au sujet de l'énoncé** — en définitive **l'existence même de l'événement** ... on ne déclare pas simplement que l'événement «est», on déclare avant tout qu'il «ne peut pas ne pas être». (An assertive affirmative clause with *do* is used not only **to assert the existence of the incidental relationship of the predicate with the subject of the utterance**, in effect **the very existence of the event** ... one does not simply state that the event exists, but rather that it cannot not exist.) (Joly and O'Kelly 1987:96–97, my emphasis)

Nexus focussing is strongly inferred from this explanation. However, further below, when returning to the subject, the authors create a paradox, claiming as follows:

> Le recours à *do* ... a précisément pour effet de **focaliser sur le contenu lexical** du verbe ... et sur **la relation prédicative** de celui-ci au sujet de l'énoncé... (Resorting to *do* ... has exactly the effect of **focussing the lexical contents** of the verb ... and **the predicative relationship** of the latter to the subject...) (Joly and O'Kelly 1987:102, my emphasis)

That is, *do* allegedly serves simultaneously to focus **both** the verbal lexeme and the nexus. It looks improbable: Focus implies contrast. For two foci to co-exist there must be two different sources of contrast, which is not the case with *do* (the contrast in point is between "I'm not accusing..." and "I *do* accuse..." [ibid. 102 no. 11], i.e., over the existence of the nexus, and not over the verbal lexeme).

Nevertheless two important statements are made in this work (Joly and O'Kelly 1987:98):
1. That this *do* is an argumentative-discoursive signal to shut off the debate between the affirmative and what is non-affirmative in favor of the affirmative. This, in a nutshell, is the semantic essence of the nexus focussing mechanism.
2. That it is highly modalized, reflecting the subjectivity of the speaker. This claim is important when the modality of the mechanism is considered.

Other related descriptions fall short of identifying the mechanism for its syntactic function. Dik et al. 1980:52–53 describe **predication focus**, as focus **on the truth value** of the utterance (for which see the following section) but they note that when the focus is on a predicate which has nothing to do with the truth (e.g., an imperative) then the focus is said to be **on the illocutionary force** of the form. Hence each such focus is different according to the various speech acts (which do not necessarily correspond to formal categories in a language). That is why the general name **predication focus** is used. In Dik et al. 1980:52–54 nexus focussing is termed *focus on the predication as a whole* while focus on the verbal lexeme is termed *focus on the predicate*. It seems hence that Dik et al. 1980 and Dik 1997 I:330–35 ignore the predicative link as a separate linguistic entity exactly by including it, together with the verbal lexeme, in **predication**, while the verbal lexeme for him is the **predicate**. This is why Dik's analysis is not brought to completion. The recognition of the verbal (or predicational) components is critical for the completion of the present analysis.

2.4.2.2 Stressing of the auxiliary in English

The present section attempts to briefly describe nexus focussing in written English in order to create some basis for comparison against the general syntactic and co-textual conditions of this phenomenon in OB.

Nexus focussing is not explicitly mentioned in the linguistic literature on English, yet spoken English has a frequently occurring mechanism which is reminiscent thereof semantically (and, after analysis, syntactically as well). This mechanism is **stressing of auxiliary** verbal forms (by nuclear, or sentence stress). Written English usually has only *do* (outside question and negation, where it is obligatory) in this function, for *do* is not dependent, as are the other auxiliaries, upon stress —*I do play* contrasts with *I play*.

However, one occasionally finds written English where nuclear stress is represented by italicizing the relevant segment. Stressing the auxiliary in English signals mostly nexus focussing. Several factors lead to this conclusion:
1. In view of the iconic relationship between nuclear stress and focus in English (Halliday 1967:203, Bolinger 1986:89, 94), when the copulative verb *be*, which generally represents the nexus, bears nuclear stress the result is literally a **focussed nexus.**
2. The syntactic and co-textual environments in which this mechanism is found at work, such as lexical resumption, having a dialogic-responsive function and finally, similar semantic values, all show great similarity with the characteristics of nexus focussing as described by Shisha-Halevy 1995:163–65, and with the characteristics of the same phenomenon in OB described below.

Jespersen 1933 §4.9_2 describes vocalic differences between stressed and unstressed forms of auxiliary verbs (among other items). The difference is that when the form is stressed it exhibits a full vowel as opposed to vowel reduction to [ə] when unstressed. The function of these auxiliaries, when stressed, is termed by him as *emphatic assertion*:

> There are in English two means by which the **reality** or the **strength of an assertion is emphasized**, namely, in the case of auxiliary verbs by using the stressed form with a full vowel. (Jespersen 1933 §28.1_2, my emphasis)

The second means is the verb *do*, about which he says:

> Stressed *do* or *did* ... emphasize the **speaker's belief in the reality of a fact stated**, often in contrast to the same verb used unemphatically. (MEG V §25.6_5, my emphasis)

These explanations of the mechanism are semantic, but take into consideration the element with which the stressed form is contrasted. Palmer 1965:19–27 proves the existence of an auxiliary paradigm via various structural tests, viz., negation, inversion, the ability to serve as carrier verbs (or pro-verb), and finally **emphatic affirmation**. The latter is achieved by nuclear stress on the auxiliary. Palmer claims that "this use of the auxiliaries is not easy to define formally. For every verbal form may have nuclear stress" (ibid. 25). These stressed auxiliaries "are used as emphatic affirmation **of a doubtful statement**, or as **the denial of the negative**." (ibid. 26). It is important to add that this emphatic affirmation has a negative counterpart — the emphatic negation, which is expressed by stressing the negative element, instead of the auxiliary form.

Describing English intonation has led Bolinger to explain nuclear stressing of the auxiliary. To explain the function of the mechanism he uses the term **truth value** (Dik et al. 1980 use this term as well, see above **§2.4.1.2**): "To affirm a proposition is to **focus on its truth value**" (Bolinger 1983:113, my emphasis). Bolinger has shown in his various works that any category, including any component of the verb, may be focussed (for example Bolinger 1983:99). The problem is this: Truth value is neither a category nor a component of the verb. The term is not precisely defined and it is problematic since the mechanism **has nothing to do with the truth**. For instance, modal verbs such as *must*, by virtue of being modal, have nothing to do with the truth. On the contrary — they usually qualify the utterance as non-factual, but may still be part of the nexus focussing mechanism. This point is exemplified by stressed *must* in the following example:

> **[2.26]** ..."You look better to *me* than most other women." "Oh, please stop it," said Mrs. Ralph. "You must be sick." I *must* be, Garp agrees, but he says, ... *Garp* 289–290[15]

In **[2.26]** *must* is used epistemically, denoting probability (and hence non-factuality), but is nonetheless (graphically) stressed.

The link linguists feel between the truth (value) and the mechanism under discussion probably lies with the type of adverbs which are habitually used with nexus focussing in English (such as *really*) or in other languages (French *bien* [=really] or spoken Hebrew *be'emet*). The nexus focussing mechanism is better characterized as **a contrast of polarity applied to the nexus**, or in other words, the contrast between the affirmative and the negative or even a mere implication of negative, such as doubt. This idea is demonstrated in the following example:

> **[2.27]** "... Do you know what's wrong with you? You've got a split personality, that's what's wrong with you."
>
> "Perhaps you're right, sir" Yossarian agreed diplomatically.
>
> "I know I'm right. You've got a bad persecution complex. You think people are trying to harm you."
>
> "People *are* trying to harm me." *Catch* 318

The stressed auxiliary *are* in example **[2.27]** is a contrastive response to the doubt expressed by *you think* (*people are trying to harm you*). In addition, there is a resumption of the segment *people are trying to harm you*, which is another characteristic of nexus focussing.

It should be added that the same mechanism may be used in agreement with something said before (the contrast in this case would be with external

15. The italics in the examples from the written English corpus are all in the original text.

factors or, in case of concessives, with the consequent clause):

[2.28] "... You used to say politics were stupid and they meant nothing to you. You were right. They *are* stupid, they *do* mean nothing." *Garp* 541

In **[2.28]** the contrast is not whether politics are stupid and mean nothing or not, but rather between what the speaker used to think about politics and what she thinks now. The next example is taken from a movie (the capitalized segments are used to mark sentence stress):

[2.29] "My God! I just sent you back to the future!"

"That's right, you DID send me back to the future, but I came back FROM the future." *Back to the Future* II [end]

Superficially there is perfect agreement regarding the facts, viz., Professor Brown sends Marty, with great effort, to the future, but the boy returns in a matter of seconds. Actually there is contrast between the different possible interpretations of these facts; the doubt is whether the shipment of the boy through time has been successful or not. This doubt is resolved by the consequent clause *but I came back FROM the future*.

Discussing the function of the mechanism, Bolinger 1983:99, 1986:101 recognizes verbal components and their relative independence regarding focussing. Bolinger is certainly right in noticing that the various verbal components are independent as far as focus is concerned. Yet, in order to illustrate focussing of the various components he uses a synthetic verbal form (*sélls*, *gíves*, etc.), despite the fact that such form, when stressed, may represent a few types of focus (and hence contrast) — verbal lexeme, tense, etc., in addition to nexus focussing. The next example shows a stressed synthetic verbal form; the exact verbal component which is focussed is not immediately transparent, and can only be determined by analysis:

[2.30] Does he sell it to them?

No, he *gives* it to them. *Catch* 72

gives is in contrast with *sell*, i.e., with another verbal lexeme, hence it is the latter which is focussed.

An analytic verbal construction (such as the progressive we find in example **[2.27]**) allows for a clearer analysis for the various components which are represented each by a different morpheme — the theme, represented by the pronoun, the rheme, i.e., the verbal lexeme, represented in the *-ing* form, and the predicative link — the nexus — represented by the verb *be*. The latter is marked for mood and tense, but has no further semantic value, as opposed to the other auxiliaries. When one of these morphemes is stressed, determining what kind of focus it is becomes simpler. Nevertheless, care should be taken lest the stressed auxiliary is contrasted with another auxiliary, or lest the tense it shows is contrasted with another tense. If there is no temporal or lexical contrast, or when the temporal difference may be explained (by *consecutio temporum*, or by shifts from narrative to dialogue, etc.), we are left with a contrast of two very similar segments, and thus it is nexus focussing.

The following examples show nexus focussing where the contrast is not strictly polar (affirmative vs. negative):

> [2.31] [teacher:] "... Now that we've talked things out I'm sure you'll stop writing those sordid little stories." [...]
>
> [Francie:] "don't you *ever* dare use that word about us!" [...]
>
> [teacher:] "... Sordid *is* an ugly word, and I'm glad you resented my using it." *Brooklyn* 263–64

In this conversation between the child and her teacher, the teacher uses a word which is abusive to the child. The teacher agrees, but this agreement is not neutral (like unstressed *you are right* would have been). It is rather contrasted with any possible doubt regarding its ugliness.

In example [2.32] the child from the former example, grown up now, has a conversation with her brother about their little sister:

> [2.32] "... And she'll never have the fun we had, either."
>
> "Gosh! we *did* have fun, didn't we, Neeley?" *Brooklyn* 383

The participants agree that they had fun. The doubt lies in the terrible poverty they had experienced as children.

The next example is more complex; the first stress (*she'll*) is focussing of the person marker *she* and need not concern us here:

> [2.33] "Call Mom," he heard himself say. "*She'll* cheer you up, she'll think of something."
>
> "Oh, she *is* wonderful," Roberta sobbed. "She always *does* think of something, but I feel I've used her for so much." *Garp* 307

Although the first stressed auxiliary occurs with no relevant co-text, it nevertheles has a context: The speaker refers to her guru, so there is no doubt whether she thinks that her guru is wonderful. The second stressed auxiliary does have a co-text, it is a resumption of *she'll think of something*. There is a perfect agreement. The contrast of both stressed auxiliaries is rather with what follows — *but I feel I've used her for so much.* Nexus focussing occurs here in a rhetorical concessive structure (discussed below in §2.5.2).

The analysis of the examples coming from an English corpus shows that nuclear stress of the auxiliary is generally an exponent of nexus focussing. There are two types of contrast. The first is the contrast to a doubt originating not only in the addressee, but possibly in the speaker himself, or even in the common *Weltkenntnis*. The contrast may be between the original utterance and the response to it — such as between *you* ***think*** *people are trying to harm you* and the resumptive response *people* ***are*** *trying to harm me* (example [**2.27**]). The second type is when there is no contrast between the original utterance, for instance *I just sent you back to the future* and the response *you DID send me back to the future* (example [**2.29**]) which refers back to it. The contrast is rather between the response, and what follows (in this case *but I came back FROM the future*). A question might come up, how it is possible for one and the same mechanism to be used for two extremes. These, however, are not two extremes; even when there is agreement it is not a neutral or factual agreement denoting reality. Such agreement is always in contrast with some lingering doubt, to which it is a response. This special expression of nexus focussing is common to both emphatic negation and agreement.

Nexus focussing may occur with no explicit co-text (and hence with no resumption):

> [**2.34**] "She means sex," Garp said. "This is classic. A lecture on what's universal by a woman who's never once had sexual desire. And the Pope, who takes vows of chastity, decides the issue of contraception for millions. The world *is* crazy!" *Garp* 227

The contrast is to something premeditated, or which was said before.

This short description of the nexus focussing mechanism in written English may now constitute a basis for comparison in discussing the OB mechanism.

2.4.3 Nexus focussing in OB

The first link between the asseverative paradigm and the general characteristics of nexus focussing is to be found in Edzard 1973:129–30, in a description of the function of the asseverative forms, namely, as an emphasis of an utterance (among other things) **as reaction to a doubt**. This description moves the discussion out of the semantic field into the context and the co-text. The observation of these in the proximity of asseverative forms yields results which enable a better and deeper understanding of the function of these forms.

2.4.3.1 Main characteristics

Shisha-Halevy 1995:163–65 discusses nexus focussing and states the prominent features of the phenomenon:
1. It is found in dialogue;
2. It serves as responsive; and
3. A resumption of the verbal lexeme in the previous co-text is habitual.
In the corpus of OB letters quite a few of the asseverative forms are found in an obscure context, or the context is altogether absent (it may be found in a former letter of a correspondence which we do not have, or it is broken, or it took place face to face and thus went unrecorded).

Dialogue environment: The most prominent research difficulty in the field of FSP in the corpus is that in OB letters there are very rarely any real dialogues. The nearest thing to dialogue is a report of dialogue by the speaker. Real dialogues are found only in the literary language, which constitutes a very different corpus. This makes it necessary to rely upon reports of dialogues and dialogue situations (such as court protocols). The dichotomy into dialogue and narrative is not suited to the letters. As a matter of fact, there is no strict narration (as found, e.g., in the epic literature of OB); what looks like narration is rather different from it and might be called 'report' or the like. It is different from a strict narrative in 1. the person sphere; 2. the personal involvement of the speaker; 3. the temporal sphere; and consequently 4. the tense system. In all these criteria the report is closer to the dialogue.

Responsive function: Since a letter is frequently a response to another, it is sometimes difficult to say with certainty what is and what is not a response. The feeling that asseveratives are responsive may originate in our applying linguistic feeling in other languages to OB. This function should therefore be independently verified in OB. The following example may serve to verify such responsive function (and illustrate the closest thing to a dialogic exchange by deliberately omitting the reporting parts between the quotations):

[**2.35**] (PN$_1$:) *ullânum* RN$_1$ *abīni aḫīni rabî*	(PN$_1$:) 'There is no other king but RN$_1$ our father, our big brother
18 *u ālik pānīni šarrum šanûm ul ibašši*	and our leader' ...
...	...
25 (PN$_2$:) *ukâ* RN$_1$	(PN$_2$:) 'And so[16] RN$_1$ is

16. The value of *ukâ* is still debated. ARM 26, 404, n. h claims it introduces direct speech, but it appears right after *ummāmi* which signals just that. It may as well be composed of *u+kâ* (a demonstrative element, not necessarily the one which marks the 2nd pers. as is suggested there).

26	*šar mātim elītim u* RN$_2$ *u* RN$_3$	the king of the uplands whereas RN$_2$ and RN$_3$
27	*mimma ul ṭeḫû ...*	do not even approach?' ...
28	(RN$_4$:) *ullânum*	(RN$_4$:) 'Besides
29	RN$_1$ *abīni u ālik pān šarrī*	RN$_1$ our father and the leader among the kings
30	*ša mātim annītim kalîša*	of this entire country,
	šum šarrim šanîm *kêm u kêm*	the name of another king
31	***lū epiš***	*is* mentioned[17] here and there'.
	ARM 26, 404:17–31	

The context for example [2.35] is a diplomatic meeting of a few of the kings of the region and their representatives. PN$_1$, a representative of RN$_1$, exalts his king, thereby offending the representatives of RN$_2$ and RN$_3$ who retire in anger. PN$_2$, a representative of RN$_2$, asks a question protesting this offense. By then RN$_4$ steps in and answers (literally: *kīam īpul* ibid. 28) him that the other kings do count. The lexical resumption is quite wide ranging, and the contrast is between *ullânum* RN$_1$ *abīni aḫīni rabî u ālik pānīni šarrum šanûm* ***ul ibašši*** (ibid. 17–18) and *ullânum* RN$_1$ *abīni u ālik pān šarrī ... šum šarrim šanîm kêm u kêm* ***lū epiš*** (ibid. 28–31).

The following example, although not situated in a dialogue, contains explicit indication of being a response:

[2.36]	*aššum mīnim annītum iqqabbi*	Why is this being said?
8	*wardum ša annītam iqbûkum*	The servant who told you this,
9	*ša ana šutelmun* GN$_1$ *u* GN$_2$	who seeks to turn GN$_1$ and GN$_2$
10	*isaḫḫuru annītam* *ina lā idîm ana pîm*	against each other, uttered this with no reason.
11	*umaṣṣi ilum lū īde ištu ūmim*	God *does* know, since the day
12	*ša niltamdu kīma awīlum* *ana* ^{f}DN *taklu*	we met, like a gentleman trusts ^{f}DN
13	*anāku ana kâšim* ***lū taklāku*** *u qaqqadī*	I *do* trust you and my head
14	***ina birkīka-ma lū ummud***	*does* lean only in your lap.
	Falkenstein 1963:59, IV:7–14	

In the edition the *lū* forms are rendered as any other predicative, the first (... *weiß*) and the third (... *ruht*) in the present tense and the second in the perfect (... *habe ... vertraut*). The response is contrasted with allegations ostensibly uttered in the preceding co-text (i.e., what the servant had

17. *epēšum* with the value of *to mention / say* is attested in ARM 26, 310:24 (*ana* PN *ippuš umma šū-ma*).

said).[18] This is an attempt to counterbalance these allegations. The doubt expected around nexus focussing lies here around the loyalty of the speaker. Such responsive function signifies that the form is not quite independent of its co-text, being analogous to an answer which, containing only the rheme, depends upon the question. This makes the syntactic slot of the asseverative a special one, being dependent upon another utterance.

Resumption of the verbal lexeme: The resumptive segment may be limited to the same verbal lexeme but can be stretched further to hold a part of a clause and even the whole clause. The resumption is attested both in contrast and in agreement with the co-text. Example [**2.37**] shows contrast:

> [**2.37**] *u išpur–ma* PN *ana* GN *anumma dūkāšu u kinnikêm* ***lā idūkūšu***
> But PN wrote to GN: 'Kill him now!' But they did *not* kill him here.
> ARM 26, 310:14–15

In n. d to the translation it is said that *ul* is expected instead of *lā*. This example, however, is deemed here to be a textbook example for the asseverative behavior and its typical co-text: The resumption is apparent in the verbal lexeme *dâkum* and the contrast is between the affirmative 2nd pers. directive *dūkā* (see **§4.3.1**) and the negative past asseverative *lā idūkū*. To show nexus focussing we need to have only one contrast between the two verbal forms, viz., polar contrast. The other detectable differences between the forms are not really contrasted and actually exist due to external reasons:

1. The referent of both verbal forms is the same, despite the difference in morphological person. There is hence no real contrast between the 2nd and the 3rd persons.
2. The difference in temporal point of view between the forms is accounted for by the textual presentation: The directive is in effect a quotation of an order uttered in the past, and hence there is no real temporal contrast between it and the past asseverative.

Polar contrast is thus established in this case as the only contrast.

The contrastive order affirmative → negative is not exclusive:

> [**2.38**] *mā kīma awīlum šū bēl nikurtika ana ūmi annîm lā tapaṭṭarušum ana mīnim lā taqbi ...*
> *mimma awâtim annêtim ina pīka ul ešme ina zumur–ma* RN *šalāssu* ***lū taqbi*** *umma atta–ma awīlum šâtu ina zumur* RN *šulṭam annītam–ma* ***lū taqbi*** *mimma šanêtim ina pīka ul ešme*

18. Both the end of column III and the beginning of column IV of this text are broken.

What! Why did you not tell (me) that this man is your enemy and that you could not liberate yourself from him for today? ... I did not hear any of these words from you. You *did* order to separate[19] him from RN himself.[20] So you said: 'Separate this man from RN'. You *did* order only that, I did not hear anything else from you. ARM 26, 391:28–30, 35–39

In **[2.38]** the contrast is between (*ammīnim*) *lā taqbi* in the first part and *lū taqbi* working the other way around, namely, negative → affirmative.

The following example is unique in that the resumption is cataphoric rather than anaphoric and the contrast is with something which is said only later:

[2.39] *ṣuḫāram annammiam ša maḫrīya an[āk]u šuāti–ma* ***lū ī[d]e*** *u[l]lûttini* (sic) *ul īde*
This servant here who is with me, (it is) him (that) I *do* k[no]w. I do not know those (who are) ours. 8, 109:6–8

Nexus focussing also occurs showing no polar contrast with the co-text, having the value of insistence or emphatic agreement. This phenomenon is hardly mentioned in the literature in which emphatic assertion has been described (only in connection with rhetorical concession, for which see **§2.5.2**), but it has been shown to exist in English as well (**§2.4.2.2** above). The similarity of this group of occurrences with the former group (which does exhibit polar contrast with the co-text) is still evident in the forms (the asseverative paradigm) and in the resumption of segments in the preceding co-text. Contrast, however, does exist, usually with a lingering doubt inside or outside the context:

[2.6] PN_1 *ṣuḫārī* ... PN_2 *imqut–ma ubtazziʾšu u yâšim magriātim ša ana eṣēnim lā naṭâ idbub ṣuḫārī–ma* ***lū ubtazziʾ*** *yâti ammīnim inazzaranni*
PN_1 my servant ... attacked PN_2 and hurt him but (the latter) has spoken insults which are not fit to smell *against me*. My *servant did* hurt (him), why does he hate *me*? . 2, 115:6–16

Example **[2.6]** shows resumption of the verbal lexeme *buzzuʾum*, but no polar contrast is found between the two forms. The contrast is rather to be found in the incompatibility between *ṣuḫārī–ma lū ubtazziʾ* and the clause which follows, reporting the way PN_2 mistreats the speaker. Such a set of contrasts is typical of rhetorical concessive clauses (discussed below, **§2.5.2**).

19. Translated *se détacher* in ARM 26, 391, n. h. It seems to be related to *salātum* (AHw:1014 *salātum* II 4), but it nevertheless has another vowel (a/u).

20. The syntagm *ina zumur–ma* RN is taken to have a focalizing *-ma* on an item in construct state which refers however to the entire syntagm.

It is interesting to note that example [2.6] starts with a typical reportative sequence (*imqut–ma ubtazziʾšu*, namely, *iprus–ma iptaras*) which accounts for the *iptaras* form. However, the asseverative form does not belong in this sequence and yet keeps the *iptaras* formation. It looks like formal attraction of the resumptive segment to the form in the co-text. The following example shows similar attraction:

> [2.40] *âm ... ša qāti* PN *ša tattadnā* ***lū tattadnā*** *ištu inanna ina êm ša ina qātīkunu ibaššû âm ... idnā*
> The barley ... in the charge of PN which you have (already) given, you *have* (already) given, (but) from now on give barley ... from the barley which is in your hands. 2, 47:6–15

The first occurrence (*tattadnā*) is reminiscent of the habitual use of *iptaras* in temporal adverbial clauses,[21] having the value of perfect. The asseverative form keeps to the same formation. Maloney 1981:186–88 interprets *lū tattadnā* as a precative form ("*may you have given* [*it*]"). This is proved incorrect both in view of the morphology (the form *lū iptaras* is not attested as precative in the corpus), and due to the fact that the form has the habitual co-text of asseverative forms. In AHw:559b, A7, *lū tattadnā* is translated "*mögt ihr auch gerade gegeben haben*", but clearly classified as **concessive**, which it is (see **§2.5.2**), but not of the precative type (for which see **chapter 5**).

The next example exhibits a peculiar type of agreement which might be explained as attraction:

> [2.41] *itti atta u šūt rēšika rēqū u bāʾirū ša maḫrīka* ***lū rēqū–ma***
> Since[22] you and your dependents are unemployed, then the fishermen with you are *surely* unemployed... ARM 1, 31:30–32

The anomaly lies in the agreement of the first *rēqū*; *atta u šunu* are usually expected to agree with *rēqātunu*. Such agreement (i.e., 2nd+3rd=3rd), although certainly irregular, is found in other places as well: ***atta u šībū*** *māt* GN *qaqqadātim* ***lipḫurū***–*ma* (ARM 28, 95:10–12). If this is attraction, then it is rather the first case of *rēqū* which is formed on the basis of either the second, *lū rēqū–ma*, or a former occurrence thereof, in line 26, also referring to the fishermen. All these cases of attraction testify to the tight link between the co-text and the asseverative forms, viz., that the resumption tends to be stronger than expected.

This analysis of both kinds of nexus focussing may help to clarify other, previously doubtful cases:

---

21. Compare example [6.20] in §6.2 *ištu ...* ***tessērā***.

22. *itti* serves as a conjunction.

[2.42] DN_1 *u* DN_2 *dāriš ūmī liballiṭūka* ***lū šalmāku*** *ana šulmika ašpuram*
May DN_1 and DN_2 keep you alive forever. I *am* well, I write to (inquire about) your health. 8, 24:4–7

Example [2.42] contains, according to the edition (n. b to the translation), a mistake for the more common *lū šalmāta*. However, in view of the features characteristic of the asseverative paradigm, it is possible now to explain this *lū šalmāku* as a reaction to a reference made (in a previous letter or oral conversation) regarding the speaker's health. Other occurrences of asseverative forms may be explained on the same basis of contrast to previous correspondence or even contrast to expectations:

[2.43] *alākī ana ṣē[r] bēliya qerub u aššum ūm waṣîya purussâm* ***[l]ā iqbûnim*** *[aššu]m kīam-ma purussâm š[a ū]m waṣîya [ana ṣ]ēr bēliya ul [ašpur]am*
My return to my lord is imminent, but they did [*n*]*ot* tell me the decision regarding the day of my departure. (It is) [fo]r that reason (that) I did not [write] my lord of the decision conce[rning the d]ay of my departure. ARM 26, 21:5–10

The edition treats *lā iqbûnim* as part of the *aššum* clause, but there is another possibility: Although in example [2.43] there is no resumption so to speak, the asseverative form *lā iqbûnim* is contrasted with an expectation of the speaker that he would be notified about the day of his departure.

Another case in point, in which it is necessary to decide whether *lū paris* is precative or asseverative, is the following example, identical to [5.20] in §5.3:

[2.44] *aššum* PN_1 *u mārī* PN_2... *ša apqidakkum u kanikšunu maḫar* PN_3 *tušēzibanni umma atta-ma kanikku* ***lū qurrum-ma*** *pûm lū šakin*
Concerning PN_1 and the sons of PN_2 ..., whom I entrusted to you and whose sealed document you had me draw up in front of PN_3, saying: 'The document *is* available but let an oral statement be made'. 11, 94:7–9

The presence of segmental resumption (*kanikkam šūzubum* vs. *kanikkum qurrubum*) makes it possible to state that *lū qurrub* is asseverative rather than precative, see discussion about this distinction in §§2.5.2 and 5.3.

2.4.3.2 Other signals for nexus focussing

Nexus focussing is a syntactic function which may be actualized in OB by other signals as well. One finds in this function paronomastic infinitive constructions and possibly even the form *iptaras*.

2.4.3.2.1 Paronomastic infinitive as exponent of nexus focussing

As is shown by Goldenberg 1971 :70–72, one kind of paronomastic infinitive construction (his type c) is a way to signal nexus focussing in Biblical Hebrew. The same is true for OB, in which certain paronomastic infinitive constructions of the type *parāsum(–ma) iprus* are used for nexus focussing. Whether it is indeed nexus focussing and not focussing of the verbal lexeme (**§2.4.1.4**) is subject to the same considerations which apply to any other mechanism of nexus focussing:[23]

> **[2.45]** [*ša i*]*štu ṣeḫrēku lā āmuru* [***am***]***ārum–ma ātamar***
> [That which] I have not seen [si]nce I was young I *have* seen now. 11, 34:5–6

The co-text in **[2.45]** clearly contains the same verbal lexeme (*amārum*) which is resumed, with opposite polarity, in the paronomastic construction. The following example lacks an explicit resumption:

> **[2.46]** *aššum* [*l*]*ā warādiya bēlī lib*[*bāt*]*iya imla anāku* [*an*]*a* GN *w*[*a*]*r*[*ā*]*d*[*am*] ***ṣummû uṣ***[***ammi***]
> My lord got [ang]ry with me for [n]ot coming down. As for me, I *did* want t[o go d]own [t]o GN. ARM 28, 52:4–7

Yet, the contrast is to be found between the anger directed at the speaker implying that he is to blame for not coming and his responsive claim that he, on the contrary, ***had*** wanted to go (and therefore is not to blame).

The construction is formally different from the asseverative forms although it exhibits the same typical features. One major difference is the syntactic flexibility exercised by the infinitive construction which enables it to occur in syntactic slots where the asseverative is excluded. The following example occurs inside a *šumma* conditional protasis:

> **[2.47]** *mārū* PN_1 *kīam ulammidūninni umma šunu–ma* 1 *amtum ša bītini qadum mārātiša udappir–ma ina bīt* PN_2 *ina* GN *ibašši* ... *šumma amtum šī* [*š*]*a mārī* PN_1*–ma* [***dupp***]***urum–ma udappir*** [*amtam*] *šiāti* [*qadum m*]*ārātiša* [*ana mā*]*rī* PN_1 *tēr*
> The sons of PN_1 have brought the following to my attention, saying: 'A maid of our family has escaped with her daughters and is now at the house of PN_2 in GN' ... 'If this maid, the one who [bel]ongs to the sons of PN_1 (and not to anyone else), ***has*** (indeed) escaped, return this [maid with h]er daughters [to the s]ons of PN_1'. 13, 18:4–12, 22–28

This example exhibits both segmental resumption (the maid escaping) and contrast between the paronomastic infinitive construction, which signals nexus focussing, and a preliminary doubt regarding the truth of the details brought to the attention of the sender of this letter.

23. For a fuller description, see Cohen 2004 §3.

2.4.3.2.2 The form *iptaras* as exponent of nexus focussing

Another possible exponent of nexus focussing is the form *iptaras*. It shows, under certain conditions which have not yet been clarified, a certain functional similarity to the asseverative paradigm and the paronomastic infinitive in this function. Whether it indeed signals nexus focussing is impossible to determine at this point in view of the small number of examples.

The first part of the following example contains a paronomastic infinitive construction, *šapārum–ma ul tašpuram* which resumes the directive *šupram* (this infinitive construction functions as topicalizer of the verbal lexeme, as can be inferred from the forced translation):

[2.48] *aw[āt eqli]m [gum]ur*	'Con[clude the neg]otiations over the [fie]ld,
kani[kkam] šūzim–ma	have a sealed docu[ment] drawn up
ṭ[ēm eqlim š]upram	and send me a re[port about the field]'.
[kīam] unaḫḫid–ma	[This way] I instructed (you) but
[ammīn]im ištu talliku	[ ][24] since you went
ṭēm eqlim ša awâtušunu	as to sending, you did not send me
lā gamrā ša unaḫḫid[u]ka	a report concerning the field over which
šapārum–ma	negotiations were not concluded
ul tašpuram	(about) which I instructed you.
awât eqlim ša lā gamrā	*Did* you conclude the negotiations
tagdamar	which were not concluded? *Did* you
kanikkam ***tuštēzi[b]***	have a sealed document drawn up?
šumma awât eqlim ša lā gamrā ***tagdamar***	If you *did* conclude the negotiations which were not concluded
[k]anikkam ***tuštēzib***	(and if) you *did* have a sealed
[k]anikkam šuāti	document drawn up, give this sealed
ana ṣuḫārtim	document to the maid
idim–ma	
...	...
ana ṣēriya šūbilam	and have it brought to me.
12, 18:7–26	

The second part of the letter contains *iptaras* forms. These forms do not occur in a reporting sequence, nor are they found in temporal clauses. The letter is sent from Babylon (AbB 12 ix b) and does not exhibit any of the neologisms of MB, namely, *iptaras* is not used as simple past. *iptaras* forms in this case resemble asseverative forms both syntactically and semantically; they are responsive (in depending upon the preceding context) and resumptive (*gumur* → *tagdamar*, *šūzib* → *tuštēzib*), first in a

24. An interrogative would not fit in very well, as is testified by *ul*.

nexus question and then inside a protasis, and are in contrast with a doubt concerning the execution of the instructions given, since the addressee had not returned an answer. Both these syntactic environments, viz., nexus question and conditional protasis, are slots where the asseverative never occurs, and so it makes sense for other exponents to step in.

Maloney 1982:77–90 examines the possibility whether the form *iptaras* may be considered modal and concludes that it is not. However, if *iptaras* can be shown to signal nexus focussing under certain restrictions then it should be considered, in this function, just as modal as the asseverative.

The following example similarly shows lexical resumption and polar contrast expressed by the *iptaras* form:

> **[2.49]** *[aš]šum sutī matī–ma sutū immērī ul išriqū inanna immērī* ***ištarqū***
> [As] to the Suteans, the Suteans have never stolen sheep. Now they *have* stolen sheep. M.11009+11010:4–8, MARI 6:263–64

A structure which has a few features in common with nexus focussing is the *-ma* conditional pattern. For a comparison of polar *-ma* conditionals and the asseverative paradigm see **§6.3.3**.

2.4.3.3 Multi-focality

A few instances of nexus focussing occur in juxtaposition to another focus marked by *-ma*. The examples are presented here again for reconsideration:

> **[2.6]** PN_1 *ṣuḫārī* ... PN_2 *imqut–ma ubtazzi'šu u yâšim magriātim ša ana eṣēnim lā naṭâ idbub* ***ṣuḫārī–ma lū ubtazzi'*** *yâti ammīnim inazzaranni*
> PN_1 my servant ... attacked PN_2 and hurt him but (the latter) has spoken insults which are not fit to smell *against me*. My *servant did* hurt (him), why does he hate *me*? . 2, 115:6–16

In example **[2.6]** *ṣuḫārī–ma* is in contrast with *yâti* and *yâšim*. The asseverative form, on the other hand, is in contrast with the fact that PN_2 is angry with the speaker rather than with his servant, who is to blame in the first place.

Another place where this double focus occurs is example **[2.36]**:

[2.36]	*aššum mīnim annītum iqqabbi*	Why is this being said?
8	*wardum ša annītam iqbûkum*	The servant who told you this,
9	*ša ana šutelmun* GN_1 *u* GN_2	who seeks to turn GN_1 and GN_2
10	*isaḫḫuru annītam ina lā idîm ana pîm*	against each other, uttered this with no reason.

11	*umaṣṣi ilum lū īde ištu ūmim*	God *does* know, since the day
12	*ša niltamdu kīma awīlum*	we met, like a gentleman
	ana ^{f}DN *taklu*	trusts ^{f}DN
13	*anāku ana kâšim* ***lū taklāku***	I *do* trust you
	u qaqqadī	and my head
14	***ina birkīka–ma lū ummud***	*does* lean only in your lap.

Falkenstein 1963:59, IV:7–14

Here, in [**2.36**], it seems that *ina birkīka–ma* it is rather the person marker *-ka* which is contrasted in any other person whom the speaker could trust. *lū taklāku* and *lū ummud*, on the other hand, are contrasted with any possibility that the speaker had not been loyal (as might have been suggested by the servant in the broken parts of this letter).

[**2.38**] *mā kīma awīlum šū bēl nikurtika ana ūmi annîm lā tapaṭṭarušum ana mīnim lā taqbi ...*
mimma awâtim annêtim ina pīka ul ešme ina zumur–ma RN *šalāssu* ***lū taqbi*** *umma atta–ma awīlum šâtu ina zumur* RN *šulṭam* ***annītam–ma lū taqbi*** *mimma šanêtim ina pīka ul ešme*
What! Why did you not tell (me) that this man is your enemy and that you could not liberate yourself of him for today? ... I did not hear any of these words from you. You *did* order to separate him from RN himself. So you said: 'Separate this man from RN'. You *did* order *only that*, I did not hear anything else from you. ARM 26, 391:28–30, 35–39

In example [**2.38**], whereas *lū taqbi* is contrasted with *lā taqbi*, *annītam–ma* is contrasted with *anything else* (*mimma šanêtim*).

The last example to be discussed in this respect is [**2.39**]:

[**2.39**] *ṣuḫāram annammiam ša maḫrīya an*[*āk*]*u* ***šuāti–ma lū ī***[***d***]***e*** *u*[*l*]*lûttini* (sic) *ul īde*
This servant here who is with me, (it is) *him* (that) I *do* k[no]w. I do not know those (who are) ours. 8, 109:6–8

lū īde is contrasted with *ul īde* while *šuāti–ma* is contrasted with *ullûttini*.

There is a double explanation for this phenomenon. First, these are two different types of foci, one pertaining to the nexus, the other to anything of a nominal, pronominal or adverbial nature. As different types they are contrasted with different entities in the text (as is pointed out for each of them separately). Second, these two foci differ in degree. One focus seems to be part of the clause which is included in the scope of the other.[25] That is, if we choose example [**2.39**], {*ṣuḫāram annammiam ša maḫrīya*} is topic whereas the rest, namely, {***šuāti–ma*** *lū īde*} is the new information referring to the topic. The rhematic clause is further analysable into focus {***šuāti–ma***} and topic {*lū īde*}. Even in this topic it is possible

25. This was suggested to me by G. Goldenberg.

to say that, whereas the nexus between the person marker and the verbal lexeme is in focus, (*anāku*) and *edûm* themselves constitute the topic. The following table might clarify this hierarchy graphically:

1	theme/topic	rheme		
2		focus/rheme	topic	
3			rheme	theme
4			(nexus	1cs+√ide)
	ṣuḫāram annammiam ša maḫrīya	***šuāti–ma***	*lū īde*	

Such multi-focality is found in the English corpus as well:

[2.50] "I don't have time to be a tourist at this point in my life," she told her son. "But *you* go ahead, soak up the culture. **That**'s what you *should* be doing." *Garp* 120

The rheme of the sentence {**That**'s what you *should* be doing} is *that*. The rest, {what you *should* be doing}, is a thematic clause, or topic, inside of which the focus lies on the nexus between the person marker *you* and the verbal lexeme in the directive *soak up* now represented by the syntagm *should be doing*. This focus is in contrast with the fact that the mother does not intend to be a tourist.

2.5 Values of the asseverative in view of nexus focussing

It is noted above (**§2.4.3.1**) that the asseverative may be in polar contrast with the co-textual segment it resumes or it could be in agreement with it. In the latter case the contrast would be with either some lingering doubt or some kind of contradiction which is found elswhere in the text or even outside it. This partition is useful in describing the link between nexus focussing and oath or concessives. Oath has to do with polar contrast with a lingering doubt, which lies, however, **outside the text**, while in agreement with the co-text. Concession, on the other hand, while similarly agreeing with the co-textual segment, is **contrasted with what follows,** which serves as a consequent clause.

2.5.1 Oath

Oath is not a linguistic term. Many languages do have special formulas to express oath, but the different formulas are mostly culture-dependent rather than language-dependent. English has quite a few oath formulas (*by X* for instance). Apart from these lexical formulas one finds the mechanism for nexus focussing expressing oath as well:

> [2.51] "... God is my witness; I'll NEVER be hungry again!" D. Selznick, *Gone with the Wind* 1939

In this famous scene, Scarlet O'Hara, standing on a hill, takes a vow. English nexus focussing in the negative is expressed by stressing the negative element, exactly as happens here with *never*. Example [2.52] is taken from real life. Here, again, it is the negative element which is stressed:

> [2.52] "I did NOT have have a sexual relationship with this woman, Monica Lewinsky." President Bill Clinton, televised public address concerning his conduct in the Lewinsky affair

Even if not strictly an oath, it is still very close to it. The situation is very similar to the one in court, where the defendant (as well as some of the witnesses) reacts to a lingering doubt on the part of the court or the jury.

The asseverative has been defined as a paradigm and shown to be an exponent of nexus focussing in OB. The present section is intended to establish the connection between nexus focussing and the oath in OB.

There are traditionally a few differences between the asseverative and the oath, namely, that in oath any verbal form may occur while in the asseverative there are mainly *iprus* forms (GAG §81f). This is quite true in OB: There are only a few asseverative examples which are not explicitly marked as oath and contain *lū iparras* forms. It can be shown, however, that asseverative forms still keep their typical characteristics in oaths as well.

The most important point is that the issue about which one takes an oath is a given, and does not constitute the new or contrastive information at the time of the oath. What is new is the oath itself, and in syntactic terms it equals nexus focussing in OB:

> [2.53] *šumma awīlum eli awīlim mimma lā īšū–ma amat awīlim ittepe bēl amtim nīš ilim i*[*zakka*]*r mimma elīya* ***lā tīšû*** *kaspam mala šīm amtim išaqqal*
> If a man is not owed anything by a(nother) man but (nevertheless) distrains his maid, the owner of the maid [will swe]ar by the life of god 'I do *not* owe you anything', he (=the distrainer) will pay silver according to the price of the maid. LE A ii:15–18

This oath has both the characteristic co-text and resumption thereof: A case is introduced in the protasis, the essence of which (*eli awīlim mimma lā īšu*) is resumed in the oath (*mimma elīya lā tīšû*). The difference of person is due to a shift into direct speech. It is important to note (resuming what is stated in §2.5) that the contrast is not with the co-text, but rather with a lingering doubt outside the text, that is, with any doubt that the owner of the maid might owe the other man after all.

The following oath is similar in its typical asseverative characteristics:

[2.54] *ālum šū ālī ina emūqim iṣbatūšu ...*
[šu]mma ālum šū ālka awīlān sinništān ... [kê]m liqbû ummāmi ālum šū ***lū ālī*** *...*
'This city is my city, they took it by force...'
[I]f this city is your city let two men (and) two women ... say [as fo]llows: 'This city *is* my city ...'. ARM 28, 95:5–6, 22–24

In example [2.54] the co-text is the complaint of a person recounting that his city has been taken by force. The rest is a sentence given by the king, in which the essence of the complaint is restated in the protasis. The oath is then about an issue which is already discussed and hence known. Again, what is new about the oath is nexus focussing itself, as against any possible doubt.

A third example exhibits a different co-text:

[2.55] *apputum karâm lā tepette tamūat ana īkim lā teggi* (*te*-NAM) *tamût*[26] *lamassam ša* PN *atma īkam šuāti ē tudannin [b]īt abīka [k]alâšu* ***lū ušmāt***
It is urgent. Do not open the silo (or else) you will die; do not be negligent regarding the ditch (or else) you will die. I swear by the protective spirit of PN, should you not strengthen this ditch I *will* put to death your entire father's family. 12, 169:15–26

In example [2.55] the threats made first contain the same verbal root as does the following oath (the different verbal lexeme [*mâtum* : *šumuttum*] is secondary and is the result of the shift in person — the agent kills, the recipient dies). The issue of what should be done regarding the ditch repeats as well (once in the first set of threats and a second time in the protasis *īkam šuāti ē tudannin*) but not within the oath itself. The addressee's possible death is no longer new information by the time of the oath — it is rather the nexus, being in contrast with any thought the addressee might have about not performing the task and staying alive.

The following example exhibits *-u* variants of the asseverative which seem to function exactly like *lū* forms:

[2.56] *[t]uša–ma werûm ša tušabbalam [an]a akāliya* ***[nit]ma*** *eḫzam u marram [an]a mānaḫāti* ***nišakkanu–ma*** *âm* ***nušelliam–ma*** *mimma ša elīni tīšû* ***[n]ippaluka***

---

26. The forms written *ta-mu-at* and *ta-mu-ut* are inconsistent. In view of the archaic script it would be better (contrary to what is suggested in the edition, n. e to the text) to consider the first (*ta-mu-at*) as normal (with no contraction: *tamuwat* <**tamawwat*) and the second (*ta-mu-ut*) as deviating from the norm.

> (You act) [a]s if the copper which you are to send me is [fo]r my own consumption. [We (hereby) s]wear: 'we *will* provide (copper) hatchets and (copper) hoes [a]s work equipment and we *will* produce barley and [we] *will* pay you what we owe you'. 9, 39:15–21

The speaker had asked for copper and despite numerous promises he never received it. The *tuša* clause is his conjecture as to why. The asseverative forms, although not having the habitual co-text which they resume, are still responsive to the *tuša* clause and are contrasted with the possibility that the copper is intended for personal use.

In those cases of oath where the co-textual features and resumption characteristic of nexus focussing are not found, it is possible to infer their existence **outside the text**. Neither in legal documents nor in letters does one find all the relevant details. The issue is not always presented before the oath is made, for it may be found in former correspondence or stated in conversation which had not been documented. Yet, the oath is not taken in a vacuum. It may be required in formal situations such as court or in other similar situations where the speaker is in a defensive position because what he says is doubted or questioned. In court one takes an oath exactly because his testimony is doubted:

> [2.1] *ina kaspim u kīsim ša tappîm eqlam bītam amtam wardam abī* ***lā išāmu*** *ina ša ramānišu–ma* ***lū išām***
> My father did *not* buy a field, a house, a maid (or) a servant from the partner's silver or (his) purse. He *did* buy only from his own (property). VAB 5, 287:18–22

The issue in doubt is the source of wealth which the accused had used. The witness is responding to this doubt, residing outside the text, by asseverative forms. These asseverative forms, despite a few differences in detail, signal nexus focussing.

2.5.2 Concession

In the cross-linguistic or typological treatment of concessives, as is found in König 1988:152–56, there are several basic types of concessives. They are arranged according to the value of the morphological constituents of the concessive marker:

1. Obstinacy, spite, contempt: *despite, malgré, trotzdem*, etc.
2. Free choice quantification: *albeit, however, allerdings, tout ... que*, etc.
3. Conditional or temporal and/or an additive or emphatic focus particle: *even if, obwohl, wenn auch, etsi, quand même, même si, u šumma*, etc.
4. Emphatic assertion of truth: *true, zwar, certes*, etc.
5. Co-occurrence or co-existence: *nevertheless, still, yet, cependant*, etc.

The fourth type is the one which is relevant here. It is said (ibid. 154) that concessive relations are expressed in many languages by **emphatically asserting the truth** of the clause in question. As is mentioned above (§2.4.2.2), emphatic assertion is the term used in referring to the semantic signifié of nexus focussing exponents. Here, however, the exponent in question, rather than the stressed auxiliary, is mainly stressed adverbials such as *true*, *indeed*, *really*, *zwar*, etc. in more than a few languages.[27]

In a later work (König 1994:681), this kind of concessive is termed **rhetorical concessive**. It is characterized not only by a contrastive relationship between two clauses (as concessives are habitually defined) but also as part of the rhetoric of an argument, where the concessive clause is resumptive.

The link between such concessives and nexus focussing is implied in the following paragraph:

> There is no point in emphasizing the truth of an 'antecedent' proposition unless this truth or the significance of this proposition as an argument is called into question. An emphatic assertion of the truth of some proposition 'p' may be called for because of a principled dissonance between 'p' and a following 'q'. (König 1988:162)

This general statement about concessives is very similar to what is said above (§2.5) about nexus focussing expressing concession: It agrees with the co-textual segment while in contrast with the consequent clause following it.

An explanation for this general notion is found in Di Meola 1997:14–16; under the title *Einräumung* (admitting to, accepting), he discusses a discourse strategy composed of accepting an argument of the opponent without drawing the expected conclusions therefrom. This acceptance of the opponent's argument makes it irrelevant, for other conclusions are drawn instead. That is, this concession (literally, which explains the use of the term concession), is contrasted not with the argument it resumes but rather with the conclusions following it, with which there exists some incompatibility. The following is an example for such concession in English:

> [2.57] "Hey, you men leave Captain Havermeyer alone," Colonel Cathcart would order. "He's the best damned bombardier we've got". [...] Havermeyer *was* the best damned bombardier they had, **but** he flew straight and level all the way from the I.P. to the target, and even far beyond the target, until he saw the falling bombs strike ground and explode... *Catch* 36.

He's the best damned bombardier we've got is the original argument made by the colonel. It is resumed (and agreed upon) by the narrator:

27. The relationship of such epistemic adverb(ial)s to nexus focussing is discussed further below, in §2.6.

Havermeyer wás the best damned bombardier they had. The differences of tense and person are due to the different perspectives: First a quotation of what the colonel had said and then a comment about *what* he had said by the narrator. Nexus focussing (*wás*) is there to show the incompatibility (or contrast) between Havermeyer's being the best bombardier (as far as the army was concerned) and what is actually meant by describing the extent of his dedication — that he endangers the lives of his crew members who would rather return alive from the mission.

Morel 1996 describes three types of concessions in French: logical, corrective, and argumentative. Only the last has to do with the type discussed here, viz., a construction of two coordinated clauses, having a fixed order, marked (in French) by epistemic adverb(ial)s:

> [**2.58**] Elle a **bien** ces yeux extraordinaires dont tu me parlais, **mais** enfin je ne la trouve pas tellement inouïe...
> She *does* have these wonderful eyes you told me about, but I do not find her that sensational after all... Morel 1996:23

One finds certain hints for this type of concession in the syntagms used for expressing concessives. The French conjunction *bienque* testifies to the basic value of *bien,* namely, when it has the value of *indeed* or *certainly.* As such it asserts the cogency of the proposition as being in doubt ("La valeur fondamentale de *bien* est de marquer que la validité d'un jugement a fait l'objet d'un questionnement dubitatif", Morel 1996:23). The Italian *sì che,* which signals nexus focussing as well, is mentioned in Di Meola 1997:259 as expressing concession as well (but no examples are adduced for such concessives).

In OB this type of concession (rhetorical or argumentative) is expressed by the asseverative paradigm. Most of the following examples have already been adduced, but not discussed for concessivity. The two following examples are classified under AHw:559b 7b as concessive occurrences:

> [**2.6**] PN_1 *ṣuḫārī* ... PN_2 *imqut–ma ubtazziʾšu u yâšim magriātim ša ana eṣēnim lā naṭâ idbub ṣuḫārī–ma* ***lū ubtazziʾ*** *yâti ammīnim inazzaranni*
> PN_1 my servant ... attacked PN_2 and hurt him but (the latter) has spoken insults which are not fit to smell *against me*. My *servant did* hurt (him), why does he hate *me*? 2, 115:6–16

Under AHw:559b 7b it is not mentioned whether the concessivity meant is precative- or asseverative-related (in GAG §158c both types are deemed to be in some kind of complementary distribution — but it is not enough to say whether they are the same linguistic entity or not). Here these examples follow the formulation of the asseverative paradigm, which is markedly different from the concessive-conditional precative (**chapter 5**).

This example, despite the difficulty of rendering the asseverative form as a concessive clause, still reflects the general criteria of such construction: 1. A resumption (*ṣuḫārī ubtazziʾšu ... ṣuḫārī–ma lū ubtazziʾ*); 2. Polar agreement; and 3. Contrast, or incompatibility, with the following segment, in this case with *inazzaranni*.

The following example likewise exhibits these criteria:

> [**2.40**] *âm ... ša qāti* PN *ša tattadnā* ***lū tattadnā*** *ištu inanna ina êm ša ina qātīkunu ibaššû âm ... idnā*
> The barley ... in the charge of PN which you have (already) given, you *have* (already) given, (but) from now on give barley ... from the barley which is in your hands. 2, 47:6–15

It should be admitted that the nature of incompatibility here between the concessive clause and its consequent is of a more general nature — since the contrast *lū tattadnā* vs. *idnā* is not enough to maintain concession. It seems plausible that the circumstantial elements (*ša qāti* **PN** vs. *ša ina qātī**kunu***) are the ones which are indicative of the incompatibility between the two clauses. Example [**2.59**] shows no resumption of the verbal lexeme:

> [**2.59**] *aššum 1/3 manā* 6 *šiqil kaspim ša aḫātī išpuram 1/3 manā kaspam–ma* ***lū tušābilam*** 6 *šiqil kaspum ul iba<šši>*
> As to 1/3 mina and 6 sheqels (of) silver (about) which my sister wrote me: 'you *did* deliver to me a *1/3 mina of silver*, (but) the 6 sheqels of silver are not ava<ilable>'... 6, 1:13–16

The resumption is partially that of the topic, viz., the amount of money about which the sister had written. This segment is repeated (26 sheqels, of which only 20 [=1/3 mina] have been received [in the concessive clause] while the rest, 6 sheqels, are missing [in the consequent clause]). The nexus regarding the shipment of the money, however, is not mentioned prior to the asseverative form, and can only be inferred.

It seems that the asseverative is indifferent to modal congruence (**§4.4.4**); this is apparent in the following example:

> [**2.44**] *aššum* PN_1 *u mārī* PN_2 ... *ša apqidakkum u kanikšunu maḫar* PN_3 *tušēzibanni umma atta–ma kanikku* ***lū qurrum–ma*** *pûm lū šakin*
> Concerning PN_1 and the sons of PN_2 ..., whom I entrusted to you and whose sealed document you had me draw up in front of PN_3, saying: 'The document *is* available but let an oral statement be made'. 11, 94:7–9

In the edition (ibid. 9) *lū qurrub* is rendered *even if ... is available*, which, in the present framework, tends to be more closely associated with the concessive-conditional precative (**chapter 5**) rather than with the asseverative. This, however, is an asseverative, since there is a conceptual resumption between drawing up a document (*kanikšunu tušēzibanni*) and its being present (*lū qurrub*). It is concessive as well because of the contrast with what follows, namely, *pûm lū šakin*.

The following pair of examples, while not exhibiting resumption, still show contrast with what follows:

> [2.12] ***lū ša ištu ṣeḫḫerēnu-ma ištēniš nirbû*** *ištu ilam taršî matīma ... šumī ul taḫsusī*
> (It) *is* (true) that we grew up together practically since we were very young, (but) since you have become lucky you never mentioned my name... 9, 15:7–11

The translation here differs from the one offered above (§2.3.3) for the same example. The former translation reflects, by and large, the traditional view. The present translation is meant to reflect the cumulative information about the asseverative paradigm at this point. This example is unique in exhibiting *lū* joined by a complex abstract *ša* clause (the fact that ...). Although there is no resumption, the acquaintance of the speaker and the addressee is a fact well known to both. The resumptive parts in nexus focussing are never new information. The incompatibility lies between the speaker and the addressee's childhood acquaintance and her having ignored him for some time. It should be noted that both examples [2.12] and [2.59] contain another focus, marked by *-ma*, similar to what is discussed above in §2.4.3.3.

Nexus focussing (here as concessive) is signaled in [2.4] by *nisniqu*, a by-form in the paradigm:

> [2.4] *aššum ṣuḫāriya šuāti u* PN_1 *museppīšu ana* GN_1 *šūrîm a[šp]ur-ma* PN_2 2 *rēdî* ***iddinam***-*m[a an]a* GN_2 ***nisniqu***-*[ma] ana bīt* PN_1 *muse[ppi] ṣuḫāriya awīlū* GN_2 ... *ana er[ēb]im ul iddinūninni*
> As to this servant of mine and PN_1 who abducted him, I w[ro]te to have (them) brought to GN_1 an[d] PN_2 *did* give (or: gave) me two soldiers and we *did* arrive [a]t GN_2, [but] the inhabitants of GN_2 ... did not let me e[nt]er the house of PN_2 who abd[uct]ed my servant. 6, 181:8'–13'

The incompatibility of *nisniqu* is with what follows, namely, *ana erēbim ul iddinūninni*. A further corroboration of the indifference of the asseverative to modal congruence is that it is found here inside a reporting *-ma* sequence (the latter co-occurs with the *lū* variants of the asseverative just as well).

Example [2.60] contains asseverative forms which are quoted as examples of concessives in AHw:559b A 7a, in CAD L 225b and also in Huehnergard 1983:572:

[2.60] *kirissum kussûm šeberum*	A hairpin, a broken saddle,
šēp imēr[i]m la[p]t[um]	an injured foot of a donkey
u ḫaṭītum ul ibši	but there was no damage.
magana ayyum–ma	Please! Anyone
ša annītam iqbû–ma	who said this and
libbam ušamriṣu	caused anger,
kussûšu ***lū iḫḫaser***	his saddle (after all) *did* break,
šēp imērišu ***lū illapit***	the foot of his donkey *was* injured,
ḫaṭītam[28] *šâti ša [i]bbašû*	should (**therefore**) report
ana pānim liqbi	the damage which occurred.
Falkenstein 1963:58, III:11–15	

In the edition, as already mentioned above (example [**2.36**]), the forms with *lū* are rendered as if the morpheme *lū* were absent. The resumption is approximate, the verbal lexemes *šebērum* and *ḫasārum* are synonymous in this context. However, the asseverative forms do not contrast, in view of the preceding co-text, with the following co-text; namely, there is no incompatibility between the saddle breaking and reporting it. The contrast is rather between the first occurrence where these mishaps are dismissed as unimportant (*u ḫaṭītum* ***ul ibši***) and the second, i.e., considering them as absolutely important (*ḫaṭītam šâti* ***ša ibbašû***) and hence one must report them. This occurrence of the asseverative, upon analysis in view of the context, is therefore not a clear-cut example for concessive.

That concession is here performed rather by nexus focussing (i.e., not only by the asseverative paradigm) is shown by the following paronomastic infinitive construction which has a concessive meaning as well:

> [**2.61**] *[ašš]um siliḫti[k]a ša libbaka [imr]aṣu–ma ta[špu]ram adi ṭēm si[l]iḫtika* PN *ištu* GN *išpuram anāk[u* ***id]ûm īdē***[29]*–ma [an]a šu[lm]ik[a] u[l] ašapparam [kīm]a* PN *[išp]ura[m]* ... *[ana šul]mika aštapram*
>
> [As t]o yo[ur] sickness (about) which you be[came] annoyed and w[rot]e me, until PN had written me (about) the matter of your sic[k]ness from GN — (you thought) I [*d*]*id* know but have not been writing to (inquire about) you[r he]alth? — [As so]on as PN wr[ote m]e, I have written [to] (inquire about) your [he]alth. 3, 27:5–12

The infinitive construction tells us that the issue is about whether or not the writer knew of the illness of the addressee. The logical incompatibility (and hence contrast) lies with the consequent clause (in this case *not writing to* [*inquire about*] *the addressee's health*).

---

28. The edition has *ḫa-ṭi-i-**tum*** (ibid. 15) but both the form *šâti* and the syntactic context prove it to be the object.

29. The plene writing signals a question in this case.

The asseverative paradigm, as nexus focussing exponent, serves to express rhetorical concession. The contrast is with the following co-text which shows some incompatibility with the asseverative form (as is typical of any concessive construction). The main difference between such rhetorical concessions and other types thereof is some kind of a segmental resumption, which is a basic feature of asseverative syntactic behavior.

2.6 Nexus focussing and modality

The asseverative paradigm, as the principal mechanism for nexus focussing in OB, is modal. This is discussed, from a purely semantic point of view, under **§2.0.1**. In this section, this modality is to be reconsidered in view of the syntactic function this paradigm signals. This syntactic function, in addition, plays a role in discourse, or rather in text linguistics — for example in responding to another utterance, or in resuming the previous co-text, thereby serving as a cohesion marker between two different parts of the text (which may be separate, yet related). The relevant issues here are whether the paradigm should be considered modal or discoursive and whether such an exponent can belong at the same time to both discourse level and modality.

It seems that the means to signal what is called in the English linguistic literature *emphatic assertion* or *counterpresuppositional assertion* have a role in discourse (for example Palmer 1986:91 [generally], Joly and O'Kelly 1987 [regarding *do*]). The modality inherent in these means is hardly ever mentioned. Joly and O'Kelly 1987 do recognize it, stating that

> Les phrases affirmatives hyperthétiques sont fortement modalisées, l'auxiliaire *do* étant porteur de la subjectivité du loc[utaire].
> (The super-assertive affirmative clauses are highly modalized, the auxiliary *do* bearing the subjectivity of the speaker.) (ibid. 98)

Palmer, discussing modality on a cross-linguistic scale, leaves the modality of these means open:

> Emphatic affirmation may be treated either as a matter of discourse or as a kind of 'strong' epistemic modality expressing complete confidence in, or knowledge of, what is being said. (Palmer 1986:92)

Palmer, it seems, does not argue with the modal value of these mechanisms. The issue he raises has to do with their classification. The answer, according to him, lies in the systems present in each language — depending upon how precise a discourse system in a language is. OB does not possess a special system of paradigms to express discourse functions while it does have an extensive system of paradigms (as well as other means) for the expression of modality.

Another point, not touched upon here until now from the OB perspective, is the use of epistemic modality markers (*really, surely, well, certainement, bien*, etc.) in nexus focussing devices. Such markers, which express subjective opinion, knowledge or belief, are used in nexus focussing as well, although with some syntactic modification, being marked as focus either syntactically or via intonation. This may be shown in spoken contemporary Hebrew:

(1) hu bétax ba	'he must have come'	(lit. 'he surely came')
(2) BÉTAX še hu ba	'SURE he came'	(lit. 'surely that he came')

(1) contains an epistemic expression pertaining to the probability of the event. In (2), on the other hand, the same adverb is both heavily stressed and set in a special cleft-like structure. As such, the structure is a responsive pattern (whereas (1) is not). As nexus focussing device it has (in this case) a polar contrast which lies in the preceding co-text.

The reason this issue has not been discussed regarding OB is that such examples, viz., with epistemic adverbs marked as focus (*kiša–ma*?) are not found with sufficient contextual information to be analysed as nexus focussing devices as well.

Tobler 1902 refers to a similar structure in the Romance languages containing such epistemic adverbs (of asseveration, oath, conjecture, affirmation, and negation) followed by a substantive *que* clause:

> Man sieht dass hier, an Stelle eines förmlichen Hauptsatzes ein adverbialer Ausdruck steht, der sonst zum Zwecke der Beteuerung oder der Beschwörung oder auch der Erinnerung daran, dass die Aussage nur den Anspruch **subjektiver Wahrhaftigkeit**, nicht den objektiver Wahrheit erhebe, ein Verbum des Sagens begleitet.
> (One sees that here, instead of a formal main clause, there is an adverbial expression, which usually accompanies a *verbum dicendi* for the purpose of affirmation or an oath or even suggesting that the statement lays claim **only to the subjective truth**, not to the objective truth.) (Tobler 1902:58, my emphasis)

The function of these constructions, as Tobler points out, is to express some **subjective truth** rather than the objective truth. In other words, such expressions are modal, for they have to do with non-factuality.

Such clauses constitute real non-verbal clauses when they occur as main clauses. Although the structure points to a cleft-like structure where the adverb is the rheme, the whole pattern is actually an exponent of nexus focussing (much like the spoken contemporary Hebrew structure):

[**2.62**] Io non intendo di cimentarvi. —*sì* che lo intendete!
I do not intend to test you. — You *do* intend it (/yes you *do*). Tobler 1902:60

The Italian example has all the features discussed above for nexus focussing, that is, polar contrast and resumption of the verbal lexeme (see Shisha Halevy 1995:165). In French one finds similar constructions (*oui que, certainment que,* etc. Grevisse 1980 §§271 and 2594). Damourette and Pichon 1911–52 Vol. 6, §2179 describe the modal adverb *certes.* They do not adduce examples structured with *que,* but nevertheless the epistemic adverb seems to work somewhat differently than usual (when marking the degree of certainty towards the clause) in that it is clearly **contrasted**, in addition, to the preceding or following co-text.

This brings us to the last point, that the type of modality inherent to nexus focussing is different from epistemic modality — for these two types of modality may co-occur (e.g., in a conditional protasis, **§2.4.3.2** example[**2.47**]). It may co-occur with deontic modality (in English,[30] **§2.4.3.3** example [**2.50**]). In all its occurrences, with whatever additional modality, its value is similar in setting contrast against some doubt. It never denotes factuality, as does the indicative. Nexus focussing marks the propositional content as initially in doubt, never actually changing the level of non-factuality inherent to doubt.

2.7 Conclusions

The asseverative paradigm, described in this chapter, is the most complicated paradigm of the OB modal system. The various precative paradigms (**chapters 4** and **5**) or the conditional paradigm (**chapter 6**), or even the modal infinitive syntagm (**chapter 7**) are all immediately recognizable as modal, all have at least some literature (specific and general) concerning them, and they all seem easier to interpret syntactically. In the domain of the asseverative paradigm, much of the descriptive work had to be started from nearly nothing. Several secondary topics had to be researched and described first in order to secure a basic understanding of the main issue. The difficulties lie both in the syntactic explanation of the mechanism underlying the asseverative paradigm, through portraying the peculiar syntactic behavior of the paradigm, linking the special characteristics of this behavior with the various semantic uses exhibited by this paradigm and finally, relating it to modality despite the fact that this is hardly ever done in the general literature. To overcome these problems a few special

30. The asseverative and the precative are mutually exclusive, for they use the same basic elements (*lū, lā,* etc.). However, a nexus focussing paronomastic infinitive construction with a directive is not unthinkable.

measures were taken: 1. Collecting examples of asseverative forms from a few kinds of texts besides letters (legal documents and a law code); 2. Extensive use of linguistic literature regarding other languages; and above all 3. Supplying a corpus-based mini-description of the syntactic mechanism of nexus focussing in English, in order to provide some basis for comparison with the OB data.

3

lū Forms in Royal Inscriptions

This short chapter is intended to be an excursus to the foregoing **chapter 2**, which contains a description of the **asseverative paradigm**. The aim is to show, based upon methodological principles, that those *lū* forms ubiquitous in royal inscriptions actually do not belong in the asseverative paradigm, despite their morphological identity with asseverative forms.

In quite a few studies describing the asseverative forms (see **§2.1** above) it is mentioned that numerous examples of *lū* forms are to be found in the corpus of royal inscriptions. The attempt to incorporate these forms within an explanation devised for the asseverative forms (e.g., Edzard 1973:29) is not convincing. Moreover, in translations of the various royal inscriptions those forms are *not* translated as one would translate asseverative forms (for instance, Huehnergard 1998:98). It is quite obvious that even semantically the inclusion of these *lū* forms in the asseverative group does not work. The very ubiquity of the forms in royal inscriptions raises questions as to their emphatic notion — for once an emphatic form is used incessantly it stops denoting emphasis.

The reasons enumerated against the inclusion of these royal-inscription *lū* forms in the asseverative paradigm are of a semantic and impressionistic order. There are, however, also formal reasons against such inclusion.

3.1 The syntactic behavior of *lū* forms in royal inscriptions

Royal inscriptions are not included in our corpus (OB letters), and for good reason — their language is substantially different from all other corpora used so far to describe the asseverative paradigm. Hence it would make sense to describe these *lū* forms independently of anything that is already known regarding these forms. First, there are three ways for a king to report his own deeds in a royal inscription:

a. 1cs. *lū aprus*
b. 1cs. *aprus*
c. 3cs. *iprus*

Most inscriptions exhibit uniform use of only one of the above possibilities. This alternation of the verbal forms between inscriptions suggests, to begin with, that the difference between the *lū* forms and the other forms is **less critical** than it would be between an asseverative form and an indicative form in other corpora. Had this been the situation throughout the royal inscriptions, it would have been nearly impossible to contrast *lū* forms with the other forms.

There are exceptions, however. In the few inscriptions which contain more than one of the above mentioned possible forms, it is possible to isolate eight occurrences of sequences composed of *iprus* forms followed by one or more *lū* forms. There are no constraints on the subject of each clause:

[3.1] DN ... *iddinam* ... ***lū*** *uwa*ʾʾ*eranni*[1] RIME 4, 381:16–24 [Samsu-iluna E.4.3.7.5]

[3.2] ... *albin* ... *ēpuš*... *ulli*... *ukīn*... ***lū*** *uṣīr* RIME 4, 382:55–61 [Samsu-iluna E.4.3.7.5] (followed by a series of *lū* forms).

[3.3] *tāḫāzam ēpuš–**ma*** ... *māḫirī* ... ***lū*** *itūr ummānī ana šalāš meattim* ***lū*** *itūr* RIME 4, 654–55:12–22 [Ašdūni-yarīm E.4.8.1.1] (=RIME 4, 656:10–20 [Ašdūni-yarīm E.4.8.1.2]) (containing different subjects).

[3.4] ... *elqē–**ma** ana ḫarrān alli[k–**ma**] mātam nakirtam **lū** ukanniš* RIME 4, 656:29–36 [Ašdūni-Yarīm E.4.8.1.2] (followed by a series of *lū* forms).

[3.5] *alwīšu–**ma** šumam* ... ***lū*** *aškun* RIME 4, 671–72:12–21 [Takil-ilissu E.4.11.2.1]

[3.6] *aḫīṭ uddi[š–**ma**]* ... ***aštakkanšum–ma (lā ušparku)*** ***lū*** *ušaškinšum* RIME 4, 673:10–23 [Takil-ilissu E.4.11.2.2]

[3.7] ... *ēpuš–**ma*** ... ***lū*** *ušēšibšunūti* RIME 4, 673:36–47 [Takil-ilissu E.4.11.2.2]

[3.8] *bābam aḫīṭ* ... *uštassiq–**ma lū*** *armi* RIME 4, 673–74:48–57 [Takil-ilissu E.4.11.2.2]

The same sequence is found in OA royal inscriptions as well (Šamši-adad):

[3.9] *ērub* ... *aššiq–**ma*** ... *utaqqin aštakkam–**ma lū*** *aqqi* RIMA 1, 64 col. II':1–11 [Šamši-adad AO.39.1001]

[3.10] *aḫḫabit–**ma*** ... *amḫaṣ–**ma*** *uṣabbit–**ma*** ... ***lū*** *aštakkan* RIMA 1, 64-65 col. III':1–13 [Šamši-adad AO.39.1001]

1. No attempt is made to translate these sequences, mainly because the corpus is radically different from the other corpora used here.

These *iprus* series and the *lū* forms that conclude them are reminiscent of the most prominent function of the **perfect** elsewhere — to end a series of *iprus* forms, representing the culmination of the actions reported and sustaining current relevance.[2] A few characteristics of the OB royal inscriptions corroborate this idea:

1. There are generally **no *iptaras* forms** at the end of preterite sequences, in contrast with other genres (letters, laws).

2. In the royal inscriptions, connection via ***-ma*** is sporadic, **except in the above series**, where it is more regularized.

3. No *lū* forms are followed by ***-ma*** (except one: RIME 4, 348:22 [Ḫammurabi E.4.3.6.12] *lū aḫream–**ma***), a feature befitting a form which tends to end a series.

4. There are practically no **negative** forms for *lū* forms in royal inscriptions (except for one: RIME 4, 673:22 [Takil-ilissu E.4.11.2.2] *lā ušparku*). Perfect forms lack a symmetrical negative form as well (the usual negative form of the perfect is *ul iprus*).[3]

3.2 *lū* forms in royal inscriptions compared with asseverative forms

Those *lū* forms found in royal inscriptions, although traditionally treated under the same heading as the asseverative forms in other genres,[4] are different from the latter in other respects as well. In fact, *lū* forms in the royal inscriptions are identical **in form only** to the asseverative forms elsewhere (letters, legal documents). This can be deduced methodically by comparing the form inventory.

As far as the form inventory is concerned, the asseverative paradigm (see §§**2.2.1** and **2.2.2**) shows, for example, negative forms, a diversity of tempora, etc., whereas the *lū* forms here show a very limited inventory (*lū aprus* / *iprus*) and do **not** have negative counterparts.

Syntactically speaking, asseverative forms are rare and appear in a well-defined environment, many times exhibiting a resumption of the preceding co-textual segment and showing contrast to some hanging doubt. *lū* forms in the royal inscriptions do not show any of these features typical of asseveratives.

---

2. Huehnergard 1997 §17.2, Maloney 1981:92.

3. Goetze 1936:313; this can be deduced from Leong 1994:168, n. 24 as well.

4. Edzard 1973:29–30; GAG §81f; AHw. 559b; Huehnergard 1997 §29.3.

3.3 Conclusions

To conclude, despite the morphological identity with asseverative forms, *lū* forms in royal inscriptions should be classified apart from the former group.

The observations made above regarding *lū* forms in the OB royal inscriptions point out that they behave more like **perfect** forms elsewhere rather than like the asseverative forms. On the other hand, there are in the corpus *iptaras* forms which seem to function much like asseverative forms (see **§2.4.3.2** above).

This resemblance of *lū* forms in royal inscriptions to the reportative or narrative form is evident semantically as well, reflected in the translation of the former — usually by a narrative tense in various European languages (e.g., the *passé simple*), rather than other devices such as asseverative adverbs (surely, certainement, gewiß, etc.) which denote asseveration.

4

The Precative Paradigms

4.0 Introduction and literature review

The precative paradigms include any form or syntagm which has a certain modal value and is in paradigmatic relationship with the precative forms in any environment in which they may occur (in accordance with the linguistic principles discussed in the general introduction, §**1.1**). Forms and syntagms which are related in other ways are accounted for as well, for example, in such environments where modality is neutralized precisely because precative forms are excluded. Such modally neutralized environments may constitute a related set of paradigms which cannot be referred to as indicative, for they are neither indicative nor modal. At the end of the chapter (§**4.5**) some space is devoted to infinitive constructions which, although not in the same paradigm with the precative (but actually belonging with modally neutralized syntagms), certainly exhibit a conditioned distribution with the precative. In this way, a full picture of the array of interrelationships between the different forms and their functions can be achieved. The view with which the forms belonging to these paradigms are described in the literature is mainly morphological, usually regarding them as independent forms rather than parts of an operational system. In such a system the interrelations and functions count the most. Many treatments tend to discuss mood in Akkadian from a diachronic point of view, or from a mixed point of view. Here, as is made clear in the methodological introduction, only the synchronic point of view prevails.

4.0.1 GAG

GAG treats all modal forms under the same heading ("der Imperativ und die Formen für Wunsch, Beteuerung und Verbot", GAG §81).

The imperative (*purus*) is set apart (§81a) and is said to be always affirmative and always active. The prohibitive (*lā iparras*) is used to express absolute prohibition and is gradually replacing the vetitive form (*ayyiprus*), which is becoming obsolete. The latter expresses a negative wish directed at a person of equal or higher standing. It is not, however, a formal prohibition.

There are two forms which are used for affirmative wish — with a verbal form, used for action (*liprus*), and with the stative, used for states (*lū paris*). The verbal precative is formed by fusion of *lū* and the preterite (that is, the *iprus* **form**). It never occurs in the 2nd person. The fusion does not conform with the regular morphophonemic contraction rules in OB. Whether the 3rd person forms convey a wish or an order can only be determined by the context. The 1st person has often a voluntative meaning. The precative of 1st person plural (i.e., *lū niprus*) exists only in OA. In Babylonian there exists the cohortative *i niprus* (this shows, beyond any doubt, that the term "precative" pertains to the **forms only**).

The volitive particle *lū* is found with a nominal clause as well. The predicate occurs with *lū*, immediately after the subject: *atta lū mutī–ma.*

The precative appears in both kinds of questions — in a word (=pronominal) question and in a sentence (=nexus) question (for which, however, see §4.3.3).

Prohibitions in the prohibitive, negative wishes in the vetitive and wishes in the precative are no different than any other verbal sentence with respect to the order of elements. Prohibitions and negative wishes can be modified by modal particles (this, however, happens but rarely; in general, modal particles such as *šumma, tuša, pīqat* or *midde* are not compatible with precative forms).

GAG §158 is devoted to using coordination for notional subordination and accounts for precative and imperative forms which are interconnected by *-ma* and their meaning.

On the whole, since GAG is a grammar covering all dialects of Akkadian, the picture of the modal system in OB which it draws is too general.

4.0.2 Edzard 1973

Edzard aims to describe mood in Akkadian in general, rather than in any dialect in particular. His point of view is synchronic and system-oriented. Despite this he hardly adduces any full-context examples and his point of departure is the morphology of the forms.

According to Edzard, the precative (including the plural cohortative, despite some reservations) denotes a desired action or state but is not used to express a strict order, meaning "I want ...", "let him ...", "he should ...", etc., whereas the imperative is a strict order (Edzard 1973:130–31). By this he separates the imperative from the precative, reasoning that they do not have the same meaning. This does not account for the prohibitive forms, and it is not clear whether these forms should be treated separately, with regard to the different persons, as well. It seems that those semantic differences between the forms are the actualization of the inherent differences between the respective persons.

The form *lū taparras* is described as a suppletive form of the imperative. Such forms are very rare, and in the few such cases where they occur in our corpus they can be established as belonging exclusively to the asseverative paradigm (see **chapter 2**).

The prohibitive means that an action or state is prohibited or unwanted by the speaker. As to the opposition between the prohibitive and the vetitive, both forms and meanings differ. The prohibitive has to do with volition and the power or possibility to execute an action while the vetitive is used with wishes,[1] where an action or state is not wanted but not ordered.

Edzard mentions the definition of "mode grammatical" ("Il arrive que la valeur propre du mode soit alterée ou supprimée par le jeu du mécanisme syntaxique..." [Marouzeau 1951:147], see n. 11 in **§7.2.2.2**), suggesting that the subjunctive may be one such mood, or in other words, he does not consider it justified to regard the subjunctive as another mood in such environments. It seems, however, that Marouzeau's basic intention was a syntactic slot where no interchangeablity is possible, resulting in a form with no value, or a neutralized value. The subjunctive is interchangeable neither with the indicative nor with any modal form and therefore has no modal value — **it is neither indicative nor modal**, or in other words it is **neutralized regarding modality**.

Edzard uses one example of the vetitive, *ayyibluṭ amēlu,* in the sense of "the man shouldn't have lived" to show that those modal forms do not have any formal temporal frame. This is correct formally, in the absence of other modal forms that indicate a different temporal reference. However, in reality, these forms, at least in our corpus, always refer to a temporal frame from the moment of utterance on. AHw:559b has a similar example (*lū ašpuraššum*) which, however, is not precative, but rather an asseverative form. Thus we find no evidence that *lū* may signal *irrealis*; there is not one convincing example (in our corpus) to establish the existence of such a function (and there is need for more than just one).

4.0.3 Leong 1994

Leong 1994:362–403 devotes a chapter to volitives (precatives, imperatives, vetitives, desideratives, etc.), describing them as a group of forms that

1. This distinction is generally correct in OB, but not in OA. See for example Hecker 1968 §133b.

share the same grammatical reality and are used to express the act of willing a situation (not) to happen. Volitive verbal forms (including the predicative) are discussed in their textual context, a procedure that is clearly justified. Some issues treated, e.g., aspectual expression (ibid. 362–63), are not usually discussed in connection with these modal forms in OB (they are with regard to peripheral Akkadian, for example Izre'el 1998:37–38). The volitives are said to express perfective aspect (like the preterite), for which see **§4.3.1.2.2** below.

According to Leong, volitives show only deontic modality, ranging from permission to obligation, a wish or a petition, depending upon the social reference and the semantic-pragmatic context. This context is the main framework in which the volitives are examined.

Leong refers to the prohibitive as follows:

> The use of *lā* (and not *ul*) as the negating particle seems to indicate that the Proh[ibitive] is marked as a grammatical form, which has **only deontic modality**. (ibid. 375, my emphasis)

The problem in this statement is that *lā iparras* is a syntagm capable of occurring in a *šumma* protasis as well as in pronominal questions, having in both these syntagmatic environments a modally neutralized value: In the protasis it is neither indicative nor modal (members of the precative paradigm are excluded from *šumma* protases and hence the opposition modal vs. non-modal does not exist, which does not contradict the fact that the whole conditional protasis is modal). For pronominal questions see **§4.3.3.1**.

Leong classifies occurrences such as the ubiquitous *lū balṭāta lū šalmāta* among the desideratives (i.e., the form *lū paris* in his terminology), apart from the vetitive forms which are said to express a negative wish and to occur only in the 3rd person. As a matter of fact, both *lū balṭāta* / *lū šalmāta* and vetitives are functionally and semantically related and actually belong to the distinct wish paradigm. As a whole, Leong's description tends to be semantic and adheres to morphology, rather than to syntactic behavior.

4.0.4 Buccellati 1996

In Buccellati 1996, two chapters are devoted to mood (chapter 28) and modality (chapter 29). Buccellati's partition is made in accordance with the structural distinction between *signifiant* and *signifié*, which are, however, two sides of the linguistic sign and should therefore be treated together (as is customary in traditional descriptions).

Buccellati states that affirmative wish for the 2nd person is not expressed by the desiderative (namely, forms of the precative, the cohortative and the vetitive) but by either the imperative or the "independent particle *lū*" followed by the present or a noun in the predicative state (Buccellati 1996 §28.3). It is understandable why, on morphological grounds only, the imperative would not be considered part of the desiderative. But "*lū* followed by a noun in the predicative state", i.e., the stative precative, is formed in a manner similar to the precative, the difference being the degree of fusion between the elements. Buccellati's description of the formal features of modality is strictly confined to morphological features, disregarding the fact that both analytic and synthetic precatives can commute, performing similarly.

Buccellati 1996 §28.6 notes that the prohibitive can occur with the 3rd person, expressing a negative command (as opposed to the vetitive, which expresses a negative wish). However, in §29.5 (both in the table and in the first paragraph), there is no mention of such a possibility. Buccellati does not mention what would be the affirmative counterpart of this 3rd person prohibitive either.

Chapter 29 is devoted to the notional categories of mood (that is, to modality). These categories override the morphological distinction elaborated in chapter 28. This happens exactly because morphological grouping does not necessarily correspond to synchronic categories, or functional groups.

The term "summons" is the notional category described under "attitude of the speaker". By "summons" Buccellati refers to "a request in the form of an order or a wish" in which he distinguishes an order ("...addressed only to a direct interlocutor") and wish ("may be addressed to all persons"). It seems that this distinction between "order" and "wish" is different than the one habitually used to differentiate between the prohibitive and the vetitive respectively (see **§4.3.2**).

4.0.5 Huehnergard 1997

Huehnergard 1997 seperates the imperative, which is "used for commands in the 2nd person" (ibid. §16.1), and the precative which

> expresses either a wish or an indirect command...; it occurs in the third and first persons (sg. and pl.), but not in the second person. Thus, with the Imperative, it forms a **suppletive injunctive** (command) **paradigm.** (ibid. §16.2, my emphasis)

The prohibitive is used for negative commands and prohibitions. The vetitive expresses a negative wish, hence it is less forceful than the prohibitive.

In a sequence of two or more clauses in which the first verb is an injunctive form (i.e., an imperative, a precative, a prohibitive, or a vetitive) and the following verb or verbs are also injunctive forms and the verbs are connected by *-ma*, the second and following clauses are often to be translated as purpose clauses.

Huehnergard (§17.2) connects the performative perfect with the precative and the imperative. However, this type of connection between the aforementioned forms is viewed here as disjunctive, and is symbolized here by // (for which see **§4.4.3**), permitting any sort of form on either side, since other forms are allowed as well in the same slot following this performative perfect.

4.1 Precative forms

This section is a survey of the forms which belong to the precative groups. The term **precative** is here used differently than in Assyriology (where it is often used only for *lū* or *l-* based forms, e.g., GAG §81). Here **precative** is a cover term for the entire group of forms, regardless of formative, person or polarity: Thus the affirmative (more or less coinciding with Huehnergard's 'injunctive paradigm', see above, **§4.0.5**) includes the forms *luprus, purus, lū parsāta, liprus, lū paris, i niprus,* etc. whereas the negative form is made up of the traditional prohibitive *lā iparras*. All these forms are henceforth regarded as **precative forms** (including the traditional **imperative**!), and the different groups they constitute are generally referred to as **precative paradigms**, especially at this point, when they are not as yet subdivided into the various (sub-)paradigms.

Dealing with these forms under *morphology* is not very convincing, for the simple reason that the use of certain forms as part of the modal system has nothing to do with morphology, but rather with syntax. More specifically, only by certain syntactic symmetry can we learn about one form being the negative of the other. An obvious example is the syntagm *lā iparras* which is recognized as *prohibitive*, the negative counterpart of *liprus*. Another example is two different forms, such as *liprus* and *purus*, which often belong in the same paradigm. Fortunately, some forms are less versatile than others (having a more limited list of functions) and can serve as a point of departure: Whereas the syntagm *lā iparras* is found in three different syntactic environments[2] (in *šumma* clauses, in pronominal questions, and in independent clauses as the negative of *liprus*), the latter form is capable of occurring in fewer environments and has fewer discrete functions and hence can better serve as an anchor.

The forms *liprus, purus / pursī,* and *luprus* (and their plural counter-

2. In even more environments when the ventive morpheme is involved, or when the forms end in a long vowel, since both neutralize the distinction between the subordination marker *-u* and its absence.

parts *liprusū / ā, pursā*, and *i niprus*) will be assumed to be forms which reflect modal value, wherever they may appear. Different values and (sub-)paradigms will be discussed further below. The inclusion of *purus* in the paradigm together with the other forms is already accepted (see above, **§4.0.5**), aided by the fact that there are actually no 2nd pers. forms for the affirmative precative (other than *purus*) in the corpus, such as the ones found in Arabic (the jussive *taf'al*), in which case it would be more difficult to include the imperative in the paradigm.

4.2 Paradigmatics and syntagmatics

The following sections show first the paradigmatic relationships between precative forms and then the syntagmatic environments in which they occur.

4.2.1 Paradigmatics

The tight connection of *liprus* with *purus* is attested in parallel constructions in which there is a shift in thematic reference:

> **[4.1]** *aššum amtim ša tašpuram ša umma atta–ma ana ṣēr* PN_1 *alik–ma* ***amtam liddikkum*** *alli[k]šum–ma umma anāku–ma a[q]a[bb]īš[um]* PN_2 *išpuranni* ***amtam idnam***
> Concerning the maid of whom you wrote to me (about) whom you (said) thus: 'Go to PN_1 and **let him give you** the maid.' I went to him and so I was s[ay]ing[3] to him: 'PN_2 sent me. **Give me** the maid'. 9, 149:4–15

In example **[4.1]** two precative forms (see **§4.3.1** below) pertain to the same issue, viz., giving the maid to the speaker. *amtam liddikkum* corresponds to *amtam idnam;* the agent in both is PN_1, whereas *-kum / -am* refer to the main speaker (the deictic shift is due to a shift in respective speakers). The following example is similar:

> **[4.2]** *šumma* PN_1 *ittalkam–ma šīpātim naši umma atta–ma* 5 *bilat šīpātim ana* PN_2 ***uṣur*** *šumma šīmam naši* 1 *šīmam* ***liṣṣuram***
> If PN_1 went away carrying wool, you (should say) the following: '**Save** 5 talents of wool for PN_2'. If he carries merchandise, **let him save** one (piece of) merchandise for me. 12, 50:23–28

Both directives (this is the function of these precative forms; see below, **§4.3.1**) are of the same verbal lexeme (for which see **§1.4**) and PN_1 is the theme of both. In addition the object of both are the wool/merchandise

3. *aqabbīšum* in this position and tense, after *umma X-ma,* is not quite regular. Compare further ibid. 17.

meant for PN_2.

That two forms, which supposedly belong in the same paradigm, do not resemble one another morphologically is of no consequence. Morphological asymmetry is quite usual even within the same paradigm: In the ancient Semitic languages the negative of the imperative form is never the negated imperative form, but rather the negated apocopate (Akk. *ē taprus*, Arab. *lā tafʿal*, Eth. *ʾi təngər*, Heb. *ʾal taʿaś*).

The interrelationship between *luprus* (the 1st pers.) and the other forms (already shown to belong together) is based mainly upon common sense. One example shows such an interrelationship but there is a slight difference between the two verbal lexemes — one is *alākum*, the other is *atlukum*, both essentially referring to the same action:

> [4.3] *umma anāku–ma ištu lā rīqu* ***luttalak*** *umma* PN*–ma* ***lā tallak***
> So I (said): 'Since he is not free, **let me go away**'. PN (said): '**Do not go**'. 7, 123:25–29

lā tallak is the negative 2nd pers. directive (§4.3.1) and thus in [4.3] the interrelationship between 2nd and 1st pers. directives is quite clear. The same interrelationship can be shown between the negative forms of the paradigm, but these first have to be established as such:

> [4.4] *šumma mû ana* GN_1 *u* GN_2 *ittabšû ina pī nārātim ša aqbûkum šiknam* ***lā tašakkan*** *šumma mû ana* GN_1 *u* GN_2 *lā ibšû [i]na pī nārātim ša aqbûkum [š]iknī* ***šukun****–ma mû–ma ... libbašû*
> If water is available to GN_1 and GN_2 **do not make** arrangement(s) in the mouth of the canals of which I spoke to you. If water is not available to GN_1 and GN_2 (do) **make** arrangements in the mouth of the canals of which I spoke to you, so that water ... may become available. 4, 80:4–17

The polar context in example [4.4] makes it incontestably clear that the negative of the 2nd pers. *šukun* is *lā tašakkan*. The negative of the 3rd pers. is *lā iparras*:

> [4.5] *šumma* ᶠPN *īdēšu ittišu* ***lillikam*** *šumma lā īdēšu (i-de-ṣi) mimma ittišu* ***l[ā] illakam***
> If ᶠPN knows him **let her come** with him. If she does not know him **let her no[t] come** with him at all. 11, 36:7'–11'

> [4.6] *nipuat* PN_1 ***lā ineppiū*** *nipuat* PN_2*–ma* ***lippiū***
> **They should not distrain** PN_1's distrainee. (It is) rather *PN_2's distrainee* (that) **they should distrain.** 9, 238:4–9

It may further be deduced that *lā aparras* functions as the negative 1st pers. of the paradigm. An important point, which is to be resumed further below, is that as the negative counterpart of *liprus*, *lā iparras* has nothing to do with *iparras*, from which it is diachronically derived. Synchronically, in this paradigm, it is nothing but the negative form of *liprus*.

As is shown above, there is an interrelationship between the 2nd pers. and the 3rd pers. of the paradigm, and it can be found in the negative as well:

> [4.7] *umma awīlum–ma šupur–ma âm* ***lā inaddinūšum***[4] *šumma ûm lā madid* ***lā tanaddiššum***
> So the gentleman (said): 'Write that **they should not give** him grain. If the grain is not measured, **do not give** him (any)'. 3, 85:5–10

Everything shown up to this point is well known; an attempt has been made, however, to show that all these interrelations between the forms are due to usage of the forms (i.e., syntactic information) rather than any semantic or morphological features inherent in the forms themselves. The forms are interrelated because they are capable of occurring **in the same syntactic environment** and hence belong in the same paradigm.

An example of the **absence of such interrelations** would be a rare form, traditionally referred to as the *vetitive*. It is generally attested in the 3rd pers. and has the formation *ayyiprus*. Although its value is similar, the vetitive **does not belong** with the negative precative (*lā iparras*), for they do not co-occur. For the systemic description of this form and its paradigm see **§4.3.2** below.

In addition, the precative paradigm includes the syntagms *lū paris* / *lū* N(ominal) and rarely *lā paris* / *lā* N (which may belong to the asseverative paradigm as well, see **§2.2**). These are analytic precative forms but they nevertheless belong in the same paradigm:

> [4.8] *daltum* ***lū birūyat*** *mādiš lā iqattin u lā ikabber*
> Let the door be medium. Let it not be too thin nor too thick. 3, 34:28–29

Example [**4.8**] both shows the formation *lū paris* and ties this form, in a kind of symmetry, to the negative precative *lā iparras* (for the distribution of analytic vs. synthetic precative formation see **§4.3.1.2.1**).

Leong 1994:378, n. 16 designates a special name for *lū paris* — *desiderative*. These forms, however, are here considered as part of the same paradigm as the synthetic precative formation, despite their different formation. This is especially apparent in a few verbal lexemes which

4. It is important to mention that this comparison is not entirely legitimate — the forms occur in slightly different syntactic conditions — the first is chained, whereas the second is not.

tend to exhibit only the analytic formation (such as *išûm, edûm, ṭābum,* and perhaps *palāḫum*). Those forms commute freely with synthetic precative forms:

> [4.9] *atta* ***lū palḫāta**–ma itaḫlalniāti ṣeḫḫerūtim*
> As for you, be fearful and crawl away from us kids. 3, 52:24–26

lū palḫāta is situated exactly where normally, due to modal congruence (see **§4.4.4**), only precative forms (of all persons, here it is the analytic 2nd pers.) fit in.

The next example shows a qualified substantive marked as a modal rheme:

> [4.10] ***lū waradka*** *ša dār[i]ātim* ***a[n]āk[u]***
> "Let m[e] be your et[e]rnal slave. 12, 175:14

Non-verbal predications are very common. Modality of non-verbal predications, on the other hand, is hardly dealt with in the linguistic literature on modality, either because this kind of modality is generally considered to be a verbal category, or because judging, in cross-linguistic research, what is verbal and what is non-verbal is impossible.[5] In OB, non-verbal predication occurs within both main modal paradigms — the precative and the asseverative paradigms. The salient point of this is that **a non-verbal clause may be either indicative or belong to a certain modal paradigm,** due to the formal opposition between both types.

The fact that in affirmative precative non-verbal clauses one finds *lū* does not mean that it is *lū* which carries the load of modal marking, although it sometimes looks that way. Modality and modality type (for *lū* is found in more than one type of modality) are marked by virtue of both syntagmatic conditions and paradigmatic constitution. Negative forms in the same paradigm never contain *lū* (in our corpus) but are still clearly a part of this functional group (see above, at the beginning of the present section). Different syntagmatic conditions and paradigmatic constitution account for the difference between the morphologically identical precatives and asseveratives as well.

The negative syntagms:

> [4.11] 1 *kur âm ana ummika idin–ma erišŝīša* ***lā wašbat***
> Give your mother a kor of barley so that she does not remain destitute. 11, 139:10–13

> [4.12] 1 *kur âm a[n]a ummika idin* ***lā ṭupullûm***
> Give your mother a kor of barley. (Let there be) no abuse! ibid. 27–28

5. Even in Akkadian there is a long-standing debate between experts about the (non-)verbal nature of the predicative conjugation — see **§1.4**.

Another point which is relevant to the paradigmatics of these forms is that they occur in the passive mainly in the 3rd pers. (see example **[4.35]** below), whereas the 2nd pers. form is never passive (GAG §81a).

4.2.2 Syntagmatics

The objective of this section is to define the syntactic environments where precative forms do and do not occur. Their non-occurrence in certain environments may at times be meaningful for modality (as in case of modal neutralization).

4.2.2.1 Syntagms in which precative forms may occur

This section ennumerates the environments where precative forms may occur, regardless of the frequency of such occurrence:

1. At the beginning of an utterance, such as the beginning of letters (# *ana* PN *qibī–ma*) or at the beginning of a citation (*umma anāku–ma* ...).
2. After *anumma,* which is a performative signal, *iptaras* forms seem to occur most readily. There are, however, a few occasions where members of the precative paradigm occur right after it (AHw:55a):

> [4.13] ***anumma*** *awīlam abī* ***ḫussis****–ma ša šulum kīsim šuāti līpuš*
> Now, remind the gentleman, my father, that he see to it that the purse is kept intact. 11, 49:19–20
>
> [4.14] ***anumma*** *ana* PN ***izissu***
> Now, go to the assistance of PN. 6, 7:12–13

It would seem better to consider *anumma* here as a particle, much like *inanna,* both of which have textual functions yet to be investigated and described.

3. Precative forms may occur after focus (whether marked by *-ma,* or by order of the elements) regardless of whether the focal element is substantival or adverbial (x–*ma* (...) *liprus* / *purus*).
4. Precative forms tolerate all coordinate connectives, *u, -ma,* and the disjunction marked by //, in different conditions for each of them (discussed further below, **§4.4.3**).
5. Precative forms can constitute the apodosis of a conditional, whether the protasis is marked by *šumma* or not. This is noteworthy because the validity of the apodosis is dependent upon the actualization of the protasis, and hence not every form can occur in the former (e.g., *iprus* does not).

6. The compatibility of precative forms with infinitive constructions is seen in a number of subgroups:

6a. Topical infinitive construction (*aššum / ana parāsim*) with the precative paradigm is rather common:

[**4.15**] ***ana*** *qemîm* ***šuṭēnim*** *nīdi aḫim* ***lā tarašši***
Do not be negligent regarding having the flour ground. 9, 14:6–7 .

6b. Infinitive complement (*parāsam / ana parāsim*) with precative forms is rare, but attested:

[**4.16**] *eqlam šuāti* ***lā epēšam*** PN ***šudki***
Convince PN not to cultivate this field. 3, 2:41–42

6c. The syntagm *ša parāsim* regularly occurs with precative forms (see **chapter 7**).

7. Precative forms in questions:

7a. Only the 1st and 3rd pers. precative forms occur in a pronominal question, to the exclusion of the 2nd. pers. For this reason the paradigmatic constitution in this environment is different and calls for a different sub-paradigm:

[**4.17**] *gimillam ša elīya taškunu* ***matī*** *anāku* ***lutēr***
When would *I* return the favor you did to me? 3, 22:6–7

7b. Nexus questions[6] with the precative are questionable because there are hardly any certain examples for them:

[**4.18**] *ina maḫrīka–ma ḫurʾussunu* ***limḫaṣū***
Should one then strike their necks in *your* presence? 1, 35:18–20

Since the features of nexus questions turn out to be similar to those in the environments enumerated in the following section, they are classified thereunder.

4.2.2.2 Syntagms in which precative forms do not occur

This section deals with syntactic environments in which precative forms do **not** occur and should ostensibly be outside the scope of modality. Such a view, however, would be mistaken, mainly from a methodological point of view but semantically as well. The point is this: Both in conditional *šumma* clauses[7] and in the attributive slot (subordination), the opposition

6. That is, with no interrogative pronoun, what is termed in GAG 154a "Satzfrage", as opposed to pronominal question (ibid. "Wortfrage").

7. To this might be added the modal particles *pīqat* and *minde* which, according to AHw:864b–65a and 655a (respectively), do not tend to co-occur with precative forms, save one occurrence of *midde* in *Sumer* 15, 14:7, 14. 20.

modal vs. non-modal (namely, *liprus* vs. *iparras*) does not exist (in contradistinction to what we find in other environments)[8] and hence the expression of modality is neutralized. Literally speaking, the forms *iparras* and *iparrasu* in these syntagms is neither indicative nor modal.

The situation inside the *šumma* protasis is semantically more transparent; von Soden (GAG §161i) states that *iparras* forms in *šumma* protases generally denote some modality ("...entweder das Tun-Wollen oder seltener -Sollen"). This is quite evident semantically:

> [4.19] ***šumma talliam*** ... *aliam*
> If you wish to/intend to/must come up..., come up. 2, 100:14–16

> [4.20] ***šumma lā talliam*** ... *šupram–ma*
> If you do not wish/intend/have to come up..., send me... ibid. 17–19

> [4.21] *ana* ᶠPN *qibī–ma* ***šumma illiam*** *līliam*
> Tell ᶠPN (that) she should come up if she wishes to/intends to/must come up. ibid. 22–23

This co-occurrence of the same verbal lexeme (*elûm*) in both protasis and apodosis compels us to interpret the verbal forms in the protasis as denoting modality, but this is not the rule. This may be explicated by the value of the *iparras* forms in the protasis, which, not being opposed to any precative forms, is neutral as to modality. As such it is able to denote both extremes of the modal scale (this modal neutralization of the forms inside the *šumma* clause does not affect the evident modality of the whole clause).

The genitive slot is very similar in this respect. In this position we find, whenever possible, verbal forms marked by *-u*. This *-u* has received ample consideration, both diachronically and synchronically. Here we are interested only in the latter. GAG §103a states that the Akkadian subjunctive is functionally different from the same term in other languages, being merely a kind of genitive ending of the verb. Reiner 1966:71 enumerates the subjunctive with the **modi**. Buccellati 1996 §28.2 considers the subjunctive as a **mood** (in the morphological sense) and contrasts it with the indicative. When discussing the notional values of the modi, however, he mentions that **it has no value**. Eilers 1968:244 regards it as **indicative.** Edzard 1973:127 considers it as **indicative** as well. As already mentioned, according to the present method it is not considered indicative, since it is not opposed to any non-indicative forms, such as *liprus*; for this reason, an *iparras* form in these syntagmatic conditions (i.e., the

8. Actually there are occurrences of precative forms after *ša* but only as quoted direct speech, constituting *style direct lié*: *u ana* PN *rēʾîm* ***ša*** *arḫam šuāti* ***amurši itaplas–ma*** *ṭēmka* ***terram***... "Moreover, as for PN the herdsman, who (was told) 'look that cow over, examine (her), and send me your report'..." (9, 174:16–18).

attributive slot) is modally neutralized.[9] The following example may show this clearly:

> [4.22] ***kīma*** *anāku* ***eppešu*** *qibīšum*
> Tell him that I intend to/will cultivate (it). 3, 2:45

This type of complementation is quite irregular in the corpus, and a more regular way would have been *qibīšum–ma anāku lūpuš,* used to convey indirect modal utterances. On the other hand, the writer might have meant to insist upon the factuality of the statement, which is why he chose this construction, rather than the precative *lūpuš* which necessarily reflects non-factuality. This is similar to a rare occurrence of *akkīma* ("so that, as") in the corpus:[10]

> [4.23] *idišam šuṭṭerī[m–ma]* ***šūbilīm akkīma*** *ina alākim ḫišeḫtam* ***našiānu*** *u atti ṭēmki lū ṣabtāti*
> Put in writing side by side and send me so that we deliver with us what is needed upon coming, and as for you, (you should) take action. 7, 17:11–15

> [4.24] ***šuprīm–ma*** *ina pānīni* ***lū našiānu*** Order (in writing) so that we deliver from what is available to us. ibid. 17–18

This is the only correspondence in the corpus between an *akkīma* clause and a sequenced precative (**§4.4**). Inside the *akkīma* clause we find the same formal modal neutralization discussed above. Actually, due to the correspondence with the modal sequence in the second part, modality is felt quite strongly. For a more detailed discussion of these occurrences see end of **§4.4.4.0.3**.

A third, altogether different, environment from which members of the precative paradigm are excluded is the reporting chain *iprus–ma ... iptaras.* Rare occurrences of precative forms here are explained only by a kind of syntactic parenthesis containing an exact quotation of what had been said. The quotation is introduced, usually marked by the direct speech marker *umma* x*–ma*, but not necessarily so:

> [4.25] *ana aḫḫātika aqbī–ma* ***erbānim ṣuḫāra ḫiṭâ*** *mamman ul īrubam*
> I told your sisters 'Come in, examine the servant', but nobody came in. 6, 38:9–12

The example contains a quotation in the middle of the reporting chain representing the content of the verb *qabûm*. The more usual slot for such

9. Methodologically speaking, so are all the other forms in the paradigm.

10. This, and the whole issue of complementation, is a domain where the OB of Mari is quite different. See Finet 1956 §§85a, 86d.

a quotation would be preceding the verb *qabûm*.

An important characteristic of such reporting chains is the expression of the original modal utterances in the form of an infinitive construction. That is, instead of the very unusual quotation *erbānim ṣuẖāra ẖiṭâ* (or the more common one marked by *umma* x–*ma*), one more often finds *ana aẖẖātika erēbam–ma ṣuhāram ẖiāṭam aqbī–ma*. These alternative models of the modal utterance are dealt with further below (**§4.5**).

The last environment from which precative forms are excluded is nexus questions. In such questions, instead of an expected precative, the form *iparras* appears (see **§4.3.3.2**). Formally this *iparras* form is modally neutralized, thus resembling in nature the situation in both *šumma* protases and the attributive slot. Discussion of the values of the forms, the problematics of nexus questions and and their interrelations with other forms is found below (**§4.3.3**).

4.2.3 Results: different sub-paradigms

Summing up the data in both the survey of forms and their syntagmatics, some conclusions can be reached as to their respective organization in different (sub-)paradigms. The **directive** sub-paradigm is the most common and is to be dealt with first and foremost. Two other sections are devoted to the **wish** paradigm and the **interrogative** paradigm.

In addition, another group, the **concessive-conditional** precative, can only be established as a distinct pattern based upon the description of larger units, namely, the precative sequence pattern. It is therefore described in **chapter 5**.

4.3 Functions and values of the different (sub-)paradigms

One letter (11, 194) seems to contain almost every construction treated in this chapter, either directly or indirectly; as such it is much more useful than any introduction:

[4.26] DN ***liballiṭkunūti*** (1)	**May** DN **keep you alive**.
6 ***aššum*** *ṭēm ipir ṣāb watrūtim* ***nadānim*** (2)	**Regarding** the report about **giving** the yearly rations to the supplementary troops
ša tašpurānim ...	about which you wrote me,
umma ṣāb watrūtim–ma ipir šattini gamram	so say the supplementary troops:
10 ***idnāniāšim*** (3)	'**Give** us our entire yearly rations;
šumma *ipir šattini gamram*	**If you do not give** us our entire
lā tanaddināniāšim (4)	yearly rations
ul nileqqe	will we not take (them)?'

...	...
16 *umma anāku–ma*	So I (said):
ana ṣāb watrūtim	'**Let** them **give** the supplementary
... ipir šattišunu gamram	troops their entire yearly rations...
liddinū (5)	(OR: **Should** they **give** ... ?)'.
20 *umma šunu–ma*	So they (said):
ipir šattišunu gamram	'**Should** they **give** them
inandinūšunūšim–ma (6)	their entire yearly rations,
ṣābum ina qāti uṣṣī–ma	the troops will go out of our control
ana pīḫat ṣābim ša ina qāti	and **we will not be able to answer**
25 *uṣṣû*	to our lord as to the responsibility
bēlni ***apālam ul nileʾʾi*** (7)	for the troops who will go out of hand.
i nillik–ma (8)	**Let us go**
	and **let them give (it) to** them
ullikīam	somewhere else
...	...
30 ***lū*** *ša 1 warḫim* ***lū*** *ša 2 warḫī* (9)	**either** (the rations) of a month **or** of two'.
liddinūšunūšim	
...	...
46 *warkassu* ***pursā*****–*ma***	**Decide** about his matter and
ana kīma birûtišu kaspam	**pay** him, in accordance with
ša apālim (10)	his diviner position, the silver
aplāšu	**which must be paid.**

An additional important point in this letter is that most of the different forms or syntagms occur with √ndn, which means the same action is portrayed differently, according to the speaker and situation:

(1) ***liballiṭkunūti*** represents the **wish paradigm (§4.3.2).**

(2) ***aššum ... nadānim*** is an **infinitive construction**, serving as topic or as an adverbial complement (**§4.5.3**).

(3) ***idnāniāšim*** is the **2nd pers. directive (§4.3.1.3.3).**

(4) ***šumma lā tanaddināniāšim*** is an example for the **modal neutralization** of *lā taparras* in *šumma* clauses (**§4.2.2.2**).

(5) ***liddinū*** is a 3rd pers. precative form, which is interpreted as a **nexus question (§4.3.3.2)** in the AbB translation, but here it is deemed to be a directive (**§4.3.1**).

(6) ***inandinūšunūšim–ma*** is the protasis of a ***-ma*** **conditional pattern (chapter 6).**

(7) ***apālam ul nileʾʾi*** is both the apodosis and representative of the **notion of ability** which is sometimes considered to be a type of modality in its own right.

(8) ***i nillik*** represents the **1st pers. plural directive** (§4.3.1.3.2).
(9) ***lū*** *ša* 1 *warḫim* ***lū*** *ša* 2 *warḫī liddinūšunūšim* demonstrates **other functions of *lū*.**
(10) ***ša apālim*** is the **modal infinitive** construction (**chapter 7**).

4.3.1 The directive sub-paradigm

Deontic modality is characterized as containing an element of will (Palmer 1986:96–125). This type of modality accommodates quite different notions, such as imperatives, auxiliary verbs of will or order and an infinitive as the object thereof (both used for reporting modal notions), and finally, a modal infinitive used substantively or attributively. All of these belong under deontic modality but are different enough to require further specification. **The directives** constitute the main body of deontic modality in our corpus. It is important to state that this group is a **sub-paradigm**, because where directives occur indicatives (mainly *iparras*, but occasionally non-verbal clauses) figure as well (this is apparent, e.g., in **§4.3.1.1.3**, where the two are compared). Within this potentially diverse paradigm, this sub-paradigm is clearly distinct in its forms and values.

4.3.1.1 Modal value

The **directives** exhibit a rather rigid functional domain, namely, to express the will of the speaker, but not in a factual manner as would an auxiliary verb (*he wants to go* can be judged as a factual report of reality) but with the intention of bringing about a change of reality in the immediate future beginning at the moment of utterance. Lyons 1977:746 defines directives as "utterances which impose, or propose, some action or pattern of behavior and indicate that it should be carried out". The (arbitrary) interrelationship between the semantic aspect (taken in full by Lyons' definition) and the formal features (i.e., the syntagmatic compatibilities and paradigmatic constitution) constitutes the object of investigation.

4.3.1.1.1 Directivity

Directivity has to do with **speaker-oriented modality**. The latter is characterized as follows:

> **Speaker-oriented modality** is meant to include all such directives as well as utterances meant to grant permission. Speaker-oriented modalities **do not report the existence of conditions on the agent,** but rather **allow the speaker to impose such conditions on the addressee.** (Bybee et al. 1994:179, my emphasis)

This group matches the functional domain of the directive sub-paradigm. This sub-paradigm manifests the above mentioned element of will originating from the speaker. The agent (viz., the one who should actually carry out the order) is not necessarily indicated. The directive feature can be isolated in contrasting a directive with a preceding infinitive construction on the syntagmatic axis:

> **[4.27]** *[š]umma ekallum–ma lā iqbi ṣuḫāru šū* ***ana wuššurim*** *... inanna šitāl–ma ṣuḫāra šâtu* ***wuššeraššu***
> If the palace itself did not order (otherwise), this servant **is to be released**... Now think (this) over and **release** this servant. 1, 74:23–28

> **[4.28]** *anumma 10 ṣābam ēpištam u 1 ṭēnšunu* ***ana*** *ūrā[t]ikunu* ***sêrim*** *aṭṭardam ūrātikunu* ***lisērū***
> I hereby send 10 skilled workers and their miller (in order) **to plaster** your roofs; **let them plaster** your roofs. 12, 17:5–9

In example **[4.27]** the *ana parāsim* construction is predicative, in **[4.28]** it is an adverbial complement of purpose. Both examples contain, additionally, directives which exhibit the same verbal lexeme as the infinitive construction preceding them. Moreover, these finite verbs are surrounded by the same participants as the infinitive constructions, namely, *ṣuḫāra šâtu* in **[4.27]** and *ūrātikunu* in **[4.28]**. A syntagmatic contrast with the preceding infinitives brings to light the essence of the directive. (To be exact, in **[4.27]**, it is a sequenced precative [see **§4.4**], rather than a directive, which is contrasted with the infinitive. The comparison is carried out on the information level where sequenced precatives and directives are often similar.) In view of all the information already communicated by these infinitives, it seems that the sole purpose of the directives in these examples is to **impose some action and indicate that it should be carried out beginning at the moment of utterance** (this being the temporal frame of directives). The rest of the information seems to be repeated for lack of any alternative.[11]

The overall temporal frame of directives, as already mentioned, begins at the moment of utterance. Within the paradigm, however, there is no temporal opposition between the various forms. This could be demonstrated by *inanna* preceding the 2nd pers. precative *wuššeraššu* in example **[4.27]** above. It seems, however, that directives are not confined to any particular time after the utterance, and they can be aimed at the less immediate future as well:

11. There is no pro-verb in OB, i.e., a semantically empty verb representing another one, as there is in English (*so let them do it*). One should not be misled by the tranlation of *lisērū* by *let them plaster*. The speaker here does not ask the addressee to permit the workers to do it but rather orders him that they do it.

[4.29] [***u***]***rra***[***m***] *ina* GN [*š*]*uṣēnšin*[*āti*]
[H]ave th[em] loaded in GN **to[mor]row**. 9, 132:10–12

[4.30] *ina kīma inanna ebūrum* ***warki ebūrim*** *i nillik*
It is harvest (time) right now; let us go **after the harvest**. 2, 33:14–16

Whether carrying out the action should be immediate or postponed is not formally distinguished, but is rather aided by the semantic context.

4.3.1.1.2 The notions of the directive scale

There are semantic differences which apply to the strength of the directive, ranging from a blunt order to a humble supplication. These may be the result of the respective social status of the sender and the addressee and possibly of other extra-linguistic factors. However, there are no formal signals for the existence of this scale:

[4.31] *a*[*n*]*a maḫar bēliya kât*[*a*] ***lullika lā amât***
Let me come to you, my Lord. Let me not die! 12, 125:20–22

[4.32] *ina ereš nadâku* ***dikianni***
Lift me from the bed in which I am lying. 12, 99:14–17

Both examples are supplications, the second (*dikianni*) is to a god, yet the forms are identical to any 1st pers. or 2nd pers. (respectively) directive forms.

Another semantic scale nuance contains the **grant of permission**, which is included in the working definition of directives in Bybee et al. 1994 (see above, **§4.3.1.1.1**). Such permission is part of the normal range within the value of directives in the corpus:

[4.33] *ša aqabbûkim mugrīnni–ma awâtum lā iḫaṭṭiā šumma ḫaṭītam eppuš* ***lā tamaggarīnni***
Agree with me as to what I tell you and matters should not fail; if I commit an error (then) **do not agree** with me. 3, 15:24–28

In the preceding example we learn about the notion of permission from the first part (*mugrīnni*), containing what the sender really wants, namely, the agreement of the addressee. The second part (*lā tamaggarīnni*) is the exact opposite of what the speaker wants and hence it is permission, denoting forced agreement, which incidentally has nothing to do with the verbal lexeme *magārum*, for any verbal lexeme could figure in that slot.

[4.34] *šumma libbaki ana šāpiriya* ***luqbī***–*ma gerseqqûm lillikakkim*
If you wish, **let me tell** (= I am willing...) my superior that a palace attendant should come to you. 6, 18:14–18

When such syntagms as *šumma libb- / digil- / niṭil-* precede it, the following directive tends to denote permission. The preceding example is even more interesting, because *luqbi* may be taken to denote ability, but this is unusual.

The following example touches upon the amodal value of *iparras* in *šumma* clauses. As is mentioned above (**§4.2.2.2**), modality inside the *šumma* clause is formally neutralized. Therefore *innaddin* may denote either notion:

> **[4.35]** *šumma ina sūt* GN *innaddin ina sūt* GN ***linnadin***
> "If it has to be / is habitually sold according to the seah measure of GN, **let it be sold** according to the seah measure of GN. 12, 70:5'–8'

The difference between an order and permission seems to be one of degree, and more specifically, the degree to which the speaker is interested in bringing about the action. Curiously enough, permission is the notion closest to the concessive-conditional precative (**chapter 5**), semantically speaking. The syntagmatic conditions and paradigmatic constitution of both precatives are different, however.

4.3.1.1.3 The directive vs. the indicative

A comparison between directives and indicatives (i.e., not in modally neutralizing syntagms) brings to light the differences between the two, since semantic value is directly dependent upon opposition (see **§1.1** above):

> **[4.36]** *šinīšu nakrum illikam–ma damqūtika ina qāti uštēṣi u ina mak rēdî ina* GN_1 *ḫalṣa[m] mamman* ***ul ukâl*** [...] *liṭrudam–ma* 500 *ṣābum ina* GN_1 500 *ṣābum ina* GN_2 *ḫalṣ[am]* ***likīl***
> The enemy came again and made (us) lose your best (men), and for lack of soldiers in GN_1 nobody holds the district. Let [...] send over [...] so that 500 men in GN_1 (and) 500 men in GN_2 may hold the district. 9, 140:5–21

In the edition, *ul ukâl* is translated (ibid. 13) "nobody can hold the district". There is a greater affinity in the corpus between the notion of ability (generally expressed explicitly by the auxiliary *le'ûm*) and the indicative, than between that notion and the (sequenced) precative. Those places in which the precative is felt to reflect this notion are either in the sequenced precative pattern (as we have here: *liṭrudam–ma ... likīl*), or in pronominal questions, which are treated below as a different sub-paradigm:

> **[4.37]** *ša kīma yâti ana kâšim mannum* ***li[dd]in***
> Who could [gi]ve you one who (is) like me? 9, 141:5–7

This also occurs in syntagms which are typical in expressing the permissive notion:

> [4.34] *šumma libbaki ana šāpiriya* ***luqbī***–*ma gerseqqûm lillikakkim*
> If you wish, **let me tell** (= I am willing...) my superior that a palace attendant should come to you. 6, 18:14–18

It should be stressed that the notions of permission and ability do not have to be mixed as they are in the English use of the modal verb *can*. In the corpus overt ability (via *le'ûm*) is perfectly distinct from overt permission (via *nadānum*, see **§1.4**, n. 19). When not overt, the notion of ability belongs more with with the indicative than with the precative.

Returning now to example [**4.36**], it can be stated that *ul ukâl* represents **factuality**, as opposed to *likīl* which is characterized by **non-factuality** (whereas the notion of ability is usually factual). This difference is apparent in the next example as well:

> [**4.38**] *ana bītišu* ***lā tašass***[*i*] *ša ana bītišu mamman* ***ul išassi*** *ṭuppaka šūbilam*
> **Do not lay claim** concerning his house; send me your tablet which (says)'**Nobody will lay claim** concerning his house'. 8, 134:10–14 (see 8, 138:17–19)

The negative 2nd pers. of the directive is here opposed to the 3rd pers. of the indicative (occurring as direct speech in a nominalized, appositive content clause introduced by *ša* reflecting the exact content of the tablet), where both pertain approximately to the same action. The first contains an order; the second a commitment — the indicative, characterized by factuality, is the choice for stating the plain truth which is not subject to any lingering doubt (as opposed to the asseverative, which is a reaction to such a doubt).

> [4.39] *anāku kīam aqbi umma anāku–m*[*a*] *ištu bēlī ṭuppam ana* PN_1 *lā iddinam bē*[*l*]*ī ṭu*[*p*]*pam ana* PN_2 ***l***[***i***]***dd***[***i***]***n****am–ma a*[*rḫi*]*š lišēšer umma* [*š*]*ū–*[*m*]*a u ṭuppam ana* PN_2 ***ul anaddin****akkum*
> I said thus: 'Since my lord did not give me the tablet for PN_1, **let my l**[**o**]**rd g**[**i**]**ve** me the ta[b]let for PN_2 so that he may qu[ick]ly go straight ahead.' (But) he (said): 'Neither **will I give** you the tablet for PN_2'. 11, 107:19'–25'

The reaction might have been *lā anaddinakkum*, namely, "I do not want to give you (...)". The same idea applies here as well, viz., directives (as well as sequenced precatives, the syntagm where *liddinam* properly belongs) have a **non-factual** value, and when factuality is meant, the choice is the indicative. Another commitment/promise is apparent in the next example:

[4.40] *qišātukunu lū naṣrā urram ina amāriya ana 1 iṣim sikiltim ša naksat awīlam bēl pīḫātim* ***ul uballaṭ***
Let your forests be watched. Tomorrow, upon my inspection, for 1 tree acquisition cut down **I will not let** the man responsible (for it) **live.** 4, 111:11–14

4.3.1.2 Other distinctions

4.3.1.2.1 Value distinctions: analytic vs. synthetic forms

The analytic precative (*lū paris*) is described by Leong 1994:378 as used in willing a situation; this could be verified by the following example:

[4.41] *umma šarrum–ma bāmassunu* ***lū wašbū*** *bāmassunu* ***[l]illikū***
The king (said) thus: 'Let half of them stay, [l]et half of them go'. 13, 104:5'–6'

wašābum is more fit to be described as a situation than is the fientive *alākum*.

This may well be corroborated by the division of verbal lexemes into three groups:

1. Verbal lexemes which occur in analytic formation only (*darûm, išûm, idûm*).
2. Verbal lexemes which occur in synthetic formation only (*alākum, šapārum, ṭarādum*).
3. Verbal lexemes (the largest group) which occur in both kinds of formations and thereby are capable of maintaining the distinction between fientive and stative anywhere, including the directive subparadigm.

This holds true as long as we remain in the affirmative sphere. Once in the negative sphere, this distinction mostly does not work. The formation *lā paris* (e.g., example [4.11]) is quite rare and instead *lā iparras* serves for both stative and fientive precative forms, even when it is clearly about stative verbal lexemes:

[4.8] *daltum lū biruyat mādiš* ***lā iqaṭṭin*** *u* ***lā ikabber***
Let the door be medium; let it not **be** (too) **thin** nor (too) **thick**. 3, 34:28–29

[4.42] *arḫātum u immerū šina* ***lā iṣeḫḫerā***
Let these cows and sheep not **be few**. 2, 58:17–18

[4.43] *līkulū* ***lā iberrû***
Let them eat so that they should not **be hungry**. 6, 39:7–8

4.3.1.2.2 Aspectual value?

In Leong 1994:362–63, under "aspectual expression", volitives (more or less the directive sub-paradigm) are said to express **perfective aspect**, much like the preterite. For this distinction to exist in the directive sub-paradigm, some opposition needs to exist first **inside this very sub-paradigm** (namely, perfective vs. imperfective). It seems that the view promoting the perfectivity of the precative is diachronically oriented, in order to explain the link between the putative historical functions of Proto-semitic **yaqtul* both as an injunctive and as punctual. However, the incorporation of an alleged imperfective form (*lā iparras*) in the paradigm would require, according to the same line of thinking, some change in the aspectual expression. As far as it is possible to say, there is no difference between the affirmative and the negative forms of the directive sub-paradigm as far as *Aktionsart*, or aspect, are concerned. Since the present theoretical framework generally ascribes no "basic meaning" to any form, and since distinction of any two values presupposes some formal difference, this distinction is not viewed as existing in the directive sub-paradigm (nor in the other precative (sub-)paradigms). The binary partition found in Huehnergard 1997 (preterite vs. durative) vis-à-vis indicative forms is not formally distinguished in the precative paradigms.

4.3.1.3 Specific values and idiosyncrasies in different persons

The different persons of the directive sub-paradigm are traditionally designated by different terms —*cohortative* for the 1st pers., *imperative* for the 2nd pers., and *precative* for the 3rd pers. (all terms apply to the affirmative only). For the negative forms, in all persons, the term *prohibitive* is used. The asymmetry is immediately apparent: Is there anything, apart from polarity, by which *lā aparras* is distinct from *luprus*? Is the interrelationship between *lā iparras* and *lā taparras* any different than the one between *liprus* and *purus* respectively? The answer to both questions is negative. Designating the different persons by different terms may be a convenient practice (not having to add the grammatical person) but it may lead to confusion in the way the system is perceived. Directives are considered here to be one group despite differences between the different persons of paradigm, which exist due to characteristics of the directive system: While two interlocutors, i.e., the speaker and the addressee, are typically a part of the dialogue sphere, the 3rd pers. is never an active participant in the dialogue.

4.3.1.3.1 The 3rd pers. directive

The 3rd pers. of the directive sub-paradigm generally conveys an **indirect order**, for reasons enumerated in the preceding section — a direct order is normally directed at the addressee (unless the vocation to the addressee is actualized as a 3rd pers. form). Traditionally at least, an indirect order presupposes an original direct order, with differences of deictics (personal, temporal or local) between them. However, if derivation is left out, there remain two related patterns, one direct, the other indirect.

In a few occurrences in the corpus we find essentially the same order uttered twice; once in the 3rd pers. and another in the 2nd pers. The former is **indirect** for it is not directly given. The latter is **direct**:

> [**4.2**] *šumma* PN_1 *ittalkam–ma šīpātim naši umma atta–ma* 5 *bilat šīpātim ana* PN_2 ***uṣur*** *šumma šīmam naši* 1 *šīmam* ***liṣṣuram***
> If PN_1 went away carrying wool you (should say) the following: '**Save** 5 talents of wool for PN_2'. If he carries merchandise, **let him save** one (piece of) merchandise for me. 12, 50:23–28

The shift in personal deixis from *uṣur* to *liṣṣur* and from *ana* PN_2 to *-am* follows a shift in presentation of the respective directives. The first (*ana* PN_2 *uṣur*) is presented as direct speech (*umma* X*–ma*), i.e., exactly as it is to be uttered. The second (*liṣṣuram*) is presented indirectly, when PN_1 (the theme of the directive) is not present. The two following examples are similar, but they differ from the preceding one in that the 3rd pers. forms in them are not directives, but rather sequenced precatives which are here regarded as a different sub-paradigm (**§4.4**). The comparison is hence strictly on the semantic level:

> [**4.1**] *aššum amtim ša tašpuram ša umma atta–ma ana ṣēr* PN_1 *alik–ma* ***amtam liddikkum*** *alli[k]šum–ma umma anāku–ma a[q]a[bb]īš[um]* PN_2 *išpuranni* ***amtam idnam***
> Concerning the maid of whom you wrote to me (about) whom you (said) thus: 'Go to PN_1 and **let him give you** the maid'. I went to him and so I was s[ay]ing to him: 'PN_2 sent me. **Give me** the maid'. 9, 149:4–15

The differentiation of both subjective and dative deictics shows that the syntagm *liddikkum* is rather an indirect order whereas *idnam* is direct. The first (*amtam liddikkum*) is indirectly aimed at PN_1 who is not present whereas the speaker (=the sender) is designated by *-kum*. The second (*amtam idnam*) is directly aimed at PN_1 while the speaker is designated by *-am*.

The following example is similar, exhibiting the sequenced precative after a *verbum dicendi*:

[**4.44**] *ša šullum kīsim šuāti* ***epuš*** *... anumma awīlam abī ḫussis–ma ša šullum kīsim šuāti* ***līpuš***
See to it that the purse is kept intact ... Now, remind the gentleman my father that **he see to it** that the purse is kept intact. 11, 49:14–20

These two precative forms contain the same idea, seeing to it that the purse is kept intact. A certain PN is the thematic referent of both *epuš* and *līpuš* (the second time this PN is referred to as *awīlam*). The appeal, however, is not made to the same man twice but first to PN_1 (by way of quotation), the thematic referent of *epuš*, and the second time to the addressee of the letter, PN_2, for him to remind PN_1 what to do.

Leong states that the 3rd pers. directive imposes an obligation on a third party while often obligating the second party as well (Leong 1994:369). This semantic statement can be backed up by a mechanical explanation, namely, that it has to do with the 3rd pers. directive being an indirect order and with vocation which is *always directed at the addressee*: The addressee has, or is given, the authority to get things done, or at least the physical ability to pass on the orders. This is felt when the 3rd pers. directive has a passive formation, in which the theme is not the agent:

[**4.45**] *eqlum linneriš*
Let the field be cultivated. 7, 55:18 [=Leong 1994 ex. 1009]

or, in the case of a non-human theme, in which case carrying out the action must be mediated by a human being:

[**4.46**] *alpū iškāram liṣbatū*
Let the oxen begin the work assignment. 12, 30:13–14 [=Leong 1994 ex. 1010]

The point is that this imposition of an obligation on the addressee is not formally marked as it is in the case of a causative 2nd pers. directive:

[**4.47**] *šupur–ma kilallīn šūriaš**šu***
Order (in writing) and have **him** bring both to me. 2, 119:14–16

In [**4.47**] the order is explicitly imposed on the addressee (the theme of both 2nd pers. directives) while the essence of it is to be carried out by an intermediary agent (designated by *-šu*). A semantically corresponding directive such as *liblam* (=let **him** bring me 12, 50:29; 2, 80:20–22) would contain the same information, save for the explicit imposition of the order upon the addressee.

This imposition upon the addressee is not formally marked in the 1st pers. directive either.

4.3.1.3.2 The 1st pers. directive

Edzard 1973:131–32 is reluctant to count the plural cohortative as belonging to the same group as the precative, considering it as a complementary mood to the precative. He regards it not only as a different form but also as a form having a different function. In addition, he is the first to raise the issue of inclusivity and exclusivity of these forms. According to him, these forms demand the presence (real or imaginary) of anyone represented by the subject. Leong 1994:372 adduces examples of both 1st pers. plural which include the addressee (showing this by the directly involved 2nd pers. forms) and examples which exclude the addressee. The 1st pers. plural is not the exact plural of the singular but rather may represent one of the following:

1. The speaker(s) and the addressee(s) (=inclusive), thereby being similar to the 2nd pers. directive in being aimed at the addressee as well:

> [**4.48**] *alkam–ma* ***i ninnamer***–*ma luttalkam*
> Come and let us (i.e., you and I) meet so I may go away. 9, 146:21–22

2. The speaker and a third party (but not the addresse, i.e., exclusive), thereby being similar to the 3rd pers. directive in containing an indirect order:

> [**4.49**] *anāku u šū ina* GN ***i nidīn***
> Let me and him litigate in GN. 2, 96:20–21

3. The speakers only (=exclusive), thus resembling the 1st pers. singular directive:

> [**4.50**] ***i ni*[*llik*]** *itti bēl*[*ini*] *i ninn*[*amer*]
> Let us [go] and me[et] with [our] lord (=the addressee). 2, 78:12–14

The complement of *nanmurum* is marked by *itti*, and is therefore not deemed included in the theme. *i nillik* too has nothing to do with the addressee. The following example is the same, leaving out the addressee:

> [**4.51**] *maḫar* D[N_1] *u* DN_2 *ana bēlini kâta* ***i ni*[*k*]*r*[*u*]*b***
> Let us pr[ay] before DN_1 and DN_2 for you, our lord. 2, 88:34'

Another example for the last type is example [**4.30**], which does not include the addresse as well. The different scopes of the 1st pers. plural **are not formally distinguished** with any consistency. The 1st pers. plural form may therefore equally express each possibility. This is important in showing that these idiosyncratic features of each grammatical person of the directive group are close enough as to reside all under the 1st pers. plural: *i ninnamer* in [**4.48**] is similar to the 2nd pers. directive in involving the addressee, in [**4.49**] it is closer to the 3rd pers. directive in involving a third party and in [**4.50**] and [**4.51**] it resembles the 1st pers. singular in expressing exhortation for the speakers.

Whether the 1st pers. singular is a directive or not may be a matter for debate, for it could be claimed that people do not order themselves. However, it certainly makes sense to consider the 1st pers. singular as a directive: The 1st pers. directive is in effect actualized as an exhortation, containing both an element of will which originates at the speaker and a directive element. The most important point is this: It may commute with any of the directives whenever they occur, thus belonging to the same paradigm. The paradigmatic interrelations with the other directives and sharing with the directives in other persons the same core characteristics make the 1st pers. singular a full-fledged member of this sub-paradigm.

4.3.1.3.3 The 2nd pers. directive

The 2nd pers. directive (*purus*), traditionally referred to as imperative, constitutes a linguistic issue in its own right. It has been sufficiently demonstrated (and thus demarcated) in opposition to the 1st and 3rd pers. of the directive sub-paradigm. It is characterized as a form which is generally not marked for certain verbal categories such as tense and person (Palmer 1986:108), having only 2nd person. In OB it is definitely marked for person both by a special pattern and by ø (which is opposed to *lu-* / *li-* / *i n-*, characteristic only of 1st and 3rd pers. forms). Palmer regards the imperative as the unmarked member of the directive system. In our corpus it would be better, setting morphology aside, to regard it as the most characteristic representative of the directive sub-paradigm. This is because the 2nd pers. directive by and large does not occur in other (sub-)paradigms (except for the sequenced precative syntagm, §**4.4**), whereas the 1st and 3rd pers. person forms are syntagmatically more flexible. This syntagmatic rigidity characterizes imperatives in many languages — typically they may not be subordinated, do not occur in questions and are referential exclusively to the point of utterance.

Palmer mentions the importance of the **syntactic** link between forms which, while clearly different morphologically, may not be so syntactically, and hence belong to one and the same paradigm (Palmer 1986:110). The example he adduces, of the Amharic jussive paradigm, has much to do with OB, not only because it is about the same historic forms.[12] In Amharic,

12. *ləngär, nəgär* and *yəngär* as formal equivalents of *luprus, purus* and *liprus*. The negation of *nəgär* is, as in most of the Semitic languages, the negated apocopate, namely, *attəngär* (< **al təngär*, the equivalent, with regard to the verbal form, of *ē taprus*).

much as in the present corpus, the forms which belong to this paradigm are tightly interrelated. The 2nd pers. forms of the jussive occur only negated, as negative counterparts of the imperative. Similarly, OB does not have any forms for the affirmative 2nd pers. other than *purus* (the analytic forms, such as *lū ṣabtāta*, are functionally identical to the synthetic affirmative 2nd pers.). For discussion of these syntactic interrelations see **§4.1**.

The main reservation regarding the inclusion of the imperative in the jussive paradigm (mentioned in Palmer 1986:111) is that the jussive can be found in deontic requests (deliberative questions) whereas the imperative cannot. Such a situation is encountered not only in Amharic — imperatives in general are not found in such an environment (in languages where we do find 2nd pers. modal forms in such an environment, these forms are not imperatives — *why* ***should you do*** *it*, etc.). This problem is one of classification. The interrelations between the 2nd pers. and 3rd pers. forms discussed in **§4.1** are not valid everywhere but only under certain syntagmatic conditions (viz., in the present sub-paradigm). Whenever syntagmatic conditions are different, the interrelations may be different as well. This problem is resolved here by postulating another sub-paradigm — the interrogative sub-paradigm (see further below, **§4.3.3**).

The speaker in the corpus, while formally addressing a secondary addressee, namely, the scribe (designated by the thematic reference of *qibī–ma*), addresses in fact the primary addressee. Speaking to the addressee is signaled via either a 2nd pers. directive (thereby ignoring or omitting the scribe), or the 3rd pers. directive, as if still channeling the information through the scribe. Here, both the 2nd pers. and the 3rd pers. directives, whose theme refers back to the addressee, are considered functionally as a 2nd pers. directive. Sallaberger 1999:49 mentions that the semantic and functional differences between using the 2nd pers. or the 3rd pers. in this context have not been resolved yet.

Table **1** summarizes the forms at play in the directive sub-paradigm:

1.

	affirmative	negative
1 sg.	*luprus / lū parsāku*	*lā aparras*
2	*purus / pursī, lū parsāta / i*	*lā taparras / ī*
3	*liprus, lū paris / parsat*	*lā iparras (lā paris / parsat)*
1 pl.	*i niprus*	*lā niparras*
	etc.	

The directive category is the predominant value of precative forms. Some precative forms, however, function in other (sub-)paradigms, showing different paradigmatic constitution, and consequently have different values as well.

4.3.2 The wish paradigm

This paradigm has a narrow semantic domain, which occurs, however, at the opening of almost every letter in the corpus. The differences between the affirmative forms of the present paradigm and those of the directive sub-paradigm are difficult to formulate exactly, for some forms are typical only of this sub-paradigm, and so are impossible to compare. The most important means to distinguish the wish paradigm, although statistically marginal, is the 3rd pers. **vetitive**.

According to GAG §81i, the vetitive expresses a negative wish directed at a person of equal or higher standing. It is, however, **not a formal prohibition**. This semantic explanation, it should be added, is directed at occurrences of the vetitive in every dialect of Akkadian, including OAkk and OA, which employ it quite regularly as a productive part of the modal system, rather than for wishes only.

Edzard 1973:132 supplies a semantic explanation, thereby pointing out the semantic difference between both groups: The prohibitive (representing the directives) has to do with volition and **the power or possibility to execute the action** while the vetitive (representing the wish paradigm) is used with **wishes**, where an action or state **is not wanted but not prohibited**.

Buccellati's view is explained in a table summarizing the notional differences between order and wish (Buccellati 1996 §29.5). As command he considers only the 2nd pers. directive (both affirmative and negative), *purus* and *lā taparras*. The rest, namely, *luprus*, *i niprus*, *liprus*, and *ayyiprus* (their negative counterpart, according to Buccellati) belong under **wish**. It seems that, for Buccellati, the difference between the various persons is more significant than it is deemed here. His wish category is therefore nothing but the other half of our directive sub-paradigm. A chapter earlier, discussing morphology, Buccellati 1996 §28.6 notes that the prohibitive **can** occur with the 3rd person, expressing a negative command (as opposed to the vetitive, which expresses a negative wish). This explanation conforms better to the accepted view.

According to Huehnergard 1997 §16.3, the vetitive expresses a negative wish, hence it is less forceful than the prohibitive.

In general, the vetitive form is described more or less in conformity with its value in the corpus, namely, as a form used exclusively for wishes. This, however, does not expose the whole picture; the vetitive form is very rare, even in wishes, and as such it occurs with very few verbal lexemes — mainly *rašûm* and one or two cases of *egûm* and *naparkûm* — occurring in the 3rd pers. only:[13]

13. The only occurrence of the 2nd pers. is conditional; see **§5.1.1**, example **[5.5]**.

[4.52] *ilum n[ā]ṣi[r]ka ṣibûtam* ***ayyirši***
May your prot[ect]ing god have no needs. 11, 105:7 (=3, 61:8–9; 6, 64:7; 6, 91:9, etc.)

[4.53] *imittam u šumēlam bēlī u bēltī ana naṣārika* ***ayyīgû***
May my Lord and my Mistress not fail to protect you on the right and on the left. 11, 106:5'–7' (see 12, 38:8)

[4.54] *maṣṣar šulmim u balāṭ[im] ina rēšika* ***ayyipparku***
May the guardian of well-being and health not cease to be available for you. 11, 105:11–12

The three preceding examples come from two closely-related letters (possibly one letter, as they are written by the same person — 11, 105, n. a to the translation). The small number of examples in which the form occurs is not in direct proportion to its importance. The vetitive form is distinct enough to compel us to propose another paradigm for wishes. The vetitive, however, is not the only structural peculiarity of the wish paradigm. The pair *lū balṭāta lū šalmāta* occurs hundreds of times. When the following occurs it strikes us as very irregular:

[4.55] *aššumiya abī atta maḫar* DN ***buluṭ***
May you, my father, live in front of DN for my sake. 1, 105:4–5

It is possible to claim that the use of the analytic formation is due to the stative nature of these verbal lexemes. But the fact remains that at least the verbal lexeme *balāṭum* is by and large attested in the analytic formation within the wish paradigm whereas the choice of synthetic formation is found **only outside it**:

[4.56] *lullik šēp bēltiya luṣbat–ma (lu-iṣ-ba-at)* ***lubluṭ***
Let me go (and) hold the foot of my lady so that **I live**. 2, 108:10–12

One dubious case is the following example

[4.57] *ana rēdîm* [...] *libluṭ–ma* 11, 61:2'

which is too broken to be certain (or to translate). To this analytic formation the expression *lū dari(āta)* should be added. This analytic form is commonly used for the 2nd pers. instead of the formation *purus* which belongs almost exclusively to the directive sub-paradigm. The 3rd pers. forms of the present paradigm are more productive than the trio *lū balṭāta lū šalmāta lū dariāta* and exhibit a richer selection of verbal lexemes:

[4.58] DN ... *qaqqadka likabbit*
May DN ... honor you. 1, 52:7; 3, 40:6–7; 3, 47:7

[4.59] DN$_1$ *u* DN$_2$ *aššumiya dāriš ūmī perʾam ša bīt abīka liṣṣurū*
May DN$_1$ and DN$_2$ guard the offspring of your father's house for my sake for eternity. 3, 22:4–5

[4.60] DN ... *qaqqadam kabtam liškunka–ma mali taqabbû limtaggarka*
May DN ... honor you and accord you whatever you say. 3, 52:6

[4.61] *ilānū rabûtum ... ana abīya kâta li[k]r[u]b[ū]*
May great gods ... p[ra]y for you, my father. 7, 118:5–6

The 1st pers. of the wish paradigm may not exist at all, which is logical; one example of it may be the following:

[4.62] *atti aššumiya lū šalmāti* ***anāku*** *aššumiki* ***lū šalmāku***[14]
May you be well for my sake and may I be well for your sake. 3, 60:12–15 (and see example **[4.65]** below)

The paradigmatic constitution of the wish paradigm is somewhat asymmetric:

2.	affirmative	negative
1	*lū šalmāku* (?)	—
2	*lū šalmāta* (/*ti*/*tunu*)	—
3	*lū šalim* / *likīl* (/*likillū*)	*ayyirši* / *ayyīg*(*û*)

The important thing is that the paradigmatic makeup is markedly different from that of the directive sub-paradigm, which makes them, despite of the partial similarity (e.g., in 3rd pers. affirmative), two distinct groups.

Another structural feature of the members of this paradigm is that they habitually occur at the beginning of the letter, right after the opening formula *ana* X *qibī–ma umma* Y–*ma*. Only rarely are they found at the end:

[4.63] *[dār]iš ūmī* ***lilabbirka***
May (DN) grant you [ete]rnal life. 1, 106:29

[4.64] *bēlī atta ina šulmi u balāṭi ana* GN *erbam–ma bunū namrūtum ša* DN$_1$ *rāʾimika u* DN$_2$ *bānika* ***limḫurūka***
You, my lord, enter GN in well-being and good health and may the pleasant faces of DN$_1$ who loves you and DN$_2$ your creator welcome you. 11, 119:27–30

[4.65] *kurbīm* ***lū šalmāku***–*ma annûm* ***lū kayyān***
Pray for me, may I be well and may this remain (so). 7, 5:17–18

The two preceding examples occur at the end of the letter. This is not the

14. Another occurrence of *lū šalmāku* (8, 24:4–7) is interpreted as belonging to the asseverative paradigm (see **§2.4.3.1** example **[2.42]**).

only peculiarity they manifest: They are connected by *-ma* as well, which is very irregular for series of wishes

Both the different paradigmatic constitution, and the fact that the members of the wish group are by and large confined to the beginning of the letter, where no other forms figure, make this group a distinct **paradigm** (rather than a sub-paradigm).

Wishes are treated independently of the verbal system in Salonen 1967, which describes greeting and politeness formulas diachronically, and in Sallaberger 1999, where they are examined in their synchronic pragmatic function in the text.

"Indirect wishes" may be expressed in example [**4.65**] above and in the following example:

> [**4.66**] *kurbī–ma ibbî* ***limaṭṭi***
> Pray that my loss be small. 3, 60:10–11

Namely, the lady who is to pray in [**4.65**] would say *lū šalmāta*. Such modal series are indeed translated many times as indirect orders (pray **that** I be healthy). This issue is to be discussed further below (§**4.4**).

A reported wish occurs only a few times in the same context. Nonetheless, one can clearly see the reflection of the model *ana naṣārim ayyīgu* (see example [**4.53**] above) inside a genitive equivalent clause, exhibiting the form *lā iparrasu*:

> [**4.67**] *ana šulmika* ***ša*** DN *zākir šumika ana naṣārim* ***lā iggû*** *ašpura*[*m*]
> I write to (inquire about) you health (namely, the idea) that DN who gave you your name does not fail to protect (you). 3, 50:5–6 (=8, 148:5–7)

The following could be interpreted as a nominalized wish, informally replacing *lū balṭāta*:

> [**4.68**] *ana balāṭika aktanarra*[*b*]
> I pray constantly for your living. 11, 105:15

The wish paradigm, although in a way a relic of a formerly more productive system (perhaps not distinct from the directive system),[15] is hardly productive anymore in the corpus, but it nonetheless is a distinct structural group, having a different paradigmatic constitution and exhibiting an important social function of its own.

---

15. See for example in an OAkk royal inscription (Narām-Sîn C1) *pān iliš*[*u*] ***ayyizziz*** (Gelb and Kienast 1990:238, 518–19), ... *zikram u šumam* ***ayyiddinā-šum*** (ibid. 523–26).

4.3.3 The interrogative sub-paradigm

Semantically speaking, a question is itself modal. It contains an expression of uncertainty (like epistemic markers expressing various degrees of certainty) and at the same time it asks for information or for an answer (in a way similar to the imperative demanding action). As such, it has to do with functional sentence perspective as well (for which see **§2.4.1** above). In addition to these general characteristics, a question can have a modal content (*liprus*, in opposition with a non-modal one, viz., *iparras*) and thus be considered a part of the precative paradigms. This is, however, a highly restricted slot which includes many neutralizations, and therefore demands a separate demarcation and discussion.

Palmer 1986:23–24, 30–31 mentions that languages such as French or German do not have any interrogative mood (i.e., the morphological expression of modality). Yet, were the definition of mood somewhat broader, that is, if it comprised (morpho-)syntax instead of just morphology, then these languages could be said to have an interrogative mood by way of inversion of subject pronoun and finite verbal form (it is of no consequence that these inversions may stand for other distinctions as well, i.e., for marking the conditional — there are enough signals to tell these two functions apart). In our corpus, a **nexus question** (**§4.2.2.1**, n. 5) is sometimes marked by plene writing, but this signal could either be missing or mark something else (word accent, vocal lengthening) just as well (the rationale behind such plene writing is not always clear). In the absence of consistent signaling of a nexus question, it is quite difficult to treat it separately as modal (for modality is here discussed only in connection with an overt and consistent signal of any order, viz., phonological, morphological or syntactic).

The following two sections describe the behavior of precatives and other related forms in connection with a question.

4.3.3.1 Modal pronominal questions

This group consists of modal pronominal questions which contain precative forms with a variety of interrogative pronouns and adverbs:

> [**4.69**] *ša kīma yâti ana kâšim mannum* ***li*[*dd*]*in***
> *Who* **could gi**[**ve**] you one like me? 9, 141:5–7

> [**4.70**] *ulazzaz–ma* (sic) *mannum* ***litēršu***
> If I do not serve, who **would pay** it **back**? 11, 27:16–17

Both preceding examples are semantically interpreted as potential (*who* ***could***...) in the AbB edition, as well as in GAG §153g (*könnte wer* ... for [**4.69**]). This notion in [**4.70**] may be the result of the form *litēršu* being the apodosis of the preceding conditional clause. In other cases, their value is closer to the deontic value of the form outside the interrogative — *should, be supposed to,* etc.:

> [4.71] *isimmānam ina mīnim* ***lišpukūnim*** *u eqlam ina mīnim* ***lūriš***
> How **should they pile up** the travel provisions and with what **should I seed** the field? 13, 4:18'

The last example, containing both 3rd and 1st pers. precatives, questions parts of the clause other than the nexus in the verbal form — specifically a question about an instrumental complement (*with what*). The main point of the question is represented here (as in any pronominal question) by the linguistic equivalent of an algebraic x — the interrogative pronoun which is the rheme of the clause. In a pronominal question, it is not the validity of the nexus, represented in the verbal form, which is questioned (as it is in case of nexus questions), but rather other parts of the clause, represented by interrogative pronouns.

The semantic value of the verbal forms in this category is considerably different compared with their value in the directive sub-paradigm. First and foremost, the forms are **not directive**. This is quite clear in [4.69] and [4.70]. In other cases, the relationship with directives is maintained by way of asking for instructions:

> [4.72] 1 *lim ummānātim ana ayyim–ma*[16] ***luddin***
> To *whom* (is it) I should give a thousand soldiers? 8, 23:21–22

Second, when an element of will is present, the precative forms in the interrogative sub-paradigm do not express **the will of the speaker**. In [4.71] and in [4.72] it seems as if **the will element has to do with the addressee**, at whom the question is directed, rather than with the speaker. Third, it seems that an element of will is not necessarily present, as is clear from examples [4.69] and [4.70] above, and from the following example:

> [4.17] *gimillam ša elīya taškunu matī anāku* ***lutēr***
> When **would *I* return** the favor which you did to me? 3, 22:6–7

It is difficult to circumscribe precisely the common value of precative forms in pronominal questions. It becomes somewhat clearer when we compare members of the interrogative sub-paradigm to an indicative form in the same environment:

16. *ana ayyim–ma* is interpreted as an interrogative and the focal *-ma* rather than as an indefinite. A similar case would be *kunuk* ***mannim–ma*** *immaḫḫar* "*Whose* seal (is it that) will be accepted?" (11, 90:29).

[**4.73**] *matī ṣābam šuātu* ***ammar***
When **will I see** this army? 7, 152:7

The difference in this case is less pronounced than it would be outside this interrogative syntagmatic environment, but nonetheless, precative forms inside pronominal questions all exhibit a common **non-factual value**.

An important structural characteristic of this sub-paradigm is that the 2nd pers. precative, *purus*, **is excluded** from it. Instead, one finds in these syntagmatic conditions a modally neutralized *taparras* form, which is not opposed to any 2nd pers. modal form. This is a phenomenon attested in other languages as well, where the imperative is nothing but a directive and hence cannot occur in an environment such as the present one (compare the English translation, where there is a modal verb instead of the imperative, which is excluded as well):

[**4.74**] *būrī idi atta ina bītika būrī ammīnim* ***tušakk****[****al****]*
Leave the calves. Why do you (**have to**) **fee[d]** the calves in your house? 8, 139:14'–16'

Example [**4.74**] contains such neutralization; *taparras* is amodal, or modally neutralized, and can generally represent either modal or non-modal notions. In example [**4.75**] the modal notion is only hinted at by contextual information, namely, the preoccurrence of modal *lušqul*:

[**4.75**] 1 *bītam amram–ma kaspam lušqul–ma lušām atta kīam tāpulanni umma atta–ma* ***ammīnim*** *kaspam marṣussu* ***[t]ašaqqal*** *šāpir ṣābim atta*
'Find me a house and let me pay silver and buy it.' You answered me as follows: 'Why **should [you] pay** a high price[17] in silver? You are (after all) an overseer of workmen!'. 13, 110:10–15

In the following example, although surrounded by modals (the rhematic *ana wuššurim* and the 2nd pers. sequenced precative *wuššeraššu*), *lā tuwaššaraššu* may denote either notions:

[**4.76**] *[š]umma ekallum–ma lā iqbi ṣuḫāru šū ana wuššurim* ***mīnu*** *ṣuḫāra šâtu* ***lā tuwaššaraššu*** *inanna šitāl–ma ṣuḫāra šâtu wuššeraššu*
If the palace itself did not order (otherwise), this servant is to be released. Why **don't/won't you release** this servant? Now think (this) over and release this servant. 1, 74:23–28

Additionally, in [**4.76**] the neutralized form is of essentially the same order as explained above, but in the negative sphere — *lā tuwaššaraššu* is modally neutralized as well. The reason for this is different: Negative

17. 13, 110, n. b to the translation.

indicative and negative precative forms are morphologicaly identical in this environment.

The following table represents the interrogative precative sub-paradigm:

3.	affirmative		negative
	modal	non-modal	modal/non-modal
(*mīnam*) 1	***luprus***	***aparras***	**lā aparras*
(*mīnam*) 2	*taparras*		*lā taparras*
(*mīnam*) 3	***liprus***	***iparras***	**lā iparras*

The asterisk marks possible forms (e.g., in other corpora, see GAG §153g). The main point remains the comprehensive neutralization of the 2nd pers. forms. A similar kind of neutralization is expected for the negative forms of both modal and non-modal forms in the 1st and 3rd pers. Those neutralized forms are **amodal**, being neither modal nor non-modal. The possibility to come across, in the affirmative 1st and 3rd pers., either indicative or precative forms requires that the modal group be regarded as a **sub-paradigm**, rather than a paradigm.

4.3.3.2 Deontic nexus questions

The second group, containing modal nexus questions, is more of a challenge. Palmer 1986:106–108 discusses a category he calls *deontic requests* where the speaker asks the addressee whether an action is necessary or permissible. This is just one possibility, where the modal element is questioned. It is not quite clear whether this is the case in our corpus. Von Soden (GAG §153g) says that the precative occurs in nexus questions, and adduces a couple of examples:

> [**4.77**] *ša*[*nītam*] *nišī ša awīlê* GN_1 [*ina* GN_2] *inaṣṣarūšunūti*[18] [*kīam taš*]*puram umma atta–ma* [*nišū* G]N_1 *ištu* GN_3 [*ikšudān*]*im nišī*[*š*]*unu* ***luwaššer***
> Sec[ondly], they will keep [in GN_2] the people of GN_1. [You w]rote me [thus], saying: '[The people of G]N_1 [have arri]ved here from GN_3. **Should I set** [th]eir people **free**?'. ARM 1, 22:34–38 (Cited in Finet 1956 §79b as well)

The answer (*inaṣṣarūšunūti*) precedes the question (*luwaššer*) which is presented in the form of a quotation. Here, the question applies directly to the nexus component of the verb (note, however, that the text is quite broken).

The following pair of examples exhibit plene writing of the third-weak

18. New reading in LAPO 17:55–56.

radical:

> [4.78] *šumi ilika u muttakilīka ša kâta u aḫāka ašariš ušēšibū libli̯*
> Let the name of your god and your trusted ones who settled you and your brother there be lost. VAB 6, 186:22–25

This example is not interpreted in the edition as a question, nor is there any apparent reason to consider it as such. Verbal forms having a third-weak radical exhibit plene writing at times. The following example is similar in this respect:

> [4.79] *awātam elīka* PN *lā iraššī̯*
> Let *PN*[19] have nothing against you. 1, 50:20–23

A precative form in a nexus question is thus conceivably possible (as can be seen in example [4.77], which comes from the ARM corpus), but there is not one convincing example for it in the AbB corpus. The following examples constitute the small group of potential precative nexus questions found in the corpus. Although they either contain vocalic lengthening or are interpreted as questions (by way of translation) none of them is an undisputable question:

> [4.18] *ina maḫrīka–ma ḫurʾussunu̯ limḫaṣū*
> Should one then strike their necks in *your presence*? 1, 35:18–20

In the preceding example there is not enough context to say whether this is a question or not; the only hint for question is the plene writing (*ḫu-ur-ú-sú-nu-**ú*** 1, 35:19). Another problem which arises is that the main point in a nexus question is the nexus, namely, the relation between theme and rheme. It means that the question here would apply to the relation between *ina maḫrīka–ma* (rheme/focus) and the rest, namely, *ḫurʾussunu̯ limḫaṣū*. The precative form, being part of the theme, is not really questioned, or in other words, as in the case of pronominal questions, the question does not directly apply to it. What is marked as question in OB is not necessarily the verbal form. The precise function of the marked part[20] inside the question is not quite clear yet. Plene writing may mislead us, as it does in the following example:

> [4.80] *awīlê lūḫuzam u anāku̯ lullikam–ma ana šigilti šālanni*
> Let me get hold of the gentlemen and let me come myself so you can ask me about willful negligence. 9, 49:36–39

anāku̯ is interpreted in the edition as a focal element, rather than a

19. PN is in focal position (see **§2.4.1.3**, examples **[2.18]**–**[2.20]**).

20. Illingsworth 1990:416 notes, regarding plene writing, that it is mostly not used for matters of emphasis.

question. The (sequenced) 2nd pers. precative is **never** part of a question.

The next two examples are interpreted in the editions as interrogative for no apparent reason:

> [**4.81**] *u annû nabrû qerbū yâti lidabbibūninni aššum ṣuḫārtim* 1, 30:19–21
>
> [**4.82**] *mali pānūki lā ku[tt]umū bītum kalûšu lillik* 7, 36:5–7

These two examples are difficult to interpret (therefore no translation is offered for them), but it does not seem that assuming that they contain a question makes the situation any clearer.

In conclusion, it seems that this category of interrogative precative in nexus questions (or, as Palmer calls them, *deontic requests*) does not have enough unequivocal examples for it to be firmly established. Such a notion, however, is not altogether missing from the corpus. There are examples where the existence of such a question is quite clear but the form is not the expected *liprus* but rather *iparras*; these examples, so it seems, formally show modal neutralization. This neutralization holds as long as the precative in nexus questions remains an uncertain phenomenon in the AbB corpus:

> [**4.83**] *ša libbiša lū <zi>kar lū sinnišat anāku̱* ***eleqqe̱*** *ammīni ṭēmki* [*a*]*nniam lā anniam* [*l*]*ā tašpurīm*
> **Should *I* take** her foetus, be it male or female? Why did you [n]ot send me your orders (namely) this or that? 7, 141:8'–13'

Here the speaker is explicitly asking for instructions, and this is the most natural use of the deliberative question.[21] It must be admitted that, at least in accordance with focal element order (**§2.4.1.3**), *anāku* is focal. The other examples of this type mostly show a nexus question which applies strictly to the verbal form.

The following example is somewhat different semantically, being similar to a moral question (but may easily be interpreted as denoting indicativity as well):

---

21. The ARM corpus has similar examples:
in[*a*]*nna šumma ṣābum awīl* GN_1 *ana* GN_2 *ulū–ma ana* GN_3 *issaniq ṣāb bēliya ina libbi ālim* ***uṣṣêm-ma̱ ittallakam*** *ulū–ma ina li*[*bbi*] *ālim* ***ikkalla*** *bēlī puru*[*ssâm ša*] *ṣābišu annītam lā annītam li*[*špuram*] "Now, if the army of GN_1 has proceeded against GN_2 or GN_3, **should the army** of my lord **exit** the city and **go away** or **should it be retained** in[sid]e the city? Let my lord [write] me his deci[sion concerning] his army, either this or that" (ARM 26, 390:12''-17''; this example is analysed and compared with a *ša parāsim* construction in **§7.2.2.3** as example [**7.36b**]).

[**4.84**] *mīnum ša* PN *warad ekallim ana ṣabāt mūšarim šâtim* (sic) *kaspam našû–ma warki ayyūtim–ma ittanallaku ašar kâti īšû annītum* ***inneppeš***
Why is it that PN, the palace dependent, carries silver and keeps following others to take possession of that garden? **Should** *this* **be** (or: **is** *this* being) **done** where I have you? 11, 160:23–28

As always in case of modal neutralization, the neutralized form may represent both modal and non-modal notions. The following example is some sort of key, denoting an unequivocal **deliberative question** which uses *iparras* forms where *liprus* forms are naturally expected:

[**4.85**] [*aššum ša t*]*ašpuram*	[Concerning what you] wrote me,
umma att[*a*]*–ma*	saying:
[*kaspam ša ri*]*bbāt būlim*	'**Should** *the ge*[*ner*]*als* **pay**
[*ša ter*]*dītim*	[the silver of the ad]ditional
wak[*lū amu*]*rrim* ***inaddinū***	[arr]ears in cattle?
waqlū ḫaṭṭim la[*pp*]*utū u rēdû*	As to the captains, ser[gea]nts
inaddinū	and soldiers, **should** they **pay**?
ṭēmam bēlī lišpuram	Let my lord send me an order'.
ša tašpuram	(This is) what you wrote me.
	Let *the* [*ge*]*nerals and captains* **pay**
[*kaspam ša ri*]*bbāt būlim*	[the silver of the ad]ditional
[*ša ter*]*dītim*	[arr]ears in cattle;
[*wak*]*lū amurrim*	
u waqlū ḫaṭṭim–ma	
liddinū	
lapputū u rêdū	**As to** the sergeants and soldiers,
lā inaddinū	**let** them **not pay.**
1, 1:4–18	

The answer, containing directives (*liddinū, lā inaddinū*), testifies to the deliberative nature of the question (*inaddinū*).

The next three examples contain rhetorical questions. The background for the first example is the pressure put on the speaker to release a distrainee. She, however, expects some barley in return, and is not willing to release the distrainee:

[**4.86**] 5 *warḫī nipûtam ušakkal–ma ša âm lā ublam nipûtam* ***uwaššar***
I have been feeding[22] the distrainee for 5 months and (you expect that) **I should release** the distrainee (to the one) who[23] has not brought me the barley? 11, 106: 30'–33'

22. Or: "Should I (be) feed(ing) ...?".

23. This *ša* clause is interpreted in the edition as a conditional clause; see ibid., n. e to the translation.

[**4.87**] *atta ana* GN *tallikam–ma ul taqbia u ana awātim annītim* ***amaggarkunūti̯***
As for you, you came to GN but did not tell me, and (you expect that) **I should consent** to this matter? 1, 33:40–43

Both examples [**4.86**] and [**4.87**] exhibit a rhetorical question rather than a request for advice or instructions. The structure is analogous to the rest of the examples here, and so the notion of modality is clearly felt. The resemblance to the ensuing example is apparent:

[**4.88**] *ana aḫātiya ul addin ana kâšum* ***anaddinakkum***
I did not give (the maid) to my sister, (you expect that) **I should give** (her) *to you*? 1, 51:34–36

Example [**4.88**] is found in a context where the addressee is advised not to agree (*lā tamaggarī*) a few times, and the example itself is the last piece of advice, what she should say (in the form of direct speech) to the messenger, in case he might be sent to convince her to give away either a maid or silver.

It seems that there are many more examples of such potentially deliberative questions containing *iparras* than there are positive cases of *liprus*. In view of these findings, the interrogative *iparras* (rather than *liprus*) is concluded hereby to be the most regular way to express deliberative questions in the corpus. However, being a modally neutralized form, **it is not a part of the interrogative precative paradigm**, although semantically it is closely related to it.

Further corroboration of the difficulty encountered with interrogative *liprus* forms may be found in the following example:

[**4.89**] *umma atta–ma ammīni unnedu[k]kaka lā illikam anāku* ***ša*** *unnedukki̯m* ***šūbulim***
Thus you (said): 'Why has your tablet not arrived here?' 'Am *I* the one who **should send** the tablet? / was *I* **to send** the tablet?'. 1, 23:7–11

For syntactic analysis of this example see below, §**7.2.2.4** and see also Huehnergard 1986:226, n. 34. The construction ***anāku*** *ša unnedukkim šūbulim*, where *anāku* is the rheme (or focus), is another way to express deliberative questions, in the absence of precative forms in such questions.

4.4 Sequenced precatives

Precative forms tend to be interconnected mainly via the connectives *-ma* and *u* or by juxtaposition of the clauses, or asyndesis (other connectives, such as *ū*, *ulū* or *-ma u* are marginal in this respect). *-ma* is the most important of all three, for reasons to be discussed below. In a manner somewhat similar to what it signals in reporting past tense sequences (*iprus–ma iprus–ma iptaras*), *-ma* marks a sequential relationship between concatenated verbal forms. The concatenated precative forms (that is, all the forms which belong in the chain, including the first one) are considered here as a different sub-paradigm. The reasoning leading to this classification is elaborated below, under **§4.4.4**. In short, these forms, although identical morphologically and very similar in their values to the directives, have a somewhat different paradigmatic constitution, as a result of the different syntagmatic conditions. This alone justifies setting this group apart from the directive group, and calling the forms **sequenced precatives.**

Infinitive constructions are sometimes related semantically to certain sequenced precatives but are not strictly interchangeable with them (for discussion see **§§4.4.2** and **4.5**) and hence are not instrumental in establishing sequenced precatives as a distinct paradigm (see **§4.4.4.0.3**).

4.4.1 General characteristics of sequenced precatives — literature review

GAG §158a mentions the peculiarity of Akkadian in the distribution of subordination and coordination compared to European languages, namely, that various logical relationships (cause, condition, consecutivity, finality, etc.) which are effected in the latter group via subordination, are many times expressed via coordination in Akkadian. As to the precative, GAG states that this may well be the only way. In §158f it is mentioned that purpose is expressed via *-ma* + precative. Structurally, it is identical to indirect command (*qibīšum–ma lillik*) and to a simple temporally consecutive order (*alik–ma tēršu*).

Edzard 1973 states that a secondary function of the precative is *finalis* — denoting purpose. Edzard does not mention that this is not always the case (it is a peculiarity of this concatenated structure, containing various notions which are more distinct when conjunctions are used — see **§4.4.4.1**). The example he adduces (**aqbī–ma līpuš*) is not really a normal manifestation of a precative sequence — and such examples are indeed rare and irregular in our corpus (and when they do occur they generally reflect conditionality rather than finality).

According to Patterson 1971:44, in interconnecting verbs in the mood of wish or command, *-ma* serves "to point to a following final clause, whether of purpose or of intended result" meaning "in order that/so that".

Leong 1994:381 divides sequenced volitives into two subgroups — indirect volitives and pseudo-indirect volitives. The former is "... accomplished through another intermediary situation ...", namely, another precative preceding the one in question. This category, described by Hebraists in connection with the modal cluster in Biblical Hebrew (Joüon 1996 §116),[24] is equated by Leong with the meaning of purpose or consequence (GAG §158f) of the connected clause. As to pseudo-indirect volitives, Leong 1994:396 mentions that there are certain syntagmatic environments[25] where what seems to be an indirect volitive turns out not to be one. These are characterized by verbs of ordering (such as *qabûm, šapārum,* etc.) whose modal content ("[the] object that constitutes the speech") is missing and is represented by the following clause. The second volitive expresses both the speech content and the purpose of the speech. The fact remains that there is no formal signal of the difference between the two types. Two precative sequences could exhibit an identical structure, and yet be semantically interpreted in two different ways — one as purpose, the other as a temporal sequence, usually depending upon the semantic relations between the verbal forms. The translation into European languages may be misleading: Had we translated such a sequence into Biblical Hebrew, it would have been more true to the original, but still would not tell us whether it is a purpose or a temporal sequence.[26] Leong is perfectly aware of this and even shows this (examples ibid. 383–84). As a matter of fact, OB does not formally differentiate between these meanings. It is stated in Huehnergard 1997 §16.4 that in a chain of injunctives connected by *-ma* (and only rarely asyndetically), the second and following clauses are often **to be translated** as purpose clauses (my emphasis).

4.4.2 The syntactic nature of sequenced precatives

The syntactic nature of clauses connected by *-ma* has been discussed since the end of the ninteenth century. A summary of this discussion is

24. Joüon 1996 §114 distinguishes *direct* and *indirect* volitives by the alleged nature of *wə-*; when *wə-* has a "purely juxtaposing value of *and*" (or when it is missing) then volitives are *direct.* They are considered *indirect* when the *wə-* "which logically has subordinating value" appears. This kind of differentiation is clearly semantic, rather than formally structure-differentiated.

25. Leong's use of the term "syntagmatic" is different than its use here — for the only difference between pseudo-indirect and indirect volitives is the use, in the former group, of a limited number of verbal lexemes in the first clause. Even when these lexemes are found, they do not consistently show a specific notion. See **§4.4.4.1** for examples.

26. For example *šāl-ma liqbiakkum* "Ask him and let him tell you" (6, 10:16), as against *šəʾal ʾāḇīḵā wəyaggedḵā* "Ask your father and let him tell you" (Deut. 32:7). The semantic neutralization is a characteristic of such sequences in both languages.

found throughout Steiner 1985. The focus of this discussion is whether clauses connected by *-ma* are subordinate or not. It seems that in the modern era no one (except Steiner) claims that clauses joined by *-ma* are formally subordinate clauses. One of the reasons for Steiner's view is what he calls modal attraction (our modal congruence, **§4.4.4**). He claims that such modal attraction indicates a syntactic dependency between the clauses. Steiner is right about this syntactic dependency, but such dependency need not imply subordination. The clauses so joined depend on each other in that together they constitute a series whose order of clauses is unalterable.

This type of connection is termed **asymmetric connection**. It is characterized by Lakoff 1971:26–31 as one which imposes an order of priority on the clauses it links. This is essentially what *-ma* does, creating a sequence of clauses whose order is linguistically pertinent. It is actually logical to regard such sequence as a **pattern**.

4.4.2.1 Comparing directives with sequenced precatives:

The following examples (the first of which is discussed by Leong 1994:387–88) enable such comparison (on a semantic level only, since the forms do not belong in the same paradigm), where both verbal forms concern the same essential action:

> [**4.90**] *aššum kallatini šumma umma abū[ni–m]a ina bītini* ***lišib*** *iqabbī–ma*[27] ***uššerši–ma*** *ma[ḫr]īšu* ***lišib***
> Concerning our daughter in law, only if [our] father says thus: '**Let her dwell** in our house', release her and **let her** (or: **so that** she) **dwell** wi[th] him. 2, 142:6–11

Semantically speaking, there might be a difference between the first and second *lišib*: As the second clause of a sequenced precative pattern, it may denote purpose as well as directivity (as the translation reflects). The difference between the two is, rather, syntactic. First, the sequenced *lišib* cannot exchange positions with the 2nd pers. form *(w)uššer*, for the latter is marked as preceding by *-ma*. The first *lišib* is not part of a sequence and hence not restricted in this way. It is not marked as temporally anterior or posterior to any other action and therefore it is independent, whereas the sequenced *lišib* depends upon *(w)uššer* (further syntactic features of the sequenced precative are discussed below in **§4.4.4.0.2**). The same holds for the next example:

---

27. This *-ma* is interpreted as the focalizing *-ma* which applies to the whole protasis (*-ma* never connects a *šumma* protasis to its apodosis).

[4.91] *šīr awīlim išḫul–ma umma awīlum–ma šupur–**ma** âm **lā inaddinūšum** šumma âm lā madid **lā tanaddiššum** appūtum*
The gentleman became annoyed and so (he said): 'Order (in writing) that they (generic) should not give him barley'. If the barley is not yet measured out, do not give (it) to him. Please. 3, 85:4–10 (compare, in the 1st pers., 2, 83:17, 37 {*-ma*} ***lā amât***)

The difference here is one of person as well. The first, a sequenced precative, is similar to what we would expect from the content of *šupur*, except that it is indirect (for it is not uttered by the addressee who is to write the order). The second is an independent, direct 2nd pers. directive.

4.4.2.2 Possible perception of a sequenced precative as an object clause

lā inaddinūšum in [**4.91**] is not the syntactic object of *šupur*. The fact that *šupur* has no other object means little, for the valency of the OB verb (which was given some attention in GAG §142–45, Finet 1956 §86 [syntactic consideration], in the dictionaries [AHw and CAD], and in the glossary of Huehnergard 1997) is not as strict as that of the English verb — namely, what can be stated regarding the OB verbal complex is how many participants are **possible**, rather than how many actually occur. After all, an OB transitive verb may occur with partial complementation or none at all, without changing its value. In addition, as a content clause one expects either an **embedded indirect speech** (*kīma lā inaddinūšum*) or, less formally, an **independent** (i.e., not formally subordinate) **direct speech** (*lā tanaddiššum*) as parenthesis (much as in example [**4.25**] above). Here one actually finds an **independent indirect speech** (*lā inaddinūšum*). There is, at least theoretically, a possibility that the object clause is simply not present and what we have is what should happen next (namely, *tell him* [*he should come*] *and let him come*, see Leong 1994:396, suggesting that the modal content of such verbs of ordering is missing and is in turn represented by the following clause).

Kuhr 1968:48 discusses this issue in Biblical Hebrew, claiming that most languages express either the content of the order or the execution thereof. According to him the Indo-European languages express the content whereas the Semitic languages express the execution. This is, however, not the whole truth: Even in OB, when this order is reported in a reporting sequence, one usually finds an infinitive (construction) representing the content of the order, a finite verb of order, and possibly a following clause reporting the (non-)execution of the order:

[4.92] *dayyānū nipâtim **wuššura**[**m**] iqbûšum–ma*
***ul uwaššer**–m*[*a*]

The judges told him **to release** the distrainees but he **did not release** (them)... 11, 158:24'–26'

Such a construction is scarcely attested for the precative sequence, as precative forms do not generally have their complements in the form of an infinitive; the following examples are the only ones clearly containing a genuine object (leaving aside those which contain *ana parāsim* in either topic role or as a substantival attribute, for which see **§4.5**, and under special conditions *ša parāsim*, for which see **chapter 7**):

[**4.16**] *eqlam šuāti* ***lā epēšam*** PN *šudki*
Convince PN **not to cultivate** this field. 3, 2:41–42

[**4.93**] *ana bīt ṭuppim* ***alākam*** *šūḫissu*
Instruct him **to go** to school. 2, 81:29

From this almost total lack of an otherwise typical form of clausal complementation (via ***kīma*** clauses [see end of **§4.4.4** for examples] or with infinitive constructions), and from the abundance of these means in conjunction with sequences containing verbal forms other than precatives, one can state that there is some kind of conditioned distribution.[28] From this distribution, where indicatives are complemented via nominalizations whereas precatives just join one another, having in principle no such complementation, it may be concluded that **the precative sequence does not express a formal deontic verbal complement, but only informally in the form of a connected indirect order** (for *ša parāsim* see **chapter 7**). One example alone reflects the co-occurrence of both kinds of complementation (in this case adverbial complementation):

[**4.94**] *kīma šanāssum-ma* 2 *awīlê ana* PN_1 ***ana qāti*** PN_2 ***ṣabātim*** *idiššum-ma* ***qāssu liṣbatū***
Just like every year, give PN_1 2 men **to help** PN_2 **so that they help** him. 3, 83:6–11

The syntagm *ana qāti* PN_2 *ṣabātim* does not seem to be adnominal, describing the two men, but rather a genuine adverbial complement of purpose relating to *idiššum*. Almost the same semantic content repeats in the form of a sequenced precative *qāssu liṣbatū*.

One prominent syntactic feature which testifies to the close juncture between the clauses in the precative sequence is the typical representation of syntactic relations via various deictic elements between the sequenced clauses:

28. "Complementary distribution" is used only when it is about two conditioned variations of the **same linguistic entity**, which is not the case here, for sequenced precatives and infinitive constructions do not constitute the same linguistic entity.

[4.95] *šupur* ***šunūšim***$^{(1)}$*–ma* ***ana*** **PN**$^{(2)}$ *liqbû*$^{(1)}$*ni[m]–ma âm* $^{(2)}$***lišābil am***$^{(3)}$*–ma nipûssu*$^{(2)}$ $^{(3)}$***luṭrussu***$^{(2)}$
Order them$^{(1)}$ that they$^{(1)}$ tell PN$^{(2)}$ that he$^{(2)}$ should bring me$^{(3)}$ the barley so that I$^{(3)}$ release his$^{(2)}$ distrainee. 11, 106: 26'–29'

Each number in superscript refers to one participant in this precative sequence. These interconnections, in addition to the particle *-ma,* show the tight syntactic link between the clauses in the precative sequence.

Other details which concern the syntactic nature of sequenced precatives are dealt with further below in conjunction with the precative sequence in **§4.4.4.**

4.4.3 Connectives and their relationship with the sequenced precative

The various connectives mentioned above (**§4.4**), being involved in the sequence, must be discussed. A thorough description of juncture in OB calls for a separate investigation, and consequently the present discussion focusses upon the important facts which are essential with regard to modality. The nature of each connective has been formulated as follows:

The connective *-ma*, according to GAG §123, connects clauses and produces a logical relation between them, meaning "and so", "and therefore", "and accordingly"; "but" is comparatively rare. In §158 it is mentioned that *-ma* between imperatives, precatives, etc. is in effect coordination which expresses (logical) subordination.

Patterson 1971:44–47 explains that *-ma* and the second clause indicate the outcome of the conditions described in the first. Such coordination shows a logical and interdependent relationship between the clauses, when the action of the second is circumstantially restricted to what is expressed in the first clause.

Buccellati 1996 §86.3 describes *-ma* as exhibiting virtual subordination: coordination in surface structure but embedded adjunct clauses in deep structure, or "undifferentiated" subordination (due to neutralization of the specific function of the adjunct). *-ma* does not allow reversibility.

According to Huehnergard 1997 §7.4, emphasis always falls on the last clause, and the order of clauses is irreversible. The clauses are logically related — the first contains the conditions that result in the action of the second. Although formally a main clause, the first is actually an "unmarked subordinate clause" to the following clause; i.e., x and so y = if / when / because x, y.

The various semantic/functional interpretations are problematic regarding one point, namely, the issue of virtual subordination. The main problem, as becomes clear from the explanations above, is that it is impossible to state in a fixed manner which clause should be considered the adjunct of the other. In certain cases, such as hendiadys, it would be the first. In other cases, such as ones translated as purpose, it would be the second. The only thing which consistently holds is Huehnergard's first formula — "x and so y". This formula, coupled with the explanation above, that the first clause contains the conditions that result in the action of the second clause (Huehnergard 1997 §7.4), is adopted here. The adopted formulation is wide enough to include every occurrence of the connective *-ma*. A related point is Buccellati's mention of value (his "specific function") neutralization of sequenced precative clauses, which is described further below in **§4.4.4.1**.

Prior to the interpretation of the function of *-ma* are the objective data concerning its syntagmatic compatibilities in the corpus. In GAG §158f it is mentioned that after the preterite or the stative one usually finds the present, hinting thereby to arrangement according to mood. According to Patterson 1971:51, 114 (= rule *-ma*$_2$), "Syndetically introduced compound sentences which show a variation of mood are connected by *-ma*". Huehnergard 1997 §7.4 states, contrary to Patterson, that *-ma* is used when both clauses carry the same mood. The data in the present corpus (which includes most of Patterson's corpus, which comprises the royal letters of Ḫammurabi and Samsuiluna)[29] contain evidence to support Huehnergard's statement: *-ma* connects clauses of the same mood. There are exceptions but they are both statistically marginal (there are fifty or so such cases in about 2500 letters containing thousands of precative sequences which do conform to this modal congruence) and most of them can be accounted for (see **§4.4.4.2** further below and in addition **chapters 5** and **6**).

The connective *u* is a wider range connective, which is able to connect almost any two linguistic entities (of the same approximate order — two substantives, two clauses, etc.). When applied to clauses, it denotes no logical connection between them (GAG §117b). It also functions as an additive particle (*in addition...*), opening paragraphs. The clauses connected thereby are reversible (Huehnergard 1997 §7.4), as opposed to those connected via *-ma*:

> [4.96] 1 *šiqil kaspam idnam–ma lūkul **u** lā atabbal*
> Give me 1 sheqel of silver so that I should eat **and** should not have to borrow. 12, 180:11–13

u is less restricted than *-ma*, in that the two clauses connected by it do not constitute a unidirectional sequence (that is, the order of the clauses *lūkul* and *lā atabbal* may be altered, causing no harm). Patterson

29. Patterson's corpus is chosen as "it would be likely to provide a source for **proper Old Babylonian usage**" (Patterson 1971:7, my emphasis).

1971:32–33 formulates the restrictions of *u* as follows (rule u_1): "In compound sentences, clauses which show a variation in mood are not coordinated by *u*". In addition, he specifies that not only a variation like **illik u līmur* cannot exist, but also **alik u līmur*, supposedly for having different modi. Patterson's corpus is apparently quite different from the present corpus in this respect (despite the fact that it is part of the AbB corpus) — the number of occurrences of such sequences connected by *u* in the present corpus is not at all small:

...***ašakkan*** *u* ... ***atlakam****-ma* 3, 2:29–30

...***kullim*** *u* ... ***aštanapparakkum*** 3, 13:13–15

dīnam ***luddinšunūti*** *u* ... ***āmur*** *u* ... ***ušābilšum***[30]*–ma* 3, 21:26–29

lā tamaššianni *u* ... ***ul anaddi*** 3, 22:36–38

uštābil *u atti* ***qibîšum–ma*** 3, 35:13–14

This is a small, randomly chosen sample. There are five such so-called exceptions in forty letters, and if these proportions are quite stable (they are, e.g., for AbB 7) the overall number of them throughout the corpus may reach a couple of hundreds. Indeed, *u* tends to connect verbal clauses of the same mood (this probably has to do with the nature of the forms themselves) but it is in no way restricted in this way, whereas *-ma* certainly is. *u* is therefore not instrumental in circumscribing the precative sequence as is the connective *-ma*.

Non-marked connection, or **asyndeton**, is given much less attention. GAG §156b mentions that clauses which belong tightly together may follow each other with no explicit connection. Huehnergard 1997 §7.5 calls it asyndeton, saying it attributes "distinctiveness, emphasis or urgency" to the clauses so joined. Patterson, on the other hand, when he mentions "asyndetically introduced sequences", aims at an altogether different type of connection, i.e., a disjunctive, or "disconnecting" type. Such non-marking of connection in the corpus is therefore a complex issue which deserves separate attention. It is characterized by juxtaposition, where the connection between the clauses is marked by their standing next to each other, which is twofold: It signals either connection or disconnection. This kind of connection is not regarded as ø for it does not meet the criteria for ø (being opposed to at least one overt signal of the same order). When occuring in the same environment as *-ma*, e.g., in between precative forms, it seems to work in a similar manner as *-ma* with the provisions of both von Soden and Huehnergard. The following examples oppose

30. Even if *āmur* is taken to be *amur* (namely a 2nd pers. directive), there is *u ušābilšum-ma* following it.

such asyndeton (henceforth noted as "→")[31] with *-ma*. It occurs in certain fixed expressions in which the two clauses are very close in meaning:

> **[4.97]** *līkulū* → *lā iberrū*
> Let them eat, let them not be hungry. 6, 39:7–8

> **[4.98]** *idin* → *lā takal[la]*
> Give, do not hol[d] back. 7, 44:9

The next example is, however, identical to the former one — but has *-ma* instead of the more habitual (in this case!) "→":

> **[4.99]** *idiššum-**ma** lā takallâššu*
> Give him, do not hold back on him. 7, 97:19–20

Other examples for this "→" may appear when it occurs inside a precative sequence and seems to be interchangeable with *-ma*:

> **[4.100]** *ḫumṭam* → *alkam-ma ana šēp šarrim muqut-ma aššatka mārīka u amātika ina nepārim šūṣi*
> Hurry, come and (/in order to) fall down at the feet of the king and(/in order to) set your wife, sons, and maids free from prison. 7, 68:12–16

> **[4.101]** *ina ūmim ša pānīšunu tammaru kaspam ša qātišunu liqē-ma* 5 *ṣubātim idnaššunūti* (sic) → *arḫiš ṭurdaššunūti appūtum*
> The day you see them take the silver which is with them and give them five garments and then send them to me quickly, please. 13, 3:9–18

The asyndeton in **[4.100]** and **[4.101]** seems to be the equivalent of *-ma*, in that it figures in the same slot when the sequential nature of connected clauses is kept. In fact, other related patterns (such as the concessive-conditional pattern and the *-ma* conditional pattern, chapters **5** and **6** respectively) contain strong evidence in favor of regarding both *-ma* and "→" as variants (see table at **§4.4.4.0.2**). For the time being, there are no convincing hints for the distribution of either signal with respect to each other (Buccellati 1996 §89.6 reaches similar conclusions, based upon Codex Ḫammurabi). The following example is similar; the juxtaposed clause is part of the sequence:

> **[4.102]** *er[i]ššīšu-ma amrī-ma ṣubātam lubbišīšu* → *eriššīšu lā illakam*
> He is naked. Look for clothes and clothe him so that he does not come naked. 12, 178:3'–6'

---

31. This "→" plays a role both in the concessive-conditional precative (**chapter 5**) and in the *-ma* conditional sub-paradigm (**chapter 6**).

Another, different type of non-marked connection, is the one which serves as a boundary of various types of sequences, which as a rule is **not** interchangeable with *-ma*, only (possibly) with *u*. Patterson refers to this type as "asyndetically introduced sequences", saying that this asyndesis is marked by a change of mood. Change of mood is indeed a powerful marker of sequence boundaries, yet one generally assumes some kind of link between clauses which are asyndetically joined, which is not the case here — for here it rather signals the lack of link (or at least a very weak one) between clauses and hence it cannot be considered asyndesis.[32] The following examples show this boundary, using the notation // to mark this type of disconnection:

[**4.103**] ... *šutamliāšu // libbī uṭīb // išariš aplāšu*
Deliver ... to him in full, he did me well. Pay him duly. 6, 126:20–22

[**4.104**] PN *dayyānum ina puḫrim magal idbubam // liššapram–ma arkat* (sic) *dabābiya lipparis*
The judge PN has spoken at length against me in the assembly. Let it be written that my complaint be investigated. 12, 2:6–8

[**4.105**] *ana mīni[m] šaḫâm telqē–ma lā tuterr[a]m // [š]upram–ma šaḫâm liddinūni // nipâtīka ušērib*
Why did you take the pig and not return it to me? Order that they give me my pig. I took in pledges. 13, 131, 4–10

[**4.106**] *annûm ša una''iduka umma anāku–ma kīma erēbika kaspam qāti awīlim usuḫ // kaspam qāti awīlim ul tassuḫ u kaspum ṣibtam uṣâb dīn* DN *epēšum annûm*
(It is) ***this*** (about) which I instructed you, saying: 'Upon your arrival, take the silver from the man'. You did not take the silver from the gentleman and the silver (now) bears interest. 12, 53:4–9

[**4.107**] *umma šū–ma allak → aḫī atarram // ul illik // qibīšum–ma lillik–ma aḫāšu litram–ma*
So he (said): 'I will go and bring my brother'. He did not go. Order him that he go and bring his brother ... 12, 44:13–18

The disjunctive function of // is clear in these examples, having an obviously different function than does *-ma* or "→".

32. There is no absolute lack of link; after all these clauses have something in common in the information which the letter conveys. But they certainly belong to different parts of the text.

4.4.4 Modal congruence — significance and implications

4.4.4.0 Modal congruence

Both the tendency of precatives to cluster together and the fact that *-ma* joins clauses of the same mood are discussed above. These data show the existence of **modal congruence** in the corpus, according to which any form joined via the connective *-ma* to a preceding precative form is a precative form as well. The same (with further syntagmatic differences) applies to indicative forms, which tend to adjoin one another.

This congruence has important syntactic implications: the existence of a distinct, well defined, **precative sequence**, leading to functional neutralization of the clauses so joined (including modal attraction, for which see example [**4.109**] in the following section). Certain restrictions which apply to the precative sequence, but not to the reporting sequence, lead to a certain complementary conditioning concerning infinitive constructions. These have to do indirectly with the sequenced precative (see **§4.5** below).

Modal congruence, such as exists in the AbB corpus, is found both in the language of thirty-six Amarna letters written in Byblos (Moran 1960:9–12), in Canaano-Akkadian (Izre'el 1998 §3.7) and in Biblical Hebrew (Orlinsky 1940–42, criticized in Joüon 1996 §116, and see further references there).

The term **modal congruence** is originally found in Moran 1960:9, whereby he describes the verbal forms which conform to the Northwest Semitic forms (*yaqtulu* / *-a* / *ø*) rather than to the Akkadian forms. The *-u* form is indicative and it is joined only to other such indicative forms, whereas the *-a* / *ø* forms are both volitives and are joined to other volitives only. Moran remarks that this congruence is strictly observed.

A similar congruence is shown by Orlinsky 1940–42 to have existed in Biblical Hebrew as well, between imperatives, cohortatives, and jussives, generally with the intermediacy of *wə-*.

The following is a common form of a precative sequence exhibiting modal congruence. The congruence is not affected by attributive or adverbial clauses (including *šumma* clauses), all of which behave as part of the clause:

> [**4.108**] *ina ṣāb* PN_1 *u* PN_2 100 *ṣābum ittišu* ***lillik–ma*** 5 *ūmī adi* PN_1 *u* PN_2 *ištu* GN *illakūnim ina ālānī* ***liptarrikū–ma*** *ḫarrānātim ša itenerrubānim* [*i*]*šteat u šitta* ***lidūkū–ma līdurā***
> Let one hundred troops from the troops of PN_1 and PN_2 go with him, and let them cause difficulties in the cities for five days until PN_1 and PN_2 come from GN, and let them strike at one or two caravans that come in regularly so that they be afraid. 11, 193:13–23

4.4.4.0.1 Modal attraction

The next is an example of modal attraction, exemplifying the obligatoriness of a precative in the sequence due to modal congruence:

> [4.109] *aššum eleppim ša taqbiam eleppam ana bēliša* ***utâr*** *// ṭuppī uštābilakkum // meḫer ṭuppiya šūbilam–ma ana tukultika eleppam ana bēliša* ***lutēr***
> Concerning the boat of which you talked to me, I **will return** the boat to its owner. I sent you my tablet. Send me an answer to my tablet and then I **will return** the boat to its owner relying on you. 9, 139:5–11

The first occurrence of the verbal lexeme *târum* is indicative (*utâr*) while the second one is a sequenced precative (*lutēr*). The reference, however, is to one and the same action (returning the ship to its owner), to be performed by one and the same person (the speaker). This difference seems to be a result of the second occurrence being joined to a preceding precative (*šūbilam*) by the connective *-ma*, and hence it is formally restricted with regard to its form — it has to be a precative as well. Such attraction is at the basis of all similar sequences in Arabic (generally denoting condition), in which, according to Bravmann 1953:127–28, all these conjoined imperatives or jussives diachronically derive from indicative forms. For other cases of the semantic neutralization induced by sequenced precative see examples [4.126] and [4.127] in §4.4.4.1 below (under **indirect oath**).

4.4.4.0.2 The precative sequence

The **precative sequence**, in which precatives are concatenated via *-ma*, is characterized differently than an independent directive. The examination of this sequence is divided into a discussion of the bi-clausal precative sequence and a theoretical discussion concerning multi-clausal precative sequences, to be complemented further below (in §6.3.4.2) by a concrete, example-based discussion.

In the **bi-clausal precative sequence** the individual clauses can be shown to have a distinct value when compared each with the few exceptions to the modal congruence. The latter are useful in being otherwise almost marginal in number compared with the immense number of the cases of modal congruence, and constitute different patterns, thereby not hampering the validity of modal congruence in the corpus. In table 4 below, a comparison is conducted between the bi-clausal precative sequence and other patterns which constitute exceptions to the modal congruence in the corpus:

4. The paradigmatic relationships of sequenced precatives

	clause I	connective	clause II	combined function	
(1)	*iparras* *iprus* etc.	-*ma*/→	*liprus*	conditional+precative	(ch. 6)
(2)	***liprus*** ***purus*** ***luprus*** **etc.**	**-*ma*/→**	***liprus*** ***purus*** ***luprus*** **etc.**	**precative sequence**	
(3)	*liprus*	-*ma*/→	*iparras*	concessive+indicative	(ch. 5)
(4)	*purus*	-*ma*/→	*iparras*	seq. precative+indicative	(§4.4.4.2)

• Pattern **(2)** represents the ubiquitous precative sequence which is characterized by an obligatory modal congruence. Each clause in this bi-clausal sequence acquires its value in opposition to other members of the paradigm, which occur only in other bi-clausal patterns. The paradigms are marked by vertical rectangles — first upwards, with pattern **(1)**, and then downwards, with patterns **(3)** and **(4)**.

• Pattern **(1)** is a representation of one recurring sequence within the -*ma* conditional pattern (described in **chapter 6**), where one may find *iparras* and *iprus* forms (among other forms) in the same slot where the sequenced precative is found, viz., in the first clause **(I)** of the precative sequence. These forms **do not** have indicative value in this pattern but rather **conditional** value, as opposed to the directivity generally found with members of the first clause paradigm of the sequenced precative.

• Pattern **(3)** represents a concessive-conditional sequence (for which see **chapter 5**).

•**(4)** represents a rare sequence (8 occurrences in the AbB corpus, see **§4.4.4.2**), in which one finds *iparras* forms interconnected via -*ma* with *purus* forms. These *iparras* forms probably have a **factual value** which is similar to the value they usually have in declarative independent clauses (this deserves mention because in pattern **(1)** *iparras* has **conditional** value).

In this array of oppositions the differences between the sequenced precative and the directive come to light: Directives are in opposition with the indicative which may figure in the same slot, whereas sequenced precatives may be in opposition with indicatives only when second. When first in the sequence, they are in opposition only with the -*ma* conditional protasis. These different oppositions are essentially the reason to regard sequenced precatives as belonging to a different linguistic group than directives. Nevertheless, semantically, sequenced precatives (especially the first clause in the sequence, but the second clause as well) are very similar to directives. Note, however, that the different paradigm (resulting from different paradigmatic makeup) accounts for the different semantic value (the 2nd sequenced precative clause may denote purpose, whereas the directive never does).

Table **4** above is not theoretical but rather based upon actual cases. The following examples are divided in four groups corresponding exactly to the abstract sequences in the table:

(1) ***iparras–ma liprus*** (conditional+precative):

> **[4.110]** 1 *pān suluppam ana bītiya̱ šūbilam* →[33] ***ul tanaddim–ma*** *ana awīlika* ***lā tašallanni***
> Have 1 *pānum* (of) dates brought to my house; should you not give (it), do not ask me about your man. 6, 120:7–10

(2) ***liprus–ma liprus*** (precative sequence):

> **[4.111]** *šāpirī išariš* ***līpulaššu–ma*** *arḫiš* ***liṭrudaššu***
> Let my supervisor pay him duly and then let him send him here quickly. 13, 119:6'–8'

(3) ***purus–ma iparras*** (2nd pers. precative+indicative, see **§4.4.4.2**):

> **[4.112]** *[k]īam* ***qibīšum–ma*** *arḫiš* ***ippalka***
> Tell him [th]us, and he will pay you quickly. 9, 1:25–26

(4) ***luprus/liprus–ma iparras*** (concessive [not 2nd pers.]+indicative):

> **[4.113]** *ummānāt aḫi<ā>tim ša ibaššû* ***lilqû–ma*** *awīl* GN ***ul anad-diššunū[t]i***
> **Even if they take** the additional troops that are available, I will not give them$_{acc.}$ (i.e.,) the people of GN. 9, 92:20–22

These patterns are not equally represented in our corpus: **(2)** prevails in more than 95% of the sequences involving precatives. The rest occur much more rarely. Yet, these rare occurrences enable us to determine the value for the individual clauses of the precative sequence and at the same time make apparent their own function in the modal system of OB, despite their scarcity.

The multi-clausal precative sequence: At first sight, in view of the strict modal congruence discussed heretofore, one would tend to conclude that the multi-clausal precative sequence must be structurally analysed as one whole whose individual parts cannot normally interchange with anything but other precative forms. This conclusion is wrong, however,

33. For "→" in this position see below, **§6.3.1**.

since it is possible to compare a small number of examples where this modal congruence is not observed with individual clauses in the multi-clausal precative sequence. Such comparison of sequences, where only one term is opposed while all other terms are equal, yields results other than expected. It enables breaking down the precative sequence into individual clauses, and ascribing value to each of them separately. Exemplifying this requires description and discussion of the *-ma* conditional paradigm and its special syntagmatic compatibilities with sequenced precatives (which is carried out in **chapter 6**).

4.4.4.0.3 Sequenced precatives and nominalized clauses

No syntactic equivalence can be shown to exist, in effect, between nominalized and adverbialized syntagms and a sequenced precative, as we can show regarding a *kīma* object clause and the infinitive (see **§7.0** examples **[7.1]** and **[7.2]**). There are several reasons for this.

First, precatives co-occur very rarely with such nominalizations (as object) or adverbializations (as adverbial purpose complementation; temporal complementation is fairly regular). GAG §177a mentions that *kīma* object clauses mostly contain a past or present action, but only rarely a future action. The latter is naturally what one expects to be in opposition with a sequenced precative, for the time frame is similar, or identical, to precatives. Rare occurrences do not really help since they cannot be considered a readily available alternative to the sequenced precative, but rather a peculiarity. The syntagm *kīma iparrasu* as object clause with those verbs which could have an indirect command clause (*qabûm*, *šapārum*, etc.), are even less frequent and there are only a handful of examples:

> **[4.22]** ***kīma*** *anāku* ***eppešu*** *qibīšum*
> Tell him that I intend to / will cultivate (it). 3, 2:45

> **[4.114]** [*nukaribbam*] *ša* [*i*]*l*[*l*]*ikam šāl–ma* ***kīma*** *minût kannim ša êm aḫum* ***izzazzu*** *liqbīkum*
> Ask [the gardener] who [ca]me and let him tell you that a *brother* should / will be ready for counting the barley vessels. 6, 179:25–28

Second, the respective syntactic position of the two is not the same: *kīma* clauses occur generally **before** the verbal form and constitute a part of the predication represented by the verbal form. Sequenced precatives, on the other hand, never constitute a nominalized part of a clause (except as quotations, where they are not formally nominalized, only embedded). There is a sequential link between these clauses but never inclusion, or embedding, of one in the other. The connective *-ma* always connects clauses of **equal syntactic status** but never **a nominalized clause with its main clause.**

The next doublet enables the comparison of an explicit purpose clause with *akkīma* (which only seldom occurs in the corpus) with a neutralized sequenced precative carrying the notion of purpose:

> [4.24] ***šuprīm–ma*** *ina pānīni* ***lū našiānu***
> Order (in writing) so that we deliver from what is available to us. 7, 17:17–18

> [4.23] *idišam šuṭṭerī[m–ma]* ***šūbilīm akkīma*** *ina alākim ḫišeḫtam* ***našiānu*** *u atti ṭēmki lū ṣabtāti*
> Put in writing side by side [and] send me so that we deliver with us what is needed upon coming, and as for you, (you should) take action. ibid. 11–15

The attempt to oppose *-ma* ... *lū našiānu* and *akkīma* ... *našiānu* suffers from the same problems enumerated above. Although both the semantic notions and the order of elements is similar, these syntagms do not occupy the same syntactic slot, and therefore are not interchangeable, and consequently not comparable, with each other.

4.4.4.1 Semantic neutralization

Precative sequences, being iconic ordering of actions, express different notions, all stemming from this structure. This semantic neutralization, or non-differentiation, is one of the most prominent features of the precative sequence. There is hardly a difference in the structure of the sequence, whether it is to be translated as a purpose, as an indirect command, as an indirect oath or as a sequence of precatives (possibly even as a condition; sequences which are concessive-conditional are treated separately in **chapter 5**). The issue is deemed worthy of discussion mainly because it evokes considerable discussion almost everywhere.

- **Purpose**

Purpose is close to a combination of two semantic notions — expression of will and causality. The sequenced precative supplies the will element while the sequence, an iconic ordering of actions, is sufficiently general in nature as to represent this relationship between clauses as well as other relationships:

> [4.115] *appūtum kunukkī anniam ina amārika mê* ***idin–ma*** *eqlam ša* PN ***lišqû***
> Please, upon seeing this sealed document of mine give (them) water **so that** they irrigate the field of PN. 9, 115:4–9

[4.116] *ana* PN *ṣuḫārim aḫīya* 1 *pān âm* ***idiššum-ma*** 5 *ūmī* ***libtalliṭ***
Give the servant PN, my brother, 1 *pānum* of barley **in order that** he may subsist for 5 days. 12, 37:6–8

[4.117] *arḫiš* ***apulšu-ma*** *šattum* ***lā izzibšu***
Pay him quickly **so that** the season does not leave him behind. 4, 154:30–31

This notion is to be found when the first precative is in other persons as well.

• Indirect command

Directives cannot be directly embedded and do not, as a rule, have an infinitive (construction) as object. For these reasons, the most typical way to express the notion of indirect command is via a sequence of precatives where the first is a verb of ordering and the second represents the order indirectly. The list of verbal lexemes in this group is quite limited: *šapārum, qabûm, nu⁾⁾udum, ḫussusum, wu⁾⁾urum* and possibly a few more. Palmer 1986:174–78 notes that purpose constructions are cross-linguistically very similar, or identical, to indirect command constructions. This is the case in OB as well, where the construction is identical:

[4.7] *umma awīlum-ma* ***šupur-ma*** *âm* ***lā inaddinūšum*** //
šumma ûm lā madid lā tanaddiššum
So the gentleman (said): 'Write that **they should not give him** barley. If the barley is not measured do not give him (any)'. 3, 85:5–10

[4.118] ***šupuršunūšim-ma*** *ana* PN ***liqbûni[m]-ma***
âm ***lišābilam****-ma nipûssu luṭrussu*
Order them (in writing) **that** they should say to PN **that** he should send me barley in order that I release his distrainee. 11, 106: 26'–29'

[4.119] ***qibī-ma liwa⁾⁾erūšu-ma littalak***
Order **that** they instruct him **that** he should go away. 7, 4:27–28

It could be argued that there is a structural difference between purpose and indirect command, apart from different verbal lexemes: In the case of the latter, the verb of order is not saturated in terms of its valency. In other words, *šapārum* is expected to have some form of object. In its absence, it can be assumed that the following sequenced precative represents the object, whereas when an object occurs the translation tends to be purpose (the object is underlined):

[4.120] *ṭēm awātim šâti* ***šuprānim-ma*** *libbī* ***linūḫ***
Send me a report about this matter **so that** my heart may be at rest. 1, 29:17–18

[**4.121**] *šulumkunu* ***šuprīm–ma lā abtanak*****[*ki*]**
Write me (about) your well being **so that** I should not incessantly wee[p]. 11, 14:21–22

There are, however, a few problems: First, as is mentioned above in **§4.4.2**, a perfectly transitive verb in OB can and does occur with no object. Second, the object can be a noun such as *ṭēmum* which can and does stand in apposition to an order:

[**4.122**] *umma atta–ma ṭēmka* ***šupram–ma*** *alpī* ***lilqûnikkum*** *annītam taqbiam*
You (said): 'Send here your order (**so**) **that** they should take the oxen to you'. This (is what) you said. 7, 132:14–17

In conclusion, there are not enough formal features to enable formal differentiation between the notions of purpose and indirect command.

• **Iconic sequence**

The following example, although containing a verb typical of directive content, cannot be rendered as such:

[**4.47**] ***šupur–ma*** *kilallīn* ***šūriaššu***
Order (in writing) **and** have him bring both of them. 2, 119:14–16

Example [**4.47**] looks the same as a sequence of indirect command — yet the 2nd pers. sequenced precative, being direct, naturally cannot stand here for an indirect command. The following example exhibits another sequence, which is semantically closer to the iconic order of actions rather than to purpose or indirect command:

[**4.123**] *šumma agurrum ṣariptum ibašši ṭēmka* ***šupram–ma*** *eleppētim* ***luṭrudakku*****[*m*]**-*m*]*a agurram liṣēnūnim*
šumma agurrum ṣariptum lā ibašši arḫiš ... agurram ṣariptam ***ṣurup–*****[*m*]*a*** *ṭēmka* [***šu***]***pr*****[*a*]*m–ma*** *eleppētim* ***luṭrudakkum***
If baked bricks are available send me your word **and then** let me (or so that I may?) send you boats [so t]hat they load baked bricks for me. If baked bricks are not available bake them quickly [**a**]**nd** se[nd] me your word **and then** let me send you boats. 12, 23:6–15

[**4.124**] *ḫitayyaṭāšunūti–ma ina simānišunu* ***linnaplū–ma*** *ana* GN ***liblūniššunūti***
Examine them continuously so that they should be picked at the right time **and then** they should bring them to me to GN. 6, 92:12–16

[**4.111**] *šāpirī išariš* ***līpulaššu–ma*** *arḫiš* ***liṭrudaššu***
Let my supervisor pay him duly **and then** let him send him here quickly. 13, 119:6'–8'

• Condition

The following example can be taken to contain a condition as well as a simple sequence, in which one thing should happen right after the other:

> [4.125] *amtī* ***šūrîm–ma*** *amatki* ***lušāriakki***
> Send me my maid and let me send you your maid. 1, 28:35–36

The notion of condition is not very common in OB, but it is more so in Biblical Hebrew and almost the rule in Arabic (for example, Bravmann 1953:128). The iconic ordering of one precative after the other roughly means that some action should take place only after another one has already taken place. This fits perfectly all the semantic notions previously discussed.

• Indirect oath

The following examples are very similar to the sequences denoting indirect command. They are different in that they neutralize not only notions, but values of a different paradigm as well, in this case, asseverative forms:

> [4.126] *nīšam* (sic) *ina šaptīšu liššakim–ma ana bīt* PN *aḫīšu* ***l[ā] uragga***
> Let an oath be put in his mouth **that he should no[t] make false claim** against his brother PN's estate. 11, 90:33–35

> [4.127] *nīš šarrim ina pī[š]u šukun–ma* ***[l]ā itâr–ma*** *eqlam* ***[l]ā i[ba]qqaršu***
> Put the king's oath in h[is] mouth **that he should [n]ot [c]laim** the field from him again. 11, 135:22–24

The second and third sequenced precative clauses neutralize a direct oath — such as we find in the following example:

> [4.128] *eqlum ša pī kunukkišu liter limṭi* ***lā aturru****–ma* ***lā abaqqaru̱***
> Should the field according to his document be more (or) be less, I will *not* claim (it) again. VAB 5, 156:1'–3" (side 1–2 and rev. 1–3)

Modal congruence is strong enough to neutralize the otherwise clear distinction between the asseverative paradigm and the precative paradigm.

• Not clear-cut

The different notions of precative sequences are not always unambiguous and are often subject to personal interpretation. The following examples are ones which are difficult to classify semantically. The next example is hardly a sequence, for both clauses refer to the same action:

[4.129] *kaspī* ***idnīšim–ma*** *u[l]ū* 1 *šiqil kaspī* ***idnīši***
Give her my silver or give her 1 sheqel (of) my silver. 6, 178:18–19

The following example contains verbal lexemes which are typical of the notion of indirect order:

[4.130] *ṭēmka arḫiš* ***šupram–ma*** *ša taqabbû* ***lūpušakkum***
Quickly send me your report and I should do for you what you (will) say. 7, 171:16–17

The object of the first clause (*ṭēmka*) seems to be in apposition with the object of the second clause (*ša taqabbû*), rather than resume the contents of the second clause (*lūpušakkum*). That precludes the notion of indirect command. Purpose is a valid option but it seems that since the object of the second clause (*ša taqabbû*) is in apposition with *ṭēmka*, the link between the clauses would be best translated as a simple sequence of clauses.

It is not clear what notions are to be ascribed the next series of 2nd pers. precatives:

[4.131] *ana pī kanikkim–ma šuāti eqlam idnāšunūšim* → *eqlam ašaršani lā tanaddināšunūti* (sic)
Give them the field precisely in accordance with this sealed document, do not give them a field anywhere else . 4, 37:21–24

The last example in this section seems to stand semantically between a sequential notion and a conditional notion:

[4.132] *ina idika annītam* ***epšam–ma*** *annûm* ***lū gimillaka***
Do this with for me according to your ability and let this be your favor. 9, 119:6'–7'

It should be underlined that all the above enumerated notions share the same pattern and hence do not constitute different structural entities, but one only.

4.4.4.2 Exceptions and their values

A language system, even an idiolect, is not expected to exhibit a perfect mathematical precision. This certainly holds in the present corpus, which comprises letters excavated over a vast area and written over a long period of time (as opposed, perhaps, to the relatively uniform language of the Ḫammurabi letters, or royal letters in general). The modal congruence discussed above has a small number of exceptions (around fifty, estimating the number of modally congruent sequences to be a couple of thousands). They can be subdivided into a few groups:

1. Cases where the alleged incongruence can be resolved by different interpretation of the material.

2. Cases exhibiting the sequence *purus–ma iparras*.

3. Cases exhibiting the sequence *luprus / liprus–ma iparras*, which belong with the concessive-conditional pattern (for which see **chapter 5**).

4. Cases exhibiting the sequence *iprus / iparras–ma liprus*, which belong with the *-ma* conditional pattern (see **chapter 6**).

5. Inexplicable cases which are deemed to be mistakes and are corrected in the editions according to the editor's *Sprachgefühl*.

6. Cases which are inexplicable.

The main point in trying to classify and explain these cases of incongruence is to see whether there is some linguistic regularity behind them, namely, a difference of function or value.

1. Resolving incongruence by different interpretation

In the examples adduced by Leong 1994:74–78, a few forms are interpreted as *iprus* forms while connected via *-ma* to a following directive. These forms, belonging to verbs I-*a* / I-*e*, may be interpreted as 2nd pers. directives (i.e., *ēsiḫ* vs. *esiḫ*, *āmur* vs. *amur*) just as well:

> [4.133] *šattam alpīya ... ušabbalakkum ebel eqel šamaššammī* ***a-mu-[ur-m]a*** *ana šamaššammī rēšam li[k]ī[l]*
> This year I will send you my oxen ... **Fin[d]** (rather than *I found*) a sesame field of one rope and let it be re[ady] for sesame. 7, 154:17–20

> [4.134] *u qemâm u mi[m]m[a] ša ana* GN *ana qātika teleqqû* ***e-si-iḫ–ma*** *rēška likīl*
> In addition **allot** (rather than *I allotted*) flour as well as anything which you took to GN in your possessions so that it will be at your disposal. 10, 32:30–32

The sequence *iprus–ma liprus* is very irregular and unless characterized as a *-ma* conditional the examples belong in the last category, cases which remain inexplicable.

Different interpretation is possible by way of supplying an alternative syntactic explanation. Such a case would be one where we find an incongruent quotative parenthetic construction, as in sequenced precatives inside a reporting sequence, as can be seen in the following example (indeed a quotation would habitually precede the *verbum dicendi* rather than follow it):

[4.25] *ana aḫḫātika aqbī–ma* ***erbānim ṣuḫāra ḫiṭâ*** *mamman ul īrubam*
I told your sisters 'Come in, examine the servant', but nobody came in. 6, 38:9–12

aqbī–ma is in effect connected with *ul īrubam* at the end.

Another example is of parenthetic direct speech in the indicative inside a precative sequence. Direct speech is generally not connected via *-ma,* but rather by //, marking it off:

[4.135] *lūriška–ma* ***ana qištim taddinaššu*** *ṭēmka* (*ṭe-ḫi-ka*) *gam-ram šu*[*p*]*ra*[*m–ma*]
Let me ask you to sen[d m]e your complete report (saying): 'you gave it to me as present' [...]. 11, 16:17–20

ana qištim taddinaššu is the exact direct content of *ṭēmka*.

2. Cases exhibiting the sequence ***purus–ma iparras***

The following cases (excluding [**4.22**]) constitute but a fraction of the number of sequences which do conform with modal congruence. Still, they imply that there is some choice in the 2nd clause of a bi-clausal precative sequence. It may be worthwhile to point out that most of these connected *iparras* forms are followed by //, marking a boundary. This choice is shown above using formal means (table **4** at **§4.4.4.0.2**). The possibility of *iparras* instead of *liprus* in the same slot implies a semantic distinction as well — all those occurrences of *iparras* have **factual**[34] value as opposed to **non-factuality** in the *purus–ma liprus* structure.

With a *verbum dicendi*:

[4.112] [*k*]*īam* ***qibīšum–ma*** *arḫiš* ***ippalka***
Tell him thus, and **he will** quickly **pay** you. 9, 1:25–26

[4.136] *u šanītam ana* PN ***qibī–ma*** *eqel a*[*ḫi*] CN *anāku* ***e*****[*rr*]*iš***
And secondly, tell PN that ***I*** **cult[iva]te** the field at the ba[nk] of CN. 9, 86:15–19

34. Almost the entire group *purus–ma iparras* may denote conditionality, but this conditionality is not clear-cut. This is in contrast with two examples of the same structure from other corpora where (concessive-)conditionality is obvious: *ina ḫumāšim ele''īka šitpuṣum* ***šitpaṣ****–ma ina šitpuṣim ele''īka* "I overpower you in the wrestling ring. Even if you choose *wrestling*, I will overpower you in wrestling" (ARM 26, 207:15–17, concessive-conditional).
iṣṣūram ***bār–ma*** *êšam* ***illakū*** *watmūšu* "(If you) **hunt** a bird, where **would** its chicks **go**?" (Gilg Ishchali:15', conditional).
Not one clear-cut (concessive-)conditional example with the sequence *purus–ma iparras* has been found in the AbB corpus. Since the resulting statement needs to be valid for the AbB corpus, we have to consider these cases a separate group, which is not necessarily related to the (concessive-)conditional pattern.

The verb *qabûm*, in sharp contrast to all its directive occurrences in similar constructions (i.e., the notion of indirect command), here has the value *say* rather than *command*. The last example is most of all reminiscent of another rare occurrence, already discussed above:

> [4.22] ***kīma*** *anāku* ***eppešu*** *qibīšum*
> Tell him that I intend to / will cultivate (it). 3, 2:45

The two preceding examples are semantically alike — both may represent an indicative content, rather than an indirect command. The difference between them originates mainly in their respective structures: The first exhibits an *iparras* form which is opposed to a sequenced precative (thus having a factual value), whereas in the second it is rather a modally neutralized *iparrasu* form.

The following examples, although containing 2nd pers. sequenced precatives which are habitually the first in a sequence denoting (notionally speaking) purpose, exhibit sequenced *iparras* with factual value:

> [4.137] 1 *ereqqam ana* 5 *ūmī ana êšu babāli* ***idiššum–ma*** *âšu ana kaspim* ***tušelli***
> Give him a wagon to carry his barley for 5 days and **you will raise** his barley for silver. 1, 65:7–10

> [4.138] *ripqātišu* ***šudud–ma*** *ša mānaḫātišu anāku* ***appalšu***
> Measure his dug-up land and ***I*** **will pay** him for his labor. 3, 2:43–45

> [4.139] *šumma taqabbi ṭuppaka* ***šūbilam***–*ma kīma artīqu̱ ana ṣērika alākam* ***eppušam***
> If you want to order, send me your tablet and **I will come** as soon as I have become available. 3, 90:24–28

> [4.140] 5 *ṣuḫārīka* ***idiššum–ma*** *ana* GN [***u***]***šq***[***el***]***lepūšu***
> Give him 5 of your servants and **they will s[h]ip** it downstream. 6, 133:9–12

> [4.141] *šīmam mali eʾēlim* ***eʾilam–ma*** *arḫiš* ***attallakam***
> Contract merchandise as much as possible (lit. as much as to contract) and **I will come** quickly. 9, 130:10–13

The last example is too fragmentary to interpret or translate:

> [4.142] [*š*]*āmam–ma* [...] [***l***]***iqē–ma*** *aklam anni*[*kīam t*]***anaddi***[***n***(***am***?)] *libbaka ul iṭ*[*īb*] 7, 90:3'–6'

This sequence is sharply distinguished from the following one.

3. Cases exhibiting the pattern *luprus/liprus–ma iparras*

The next two examples seem to have a concessive-conditional relationship between the clauses (see **chapter 5**):

[4.113] *ummānāt aḫi<ā>tim ša ibaššû* ***lilqû–ma*** *awīl* GN ***ul anaddiššunū[t]i***
Even if they take the additional troops that are available, I will not give them$_{acc.}$ (i.e.,) the people of GN. 9, 92:20–22

[4.143] 10 *šiqil kaspam anniam* ***luqerribšunūšim–ma*** *ina matī–ma ina eqlim u kirîm* ***eleqqe***
Even if I bring them 10 šeqels (of) this silver, when will I get (a return) from the field and the garden? 3, 88:9–12

The following is a rare occurrence of hendiadys, which is characterized elsewhere by two verbal forms exhibiting the very same mood and tense:

[4.144] *urram ana kaprim* GN ***lušēram–ma allak[am]***
Let me com[e] early tomorrow to the village GN. 3, 25:10–12

No interpretation or translation is offered for the last example:

[4.145] *lilliḫ–ma* (sic) ***līpussu–ma*** [*ša*] *nadānim* [*in*]***addinūnikkim*** 7, 21:29–31

4. Cases exhibiting the pattern *iprus/iparras–ma liprus*
Such cases are given ample consideration in **chapter 6**. Their importance in the context of precative sequences lies in the fact that they constitute a distinct pattern in opposition to which the value of the first precative in a bi-clausal structure is determined.

5. Emended sequences originally deviating from modal congruence
The following group of examples is indicative of the tendency of text editors regarding modal congruence. When the sequence does not feel right (according to the editor's Akkadian *Sprachgefühl*, namely, due to the feeling that the sequence does not abide by this modal congruence) emendations are sometimes offered. No translation is attempted for these examples. In the following example, the form *ittalkūnim* is emended to <*l*>*ittalkūnim* in the edition, for it is sequenced with a preceding 2nd pers. precative *idnānim*:

[4.146] *idnānim–ma* **<*l*>*ittalkūni*[*m*]** *ana ṣēriya šūriaššunūti* 6, 88:22–23

A second case is where *išpur* is emended to <*l*>*išpur* as it starts a sequence ended by *likīl*:

[4.147] *bēlī* **<*l*>*išpur***–*ma ḫarrānam šuāti likīl* (*li-di-il*) 8, 24:23–24

The next occurrence is of *išpurā* is not emended, but rather *interpreted* as *šuprā* (n. c to the translation):

[4.148] *ittišu mitgurā–m*[*a*] *u kaspam* ***išpurā***–*ma* PN *u* PN$_2$ … *liḫmuṭūnim* 9, 37:18–22.

The next sequence cannot be emended to a precative, so the other way around is chosen:

[4.149] [*l*]***i***-[***i***]***b-ti-ru-ú***–*ma š*[*e*]-*ạ-am t*[*ạ-ạ*]*t-ta-*[*d*]*i-in* 12, 190:2'–3'

N. a to the translation says: "The precative is awkward, emend possibly to <<*li*>>-[*i*]*b-ti-ru-ú–ma*, 'they were starving'."

6. Inexplicable cases (no translation is attempted)

[4.150] *ī*[*l*]*ī–ma* ***i***[***d***]***bubši–ma šupram***–*ma lullikam–ma ittiša ludbum–ma*... 7, 122:14–17

[4.151] *tēršum–ma* 3 *uṭṭātim* ***šuddiššum–ma*** *rēšī* ***tukīl*** 8, 109:26–28

[4.152] *eqlam kalâšu* ***agdamar–ma*** *appūtum šumma m*[*ār*]*ī att*[*a*] ***lā teggi*** 9, 250:4–9

4.5 Infinitive constructions

Infinitive constructions are different models which indirectly have to do with the notions of the sequenced precative (finite complement clauses are discussed in this connection above, under **§4.4.4.0.3**). They are indirectly related because, although there are never paradigmatic relationships between them and the sequenced precative,[35] they are to be found in a certain conditioned distribution with the sequenced precative and have a certain textual relationship with it. This conditioned distribution was hinted at in various parts of this chapter: Whereas the use of both object *kīma* clauses and infinitive constructions (*parāsam* / *ana parāsim*) with directives is highly restricted, it is the rule with indicatives (see **§§4.2.2.1–4.2.2.2**). More precisely, sequenced precatives are joined by other sequenced precatives actually standing for sequence or result but notionally translated as object or adverbial complements involving will, or in other terms, as indirect commands or purpose clauses. Indicative verbal forms serialize as well but take either infinitives or substantivized and adverbial clauses quite readily.

It should be emphasized that these models are modally and temporally neutralized. They usually constitute an argument of the verbal lexeme — in contradistinction to sequenced precatives, which always constitute the clause itself, rather than a part of another clause.

The following example shows neutralization of asseverative modality by way of an infinitive construction:

35. The construction *ša parāsim* does have a paradigmatic relationship only with directives, rather than with sequenced precatives. It is therefore treated separately as a syntagm having a formal relationship with directives. See **chapter 7**.

[4.153] *u* PN ***ana*** *eqlim* ***lā erēšim*** *nīš šarri utammi*
And I bound PN by oath on the life of the king **not to cultivate** the field. 11, 189:20–22

4.5.1 *parāsam*

The infinitive constructions discussed hereunder are only those whose meaning is similar to the sequenced precatives, and more specifically, those which occur second and semantically represent the object clause.

qabûm is a noteworthy example; it is ubiquitous in both models, as a sequenced precative and in a reporting sequence, both of which may refer to one and the same action. In the following pair of examples, the first occurrence consists of a precative sequence, whereas the second has an indicative verbal form having an accusative infinitive object:

[4.154] ***qi[b]ī–ma*** *ma[mman* ***l]ā udabbabšu***
O[r]der that n[o one] should harass him. 12, 13:17–18

[4.155] *mamman* ***lā dubbubšu*** ***[i]qtabī****šunūšim*
[He] ordered them that no one should harass him. ibid. 12–13

Despite the obvious semantic similarity, *-ma lā udabbabšu* is not interchangeable with *lā dubbubšu*, for they do not occur in the same syntactic slot. The first is a clause which does not formally constitute a part of another, whereas the second is the formal object of a clause. Moreover, even the structures as a whole (namely *liprus–ma liprus* and *parāsam iprus*) are not really interchangeable, for they are found in different sequences: One is a bi-clausal precative sequence, **issuing an order** at the moment of utterance, whereas the second is a single indicative clause **reporting** what was ordered.

The relevant infinitive constructions, namely, those which express indirect command or purpose, are *parāsam* (or *parāsum*, in the case of a passive construction), *ana parāsim*, and more rarely *aššum parāsim*. None of these is necessarily modal, as opposed to the syntagm *ša parāsim* (for which see **chapter 7**). Whether modal notion should be attributed to these constructions depends upon the nature of the lexeme of the main verbal form.[36] Only with verbs which are susceptible of taking an indirect command for an object does the expression of the latter denote modality:

[4.156] *âm* ***šarāq****[šunu] nīmu[r]*
We sa[w their] stealing barley. 3, 70:19–20

36. According to the lists supplied by Aro 1961:74–77 (for verbs taking an accusative infinitive) and 119–24 (for verbs taking *ana parāsim*) some verbs are attested only with the first option, other verbs with the second, and yet another group with both.

amārum here has the value "to see", and what was seen is factual.[37] *amārum* may have an object denoting modality, but then the object is of a different construction (and so is the value of *amārum* — "see to it that"):

> [4.157] ***ša napāṣi*** *amrī*
> See to it that it (=sesame) should be crushed. 4, 141:20

The problem of neutralization is more acute in the following examples, where there is no formal difference between the infinitives to indicate whether they denote modality or not:

> [4.158] ***wašābšu*** *ina ālim maḫrīka iqbûnim*
> They told me of his staying with you in the city. 9, 62:18–19

wašābšu refers to the **fact that he dwells** in the city.[38] The same construction could have meant "they told me he should stay" just as well, and were it not for the context, we would not have been able to tell. The following example exhibits *qabûm* with an infinitival object denoting a reported indirect command:

> [4.159] *ina atta–ma tuštaḫḫûšunūšim adi inanna ibrû // inanna pūḫti eqlim šuāti* ***nadānam*** *bēlī iqtabi // ... pūḫ eqlim kurummatišunu* ***idiššunūšim****–ma lā iberrû*
> They went hungry until now since (it was) *you* (who) were negligent towards them. Now *my lord* has ordered to give (them) a substitute for this field. ... give them a substitute for their subsistence field so that they do not go hungry. 3, 74:26–33

It can be stated then that **the accusative infinitive is modally neutralized**. In addition, it seems that when denoting modality it can interchange with *ana parāsim*. Incidentally, the rare abstract *nomen actionis* (***wašbūssu*** *iqbûnim* 13, 21:13, ***ḫalqūssu*** *iqbûnim–ma* 2, 128:6'–7') in object position is always indicative.

4.5.2 *ana parāsim*

A construction somewhat similar functionally is *ana parāsim*. In the next example *ana epēšim* denotes, as is clear from the context, an indirect order:

37. As is clear from the context: *awīlû bītam iplušū–ma ina êm zabālim ālum ukīnšunūti* "The men broke into the house and the city convicted them of carrying barley" (3, 70:8–10).

38. PN *aḫšu* (sic) [*ina*] GN *īmuršu–ma* "PN his brother saw him [in] GN..." (ibid. 13–15).

[4.160] *ana* PN *aḫīya ṣibûtam* ***ana epēšim*** *aqbīšum ...* [*ša*] *aqbûšum* ***līpuš***
I told PN my brother **to do** what is necessary. ... **let him do** [what] I told him. 11, 115:3–10

ana epēšim is a reported command corresponding *līpuš*, the actual directive. Another example which shows the same idea of a reported indirect command is the following:

[4.161] *awīl* GN ***ana*** *kaspim* ***nadānim*** *aqbīkum–ma annam tāpulanni–ma ēzibakkuššu // ana mīnim adi inanna lā taddinšum–ma kasapšu lā tušābilam // arḫiš* ***idiššum***–*ma kasapšu šūbilam*
I told you **to sell** the man of GN for silver and you agreed so I left him to you. Why did you not sell him and send me his (worth of) silver until now? **Sell** him quickly and send me his (worth of) silver. 6, 19:7–16

Here the principal action is represented in three different ways: As an indirect order in the form of the infinitive; in a question where it is reported to have not been accomplished (the question itself concerns the reason for this); and finally as the (reissued) directive.

ana parāsim is different from *parāsam* in a few respects: First, it can denote purpose, in addition to indirect order, for it occurs with *verba movendi* (whereas *parāsam* does not):

[4.162] ***ana*** *šīmātim* ***epē[šim]*** [*a*]*ṭṭardaš*[*šu*] // [*šīm*]*ātim* ***līpuš***
[I] sent [him] **to ma[ke]** purchases. **Let him make** the [pu]rchases. 7, 1:7–9

This example is very similar to the previous one, except that *ana epēšim* is not the object but rather an adverbial complement of purpose tied to a *verbum movendi.*

Second, it occurs (very rarely) predicatively, thereby resembling *ša parāsim* in being deontic (denoting will):

[4.27] [*š*]*umma ekallum–ma lā iqbi ṣuḫāru šū* ***ana wuššurim*** // ... *inanna šitāl–ma ṣuḫāra šâtu* ***wuššeraššu***
If the palace itself did not order (otherwise), this servant is **to be released** ... Now think (this) over and **release** this servant. 1, 74:23–28

Third, *ana parāsim* is sometimes on the border between topicality and indirect object, very much like *aššum*, regularly so with verbal lexemes denoting negligence:

[4.163] ***ana*** *šūmim u šamaškillim* ***šūbulim*** *nidi aḫi lā tarašši*
Do not be negligent about sending garlic and onion. 1, 123:11–13

[4.164] ***ana*** *a*[*girtim*] ***agārim*** *lā tu*[*m*]*a*[*qq*]*î*
Do not be w[ear]y towards hiring the h[ireling]. 7, 112:23

Indeed, the complement of such an expression, whether an infinitive or otherwise, is formally marked by *ana*. There is one peculiar thing about these expressions: This is just about the only regular situation where directives take *ana parāsim* as complement.[39] Topicality is one possible explanation for this phenomenon. This is one of the functions of *ana*:

[4.165] ***ana šūbul*** *kanikki šuāti abī atta anna tāpulanni–ma*
As to sending this sealed document, you, my father, answered 'yes' to me... 1, 15:10–11

Topicality can be established by pointing out that both slots of object are filled out by *anna(m)* and the pronominal suffix *-anni* respectively. Hence *ana šūbul(im)* is "extra" and is used in effect to set up a point of reference, i.e., the topic. An analogous example would be:

[4.166] ***ana*** *alpī* ***ṭarādim*** *kīam taqbiam*
As for sending the oxen, you told me thus: 7, 132:12–13

The importance of this topicality (both in these clear-cut examples and with verbs which denote negligence) is that it seems to neutralize the modality which is otherwise quite clear (both in purpose infinitive clauses and when *ana parāsim* is used predicatively).

The following example contains *ana parāsim* either in the role of an appositive content (much like *ša parāsim*) or as topic:

[4.167] *u* ***ana lā târim–ma lā baqārim*** *kanikkam nušēzibšunūti*
In addition, we had a document made out for them **(as to) not to lay claim again**. 1, 14:27–29

This example leads to the fourth point in which *ana parāsim* is different from *parāsam*. *ana parāsim* is attested in the vicinity of directives when it is used adnominally (again, much like *ša parāsim* — namely, serving as a functional adjective rather than a functional adverb, as it would when describing the nexus), which is impossible as far as *parāsam* is concerned:

[4.168] *ana awīltim šuprīm–ma eleppam* ***ana rakāb ṣuḫārtim*** *liskipam*
Write to the lady (an order) that she should dispatch a boat **in which the servant can/will sail**. 1, 117:10–12

[4.169] *maturram* ***ana rakābiya*** *idnaššu*
Give him a small boat **in which I can/will sail**. 3, 23:16–17

In both preceding examples *ana parāsim* is chosen, rather than *-ma liprus* (for *ana rakāb ṣuḫārim*, **-ma ṣuḫārum lirkab*, and for *ana*

39. There are sporadic cases which are more relevant to directives, for which see §4.4.2.

*rakābiya, *-ma lurkab)*, probably to maintain the attributive link with the boat, rather than to make the adverbial modality explicit. Modality could have been made explicit using the *ša parāsim* construction as well, but the latter is never used for denoting purpose.

4.5.3 *aššum parāsim*

Topicality and modal neutralization concern the *aššum* construction as well:

> [4.170] ***aššum*** PN_1 *mamma[n]* ***lā dubbubim*** *ana* PN_2 PN_3 *u* PN_4 *ina tamlītim awīlum iqbī–ma* [4.155=] *mamman lā dubbubšu [i]qtabīšunūšim // pīqat mamman illakam–ma* [... *uda]bbab* [4.154=] *qi[b]ī–ma ma[mman l]ā udabbabšu*
> At the relief[40] the gentleman spoke to PN_2, PN_3, and PN_4 about not harassing PN_1 (lit. *about no one to harrass), and [he] told them that no one should harass him. In case anyone comes and [har]asses (him) ... or[de]r that n[o one] should harass him. 12, 13:6–18

The context for this *aššum parāsim* is the two examples already adduced, [4.155] and [4.154], which are explicit about the orders given. The *aššum parāsim* construction preceding them is there just for the sake of announcing the topic.

4.5.4 Concluding remarks

The various infinitive constructions have been shown to be informally related to the sequenced precative. They occur in a conditioned distribution with it, namely, to denote indirect command or purpose mainly with indicative forms. These constructions are treated apart from *ša parāsim* for they are modally neutralized, as opposed to the latter, which is modal throughout (see **chapter 7**).

4.6 Conclusions — the precative paradigms

The precative paradigms are revealed to be quite a complex issue. Despite the relatively small number of different morphological forms, the various (sub-)paradigms which constitute this system are not few at all. The (sub-)paradigms found to be operative in OB are **1.** the **directive** sub-paradigm; **2.** the **interrogative** sub-paradigm; **3.** the **wish** paradigm. In addition, **4.** the **sequenced precative** in a bi-clausal precative pattern is found to constitute a sub-paradigm in its own right by being opposable

40. N. a to the translation.

with other forms in different patterns. One such pattern is **5.** the **concessive conditional** precative sub-paradigm. The other pattern is the ***-ma*** **conditional** pattern which does not quite belong with the precative (sub-)paradigms and is considered separately in **chapter 6**.

These groups have been arrived at by analysing the syntagmatic compatibility and paradigmatic constitution of precative forms. In addition to this syntactic investigation, semantic information was extracted as well by comparing forms belonging to the same paradigms and also by ascribing, whenever possible, a range of notions to modally neutralized environments and syntagms. Infinitive constructions and substantivized clauses, being indirectly and informally related to precative forms, and their various functions have been discussed as well.

5

The Concessive-conditional Precative

5.0 Introduction

In a small number of examples (both inside and outside our corpus) the precative is used not for injunction, but rather for representing a potential situation which may or may not happen. Such a precative is taken to represent either a conditional protasis or a concessive-conditional clause. This precative is devoid of its characteristic injunctive value when it is a directive. It is opposed to the bare 2nd pers. directive in that the latter presupposes the ability to perform the task and demands completion thereof. The element of will which lies with the speaker in most other manifestations of the precative is somewhat weakened as well.

Such patterns as are used for concessive-conditionals and for *-ma* conditionals (**chapter 6** below) are briefly mentioned above (**§§4.4.4.0.2** and **4.4.4.2**) in conjunction with the **sequenced precative**, rather than with independent directives. The reason for this is not semantic (for it has been shown above, in **§4.4.2**, that there is no necessary semantic difference between a directive and a sequenced precative), but rather syntactic. Sequenced precatives, concessive-conditionals and *-ma* conditionals are all bi-clausal patterns and are hence tightly related vis-à-vis their respective structures.

That the concessive-conditional precative shows a discernible notional difference compared to a directive is not enough to classify it in a different (sub-)paradigm. To do that one has to show that it is distinct in its paradigmatic constitution. This chapter is an attempt to isolate this type of precative structurally and to describe the way in which it is different from the more frequent occurrences of the sequenced precative.

The use of a form otherwise denoting directivity as a conditional is found in other languages as well — in French for example. Treatment of the **independent** subjunctive (as well as the imperative) expressing a conditional clause is found in Sandfeld 1965:354–55 (***Que je ferme** les paupières, **et** je revois l'hôpital* "If I close my eyelids I see the hospital again") and in de Boer 1947:322–24 as well, who explains it as a weakening of the original force of the injunctive:

> Leur fonction primaire est à tel point affaiblie, que le subjonctif et l'impératif n'y font plus qu'inviter à supposer la situation hypothétique voulue. (Their primary function has weakened to such a degree that the subjunctive and the imperative only imply the required hypothetical situation.) (ibid. 323)

De Boer's statement combines diachrony and synchrony. Yet, the synchronic statement which may be extracted (viz., that the subjunctive and the imperative only express a hypothetical situation) could be made regarding the cases in OB as well, but in the present framework a syntactic (rather than semantic) approach, involving the paradigmatic and syntagmatic axes, is employed.

5.0.1 The notion of concessivity

The concessive relationship in general is treated as an adverbial one, much like the causal, conditional, and temporal relationships. This relation, however, as well as others, may be realized in other syntactic strategies — e.g., the OB asseverative (**§2.5.2**), or, with regard to conditionals, the *-ma* conditional structure in the following chapter — in both cases no subordination whatsoever is involved. The main idea in concessives is some logical incompatibility between or around the two interrelated clauses. According to Di Meola 1997:17–32, the logical notions involved in it are concession (literally, that is, admitting to an argument, for a discussion of which see **§2.5.2**), conflict between the two parts of the construction, hinderance, disappointment due to an unfulfilled expectation, deviation from the expected norm, and finally the negation of the causal relationship.

Bybee et al. 1994 formulate efficiently and clearly the notion of concessivity:

> The main clause is, as usual, asserted, while the concessive clause describes a situation which would ordinarily lead to a negative implication about the main clause. The function of the concessive clause is to say that in spite of the negative implication, **the main clause assertion stands.** (ibid. 225, my emphasis)

This applies when there is a clear, unequivocal concessive marker such as *although, bien que, aunque,* etc. However, one finds in various languages the very familiar combination of a conditional marker accompanied by a particle, together used for expressing the concessive-conditional — ***even*** *if, wenn* ***auch***, ***même*** *si,* ***u*** *šumma*, etc. In certain languages this combined marker serves to express both concessives (*even though*) as well as concessive conditionals (*even if*). Occasionally the means to express conditionals and concessive-conditionals are alike, as is the case of the present sub-paradigm.

5.0.2 Concessivity in Akkadian

In OB there is no uniquely designated marker of concessivity, such as specialized verbal forms (asseverative and precative forms have other values as well) or a specialized conjunction, although *u šumma*, mainly in the Mari texts, sometimes plays this role.[1]

GAG §158c is devoted to concessivity, and the two means described therein are the precative and *lū*+preterite, the past asseverative in the present terminology. These two options of signaling the concessive relation are not specialized means, as they are mainly found performing other tasks rather than this one (regarding the precative, see the present chapter; for the asseverative, see **§2.5.2**). Von Soden defines the difference between the two as a temporal one — the precative is used for expressing future reference concessive and the past or stative asseverative for past reference. Von Soden may well have been right about this temporal complementary distribution, but in the present framework it is proposed that the difference between these verbal forms is much more fundamental (despite the occasional formal similarity, they belong to two distinct paradigms).

Besides the above enumerated means there are many occasions where a concessive or adversative relationship is implied but no specialized signals are present to express it:

> [**5.1**] *ištu* 3 *šanātim* ... *aštanapparakkum–ma ul âm ul kaspam tušabbalam*
> I have been constantly writing to you for three years ... **but** you send me neither barley nor silver. 7, 155:1–6

These cases are structurally identical to other chains where the clauses are interconnected by *-ma*, a connective which neutralizes various notions. There is no distinct way in OB to express "but" (Huehnergard 1997 §7.4),

1. ***u šumma*** *atta mīšātanni anāku elīka aḫabbuṣ nakrīka ana qātika umalla* "**Even if** you disregard me I will (still) kill for you (and) deliver your enemies into your hand" (ARM 26, 214:9–14). GAG §179d mentions the rare *iššā* (Mari letters) as well. In addition, one rarely finds the syntagm *ana ša* expressing (factual) concessivity: ***a[n]a ša*** *ina pānī ḫiṭṭīšunu* ***iḫliqū innābitū*** *ul išḫuṭū ul īdurū* "**Although** they **disappeared** (and) **fled** because of their crime, they showed neither respect nor fear" (13, 60:45–46).

and different connectives may, at times, express such a notion.[2]

5.1 Concessive, concessive-conditional or conditional?

The syntactic pattern to be discussed in this section is the precative when serving as a concessive-conditional clause with its apodosis/consequent clause. Although the pattern in which such a precative occurs is rather heterogeneous, an exact formulation of the pattern seems feasible.

5.1.1 Conditional clauses

GAG §160c mentions that "nur im aB Dialekt von Ešnunna bisher ist der Prek[ativ] in einer Art von konditionaler Funktion nachweisbar". The following example is adduced there as evidence:

> [**5.2**] 5 *šiqil kaspam* ***libil–ma šiqil idūšu***[3] 10 *šiqil kaspam* ***libil–ma*** 2 ***šiqil idūšu***
> **Should he bring** 5 sheqels of silver, his hire is 1 sheqel; **should he bring** 10 sheqels of silver, his hire is 2 sheqels. LE B i:8–9

Another example from the same corpus is mentioned, but not cited:

> [**5.3**] *mār awīlim ina bīt emim terḫatam* ***libil–ma*** *šumma ina kilallīn ištēn ana šīmtišu ittalak kaspum ana bēlišu–ma* ***itâr***
> **Should** a son of a man **bring** bride payment to the house of his father in law, if one of the two dies (it is) *to the owner* (that) the silver will return. LE B i:13–15

Example [**5.3**] serves as the opening of a law, so there is hardly a doubt that it serves as conditional. In both [**5.2**] and [**5.3**] it is *-ma* which interconnects the protasis and the apodosis. Another precative conditional, mentioned at Whiting 1987:14, n. 42, occurs within a string of asseverative forms:

> [**5.4**] *šaptīya lā inaššiqu–ma ša zikarim u sinništim lā amaggarušu–ma ana utūl sūnī* ***liqrianni*** → *šībūt ālim u rabiānam* ***lū ušedde***
> He shall *not* kiss my lips and I will *not* consent to sexual relations and **should he call** me to lie in (my) lap, I *will* notify the city elders and the mayor. BM 13912:8–12, Anbar 1975:121

2. Under the subtitle "Some Cross-Linguistic Generalizations", König 1988:151 states that "all [languages] seem to have a counterpart for the adversative conjunction *but*". OB is one clear case which refutes this universalist statement.

3. The apodosis (or the consequent, when a concessive clause precedes) is boldfaced as well for the consideration of the bi-clausal structure in its entirety, exactly as has been done in §**4.4** above.

This example is found in Larsa, which broadens the geographic domain in which these conditionals are found (W. Mayer, in his additions to GAG §160c, mentions that such precative conditionals are found elswhere as well). In example [**5.4**] it is "→" (representing non-marking which is deemed equivalent to *-ma*), rather than *-ma*, which interconnects the protasis and the apodosis (see **§4.4.3** and, further below, **§5.2**).

The following example is of an analogous structure — first a precative form and then an asseverative form used for an oath. The uniqueness of the example lies in the fact that it contains a vetitive form as protasis, unattested so far (in OB; AbB 12:169 n. c to the translation). The vetitive form is mostly used in OB letters for negative wish (**§4.3.2**):[4]

> [**5.5**] *lamassam ša* PN *atma īkam šuāti* ***ē tudannin*** → *[b]īt abīka [k]alâšu* ***lū ušmāt***
> I swear by the protective spirit of PN, **should you not strengthen** this ditch, I *will* put to death your entire father's family. 12, 169:20–26

Here too, there is no doubt as to the conditional notion of the precative form. It is the only example of the (concessive-)conditional precative which is negative and is in the 2nd person, yet it exhibits a pattern very similar to [**5.4**].

A unique example from literary OB has a similar structure (the protasis is 2nd pers. precative form) with an uncontestable conditional notion.[5] However, as is explained above, **§4.4.4.2**, n. 34, this example does not work the same as the examples in our corpus that have the structure *purus–ma iparras* (see **§4.4.4.2** under 2 for the examples), which *may* be interpreted as conditionals, but not necessarily so. Since this description is intended to hold for the AbB corpus, there is no choice but to consider this sequence as a non-specialized, or neutralized structure (see below, example [**5.22**]).

It should be emphasized here that the interpretation of the last four examples is **conditional, rather than concessive-conditional**. These two notions are treated separately in GAG (§160c and 158c respectively). The following example is mentioned as another example for a **precative condition** in Whiting 1987:14, n. 42 (as well as in the commentary referring to the text, SLB:133):

> [**5.6**] *nakrum* ***lītiq–ma aliam–ma*** *nikassam–ma* ***epuš***
> (**Even**) **if** the enemy **advances**, come here and do *the accounting*. 3, 38:31–32

4. See, e.g., example [**5.21**] further below.

5. *iṣṣūram* ***bār–ma*** *êšam* ***illakū*** *watmūšu* "(If you) **hunt** a bird, where would its chicks go?" (Gilg Ishchali:15').

This example, however, is dubious in this respect. The interpretation of this sentence is equivocal, and without enough context it could just as well be interpreted as concessive-conditional (i.e., *even if* as opposed to *if*) and possibly even as a precative sequence (i.e., "let the enemy pass and then come up...").

Another so-called conditional is drawn from the archaic OB of Ešnunna:

> [5.7] 10 *šanāti[m] Amurru[m]* ***likk[ir(?)–ma(?)]*** ... ***liblam*** → *ina āliya* ***dannāku***
> **Even if** the Amorites **make w[ar]** for ten years [and] **bring** ... I will remain secure in my city. Whiting 1987:14, n. 42 (=ibid. 9:8–16)

This example is considered in the edition to be conditional as well — but it is actually **concessive-conditional**, as is the following example:

> [5.8] *ummānātim aḫi<ā>tim ša ibaššû* ***lilqû–ma*** *awīl* GN ***ul anaddiššunū[t]i***
> **Even if they take** the additional troops that are available, I will not give them$_{acc.}$ (i.e.,) the people of GN. 9, 92:20–22

In the edition *lilqû* is translated "let them take", rather than as concessive-conditional. Here it is deemed to be concessive-conditional because of the **pattern** which predominantly signals this value.

In order to clarify the differences between the two notions, some principles, or the basic characteristics of these notions, should first be provided.

5.1.2 Concessive and concessive-conditional

The formulation of the concessive notion given above (Bybee et al. 1994, see **§5.0.1**) does not differentiate between concessive and concessive-conditional. The difference between the two notions is sometimes subtle, but can be formulated. A clear example of such formulation is found in Kjellmer 1989.[6] There, dealing with the differences between *even if* and *even though*, he states that in general the first covers **non-factuality** while the latter covers **factuality** (at least in British English). That is, the use of *even if* (as opposed to *even though*) implies that the concessive-conditional clause is not asserted (*I'll go for a swim* ***even if*** *the water is freezing* = the water **may or may not be** freezing, Kjellmer 1989:259).

---

6. This paper is important in that **it relies on real corpora**, which is quite unusual for the neo-linguistic treatment of English.

5.1.3 Conditional and concessive-conditional

As to the opposition *if* : *even if*, which is more important in the present context of the precative (the point being the difference between a conditional interpretation of the precative form as against concessive-conditional one), Kjellmer 1989:257 quotes Fraser 1971 who describes the peculiarity of *even if* as against *if*:

> *Even if* sentences are not normally conditional in the sense that the subclause determines the truth conditions of the sentence; **the proposition of the main clause is valid irrespective of what is contained in the subclause.** (ibid. 158, my emphasis)

Whereas the apodosis in a conditional sentence may be valid or not, depending upon the the eventual actualization of the protasis, the consequent clause of the concessive(-conditional) sentence is valid no matter what.

There is a connection between a conditional and a concessive-conditional interpretation of a conditional structure, which may be resolved according to this principle:

> [**5.9**] *urram apālam ul eleʾʾi* ***šumma*** *ana bīt ilim*
> ***išap<pa>rūninni*** *apālam ul eleʾʾi*
> I will not be able to pay tomorrow. (**Even**) **if they send** me to the temple of god I will not be able to pay. 6, 4:12–15

[**5.9**] has the exact structure of a condition. Yet, due to the repetition of *apālam ul eleʾʾi*, it reflects no ordinary conditional but rather a concessive-conditional. The repetition of this phrase shows it is valid no matter what, whereas such validity would have been absent in a conditional apodosis. Thus, one way to determine whether we have a conditional or a concessive-conditional would be to decide whether the consequent clause holds anyway or just in the case of an actualization of the conditional protasis. So, in the case of [**5.4**] above (*ana utūl sūnī liqrianni* → *šībūt ālim u rabiānam lū ušedde*), the woman will notify the mayor and the city elders **only** if her ex-husband calls on her to sleep with him, and hence we have a conditional. On the other hand, in [**5.7**] (10 *šanāti[m] Amurru[m] likk[ir(?)–ma(?)]* ... *liblam* → *ina āliya dannāku*), the consequent clause *ina āliya dannāku* holds whether the *Amurrum* attack or not.

König 1986 accounts for the contextual conditions which lead to neutralization of the (normal) distinction between conditionals and concessive-conditionals:

> Whenever a conditional protasis contains an expression marking a suitable extreme value on some scale for some propositional schema, the conditional is interpreted as a concessive conditional. If the consequent is asserted to hold for a given extreme antecedent, it can also be assumed to be true for less extreme cases. (König 1986:238)

That is, the concessive-conditional contains some extreme value whose very existence will not change the validity of the consequent clause, and neither will less extreme values. An illustration of this can be found in example [5.7], where the extreme is 10 *šanātim*. The consequent clause, i.e., *ina āliya dannāku*, will also hold for less extreme cases, for instance five years. Another example of such an extreme is [5.10], a well-known example, cited **as concessive** in GAG §158c:

> [5.10] *ūmī šattim išteat ina bītišu* ***lišim–ma ul aššat***
> **Even if she lives** in his house for one whole year, she is not a married woman. LE A ii:33–34

This law states that a woman is not considered married no matter what, so long as certain legal conditions have not been fulfilled. The period of time in the protasis serves as an extreme — the consequent clause legally holds for a shorter time period just as well.

It is worthwhile to mention here that the same corpus (LE) contains examples for both conditional and concessive-conditional precatives. Moreover, the respective syntactic patterns are the same:

> [5.2] *libil–ma šiqil idūšu* (conditional)
> [5.3] *libil–ma ... itâr* (conditional)
> [5.10] *lišim–ma ul aššat* (concessive-conditional)

That the consequent clause, or apodosis, may contain different forms is of no consequence — it may contain any form which is compatible in any conditional apodosis. The most prominent feature of the syntactic pattern is the interconnection via *-ma* (or, in other cases, the equivalent "→") of two forms **which do not tend to connect thus**, such as precative and indicative (non-verbal clauses may be marked as either indicative, asseverative or precative; for the latter see examples [4.10]–[4.12] in §4.1 above).

The next example is cited by Whiting (1987:14 n. 42), as an instance of a conditional:

> [5.11] *ištu inanna 10 līmī nakrum* ***lillikam–ma*** *atappulšu* ***ele***^{ʾʾ}***i***
> From now on, **even if** ten thousand enemy (soldiers) **should come**, I will always be able to stand up to them. ARM 4, 68:14–16

Judged by the same parameters as above, the precative in example [5.11] would seem to be a conditional, since being able to stand up to the enemy is valid only if the enemy should come. However, this is not the point. The range of extremes discussed above lies in **the number of soldiers** (and not whether the enemy comes or not), and the speaker claims to be able to stand up to them **no matter how numerous they might be**.

To sum up, there are two semantic characteristics which distinguish between the conditional and the concessive-conditional notions. The first is that the consequent clause in the latter is valid, irrespective of what is expressed in the protasis. A conditional apodosis, on the other hand, is fully dependent upon the actualization of the contents in the protasis. The second characteristic is that the concessive-conditional has some extreme, absent in conditionals, despite which the consequent clause still holds.

5.2 The syntactic and semantic nature of the concessive-conditional precative

The syntactic pattern under discussion is statistically marginal but deserves treatment because it is clearly different in value from the other precative (sub-)paradigms. Contrary to the rhetorical concessives treated in **§2.5.2**, the concessive-conditionals precatives have to do with the notion of possibility or potentiality. The two kinds of concession express different kinds of non-factuality (for the former, see **§2.6**).

The following example is a legal formula that appears in a number of texts:

> **[5.12]** *u mārī* PN_1 *u* ᶠPN ***liršû–ma*** **PN_2*–ma aḫūšunu rabûm***
> And **even if** PN_1 and ᶠPN have sons, *PN_2* (rather than anyone else) will be their elder brother. VAB 5, 8:9–12 (and similar cases in VAB 5, 9:7–9; ARM 8, 1:21)

The text is a child-adoption legal document and it typically assures the rights of the adopted son as heir. The form *liršû* is clearly not a directive and the close syntactic juncture with the (indicative) non-verbal consequent makes the concessive-conditional interpretation quite obvious.

Ordinarily in concessives of the present kind, only one extreme is explicitly mentioned. The next example, however, exhibits two extremes:

> **[5.13]** *eqlum ša pī kunukkišu* ***līter limṭi*** → ***lā aturru–ma lā abaqqaru***
> **Should** the field according to his document **be more** (or) **be less**, I will *not* claim (it) again. VAB 5, 156:1'–3'' (side 1–2 and rev. 1–3)

The syntactic pattern is most closely associated with examples **[5.4]** and **[5.5]** above, in having an asseverative for a consequent clause. Those two examples are, rather, conditional, and it may be contended that each precative form in [5.13] is in itself conditional just as well. What makes the whole protasis concessive-conditional is the fact that each precative form stands for one extreme. The two verbal lexemes *watārum* and *maṭûm* are considered a *Koppelung* ("more or less") and as such must be found together. Yet, the choice of the precative form of all other possible verbal forms makes it possible to regard *līter limṭi* as a concessive-conditional clause.

> [5.14] *šum[ma lā] ḫa[šḫāta] ak[ālam] ištu bīt[iya]* ***liblūnikku[m]*** → ***lā tamaḫḫar***
> I[f you have no n]eed, **even if they bring** you fo[od] from [my] house — do not accept (it). 9, 260:10–15

Example [**5.14**] is interpreted as a concessive-conditional due to an incompatibility which would otherwise lie between the directives "let them bring you" and "do not accept". In addition, the form *liblūnikkum* cannot be interpreted as having a directive value for it is definitely incompatible with the conditional *šumma lā ḫašḫāta*. It makes sense only as representing some possibility or potentiality.

The next two examples contain the 1st pers. of the precative:

> [5.15] *mīnum epēšum annûm ana ūsī* ***lušpurakku*** → *meḫer ṭuppiya* ***ula tušabbalam***
> What is this behavior? **Even if I write** to you according to the rules, you do not send me a response to my tablet. 9, 264:4–8

The concessive-conditional pattern in [**5.15**] resumes *epēšum* as its appositive content. *lušpurakku* is not interpreted as a question since precative nexus questions hardly exist in the AbB corpus (see **§4.3.3.2** above).

An important point is that "→", used to connect the concessive-conditional clause with its consequent clause, is very different (both semantically and syntactically) from "//", representing disjunction between clauses, despite their identical material form (i.e., non-marking). The two preceding cases, [**5.14**] and [**5.15**], as well as other cases adduced above ([**5.4**], [**5.5**] and [**5.7**]), all exhibit a "→" connective — and in all of them the link between the concessive-conditional clause and the consequent clause is a tight link, as one finds in examples [**4.97**]–[**4.99**] in **§4.4.3** above (where this "→" is shown to be a variant of *-ma*). This kind of link is viewed here as **part of the pattern**.

The following unit of text contains two concessive-conditional precatives. Whereas the second (**b**) is well recognized as such (quoted in GAG §158c), the first (**a**) is not, as it may have alternative interpretations, possibly because the background has been considered differently:

[5.16] [*û*]*m šakin ina lā rīqūtim–ma*	There is [bar]ley.[7]
ul ušābilakkim	I did not have it sent to you only due to scarcity of time.
(a) *kaspam* ***lušābilakkim–ma***	**Even if I have** silver **sent** to you
âm ***šāmī*** → *ûm ša tašamm*[*ī*]	so that you buy barley, the barley you will buy
kīma yāʾim ***ul d*****[*ami*]*****q***	will not be as g[oo]d as mine.
(b) *u pūḫātim*	And **even if they**
liddinūnikkim →	**give** you substitutions,
ul damiq	it will not be good.
kīma taḫabbatī	Borrow (as much) as you (need to) borrow,
hubtī lā tātana[*šš*]*ašī–ma*	do not keep being wo[rr]ied, and
kīma artīqu	as soon as I have become free,
âm damqam ana rēšiki	let me bring you good barley,
lublakkim–ma lā tanazziqī	so that you do not worry.
11, 40:9–21	

The sender was unable to provide the addressee with barley because he had been busy. Concessivity in **(a)** originates in the incompatibility between the alleged willingness of the writer to provide silver (in order for the addressee to buy barley) and the fact that he does not recommend it, as reflected by the consequent clause of **(a)** *ûm ša tašammī kīma yāʾim ul d*[*ami*]*q* and by the end of the letter where the sender encourages the addressee to wait for his barley. The bi-clausal nature of the protasis in **(a)** (*lušābilakkim–ma âm šāmī*) is unique as well. An almost identical incompatibility lies at the basis of **(b)**. The concessive sense (mainly of **(b)**) is close semantically to the permissive notion, which is one extreme of the directive scale of notions (see §**4.3.1.1.2**). Yet, the concessive precative, having to do with a pattern, belongs in another sub-paradigm.

So far, the value of the protasis, its logical incompatibility with the consequent clause and the *-ma*/→ juncture between them have been discussed. The nature of the consequent clause is discussed further below.

5.3 The limits of the concessive-conditional precative

The morphological neutralization of the syntagms *lū paris* and *lū* N, belonging to either the asseverative or the precative paradigm, is mentioned

7. For the preceding lines ([5]*aš-šum še-im ša ta-aš-pu-ri-im* [6][*at-ti ti*]-KI *ki-ma ša še-um-ma* [7][*la i*]-*ba-aš-šu-ú* [8][*a-we*]-*lu*[*m*] *ú-za-ab-ba*-[*a*]*l-ki*) the AbB edition has "[6]you know that [7]no barley is available". It could, however, be interpreted differently: "[8]The [ma]n keeps you waiting [6]**as if** there were [no] *barley*". The second interpretation spares us the need to interpret *ûm šakin* as an ad hoc counterfactual conditional (had there been ...), as the edition in fact does.

in §2.2 above. This neutralization is an acute problem when the syntagm exhibits a concessive notion, and a decision should be made whether it belongs to the asseverative paradigm or to the precative paradigm (since forms belonging to both paradigms may constitute concessive clauses). There are various considerations in making these decisions, both structural and semantic. The following examples have such a construction:

> [5.17] *kunukkī ina amārika lā tuḫḫaram ṣibātuka* ***lū ḫamiš*** → ***kušdanni***
> Upon seeing my document, do not delay. **Even if** you have **five** (other) **things to do**, reach me. 11, 167:16–17

lū ḫamiš is here interpreted as precative, for it is merely implying a possibility that the addressee might have something else to do. Another factor is the extreme, typical of concessive-conditionals, expressed by *ḫamiš*. Example [5.18] contains the syntagm *lū* N–*ma*:

> [5.18] *šā[r]um kīma ištaknu* ***lū mūšum–ma nušerreb–ma*** *ṭēmam* ***nišapparam***
> As soon the wi[n]d has subsided, **even if it is night**, we will take (the barley) in and send a report. 7, 84:6'–8'

Since it is not yet known, at the time of utterance, *when* the wind will quiet down, it would make sense to consider the syntagm *lū mūšum–ma* as a precative. The precative is always prospective, facing the future, whereas the stative asseverative has a non-future reference (see §2.2.2). In other words, the possible subsiding of the wind at night is yet to happen, and hence precative is more likely. This example is unique in that the syntagm *lū* N(*–ma*), contrary to verbal forms (including the predicative which is generally identical to the latter as far as juncture is concerned), are not followed by the connective *-ma* or by "→", as far as can be established (but this case may turn out to be an exception, compare 10, 23:18–19).

The following example is quite similar:

> [5.19] *upnāšu sāmam* ***lū malâ*** → ***ul aḫaššeḫšu***
> **Even if** both his palms **were filled** with rubies (or red gold?), I do not need him. 9, 181:17–18 (n. c to the translation)

The protasis in [5.19] contains a remote possibility, serving as an extreme. Moreover, this form is not resumptive (for resumption is a characteristic of asseverative forms, see §2.4.3.1). In view of these considerations, *lū malâ* is interpreted as precative.

In contradistinction to examples [5.17]–[5.19], the following example, even though it is of an analogous structure to a precative sequence, actually belongs with the asseverative paradigm rather than to the concessive-conditional precative:

[5.20] *aššum* PN_1 *u mārī* PN_2 ... *ša apqidakkum u kanīkšunu maḫar* PN_3 *tušēzibanni umma atta–ma kanīku* ***lū qurrum–ma*** *pûm* ***lū šakin***
Concerning PN_1 and the sons of PN_2 ..., whom I entrusted to you and whose sealed document you had me draw out in front of PN_3, saying: 'The document *is* available, but let an oral statement be made'. 11, 94:7–9

In the co-text of the clause in question (*kanīku lū qurrub*), it is mentioned that a document had been made out (*kanīkšunu ... tušēzibanni*), and therefore it was present at the point of utterance. Referring back to the presence of the document at the point of utterance serves as resumption, hence *lū qurrub* is analyzed as asseverative. In addition, semantically, since a document is already made out and hence a fact, future possibility is out of the question. This example is therefore considered as belonging to the asseverative paradigm, reflecting a rhetorical concessive rather than a concessive-conditional.

The next example resembles a saying and contains the syntagm *lū* N–*ma* as does **[5.18]**:

[5.21] *atta* ***lū šamšum–ma*** *ṣētka luštaḫan atta* ***lū erēnu[m]–ma*** *ina ṣillika ṣ[ētum]* ***ayyiḫmuṭanni***
Be the sun (so) I may warm myself in your bright light. Be a cedar (so) the h[eat] may not scorch me in your shadow. 9, 228:16–20

The clauses in question are translated in the edition as asseverative (*you truly are the sun so...*). However, in view of the criteria developed heretofore, now used to distinguish allegedly identical structures, and of the careful characterization of each and every modal paradigm, there are more possibilities: As the translation here shows, the clauses may be interpreted as 2nd pers. directives (or even better, as sequenced precatives); they could, just as well, be interpreted as members of the wish paradigm or as if they are a conditional precative. As a matter of fact, it is impossible in this case to determine the exact syntactic nature of these forms. A saying may reflect a former, rather than a synchronic, set of rules.

One more example, structurally analogous to the one adduced in n. 5 above, has a 2nd pers. precative form which denotes concessive-conditionality:

[5.22] *ina ḫumāšim eleʾʾīka šitpuṣum* ***šitpaṣ–ma*** *ina šitpuṣim* ***eleʾʾīka***
I overpower you in the wrestling ring[8]. (Even if you) **choose** *wrestling*[9], then I will overpower you in wrestling. ARM 26, 207:15–17

8. See AHw:1412b and LAPO 18:323.

9. For the paronomastic infinitive constructions, see Cohen 2004.

As explained in **§4.4.4.2**, n. 34 above, this example (which is unique in the ARM corpus) does not fit together with the same structure in the AbB corpus. The structure *purus–ma iparras* is not an obvious (concessive-)conditional in our corpus, and therefore cannot be included in the present pattern, which is formulated with regard to the AbB corpus.

5.4 Conclusions

The following table summarizes the formal characteristics of each example of the concessive-conditional precative. Since this type of precative is pattern-related (as are the sequenced precatives and *-ma* conditionals), the connective and the apodosis/consequent clause are considered as well:

1a. Concessive-conditional cases

ex.	source	text	protasis	connective	apodosis/consequent
5.7	Whiting	letter	*lipr[us-ma] liprus*	→	*parsāku*
5.8	AbB	letter	*liprus*	***-ma***	*ul aparras*
5.10	LE	legal	*liprus*	***-ma***	*ul parsat*
5.11	ARM	letter	*liprus*	***-ma***	*aparras*
5.12	VAB 5	legal	*liprus*	***-ma***	non-verbal clause
5.14	AbB	letter	*liprus*	→	*lā taparras*
5.15	AbB	letter	*luprus*	***-ma***	*ula taparras*
5.16a	AbB	letter	*luprus–ma purus*	→	*ul paris*
5.16b	AbB	letter	*liprus*	→	*ul paris*
5.17	AbB	letter	*lū pāris*	→	*purus*
5.18	AbB	letter	*lū* N-*ma*[10]		*niparras-ma niparras*
5.19	AbB	letter	*lū paris*	→	*ul aparras*
	AbB	letter	*luprus*	***-ma***	*aparras*[11]
	AbB	letter	*liprus*	→	*aparras*[12]

10. As is mentioned above (**§5.3**) *-ma* in the vicinity of a noun is not considered as the connective ***-ma*** (and in consequence the absence of *-ma* cannot be considered as "→").

11. 10 *šiqil kaspam anniam* ***luqerribšunūšim–ma*** *ina matī–ma ina eqlim u kirîm* ***eleqqe*** "**Even if I bring** them 10 sheqels (of) this silver, when will I get (a return) from the field and the garden?" (3, 88:9–12, not discussed above).

12. *gimrī mala tagammarī* 1 *šiqil kaspum* 2 *šiqil kaspum* ***libbašû*** → *anāku* ***appalki*** "Use up as much as you need, **be** (lit. become) **it** one (or) two sheqels (of) silver, I will pay you" (11, 154:15–18, not discussed above).

1b. Conditional cases

5.2	LE	legal	*liprus*	*-ma*	non-verbal clause
5.3	LE	legal	*liprus*	*-ma*	*iparras*
5.4	RA 69	legal	*liprus*	→	*lū aparras*
5.5	AbB	letter	*ē taprus*	→	*lū aparras*

1c. Undecided cases

5.6	AbB	letter	*liprus*	*-ma*	*purus–ma purus*
5.13	VAB 5	legal	*liprus → liprus*	→	*lā aparrasu–ma lā aparrasu*[13]

A few points become immediately apparent:

- The connective is always *-ma* / →, testifying to a close juncture between the connected clauses (see **§4.4.4.1** above).
- The apodosis/consequent clause is mostly indicative (including non-verbal clauses) but occasionally precative or asseverative. No apodosis/consequent clause has past reference.
- There are no ***purus*** forms for protasis (except one **sequenced** 2nd pers. precative in **[5.16a]**, which is syntactically different from the 2nd pers. directive — see **§4.4.4.0.2** above). This is especially evident in view of the sequence *purus–ma iparras* (examples **[4.136]–[4.142]**, **§4.4.4.2**) where *purus* does not have an incontestable concessive-conditional notion, and may imply directivity just as well. Having another form *and* a somewhat different meaning, this sequence is classified here separately. It is important to note that in these syntactic conditions ***purus*** is opposed to ***luprus* / *liprus*** despite the fact that in other (sub-)paradigms they belong in the same category. (In fact, different groups are proposed exactly on these grounds.)

In table 2 the forms are organized so as to show the pattern, which is composed of a. the protasis paradigm and b. the apodosis/consequent paradigm, both interconnected by *-ma* / →:

2a. The conditional protasis and apodosis paradigms:

protasis	**connective**	**apodosis/consequent clause**
liprus *ē taprus*	***-ma*** / →	*lū aparras* / *lā aparrasu* *iparras* non-verbal clause

13. This abstract structure represents example **[5.13]** discussed under **§5.2** above. As far as structure is concerned, it resembles conditionals; as far as notion and other characteristics go, it is concessive-conditional. Therefore, it is here left undetermined.

b. The concesssive-conditional protasis and consequent paradigms:

liprus	***-ma* /→**	(*ul*) *iparras*
luprus		(*ul*) *paris*
lū paris		*lā iparras*
lū N-*ma*		non-verbal clause

- The connective is not a paradigm but rather a free variation of *-ma* /→ which are equivalent (as is explained above in §§**5.2** and **4.4.3**).
- *ē taprus* in the conditional protasis (example [**5.5**]) is irregular not just for the AbB corpus, but for other OB letter corpora (ARM, the archaic OB of Ešnunna in Whiting 1987). It does, however, have similar functions in OA (see various examples throughout Hecker 1968 §135). The occurrence of this form is one of the reasons to provide for two protasis paradigms, one conditional, the other concessive-conditional.
- The paradigmatic constitution of the concessive-conditional protasis is easy to formulate, containing a few **1st**, but mostly **3rd pers. affirmative precatives.**
- The apodosis paradigm (for the conditional pattern) contains future asseverative (affirmative and negative) forms, an indicative form and one non-verbal clause.
- The paradigmatic constitution of the consequent clause (for the concessive-conditional pattern) is different and contains affirmative and negative indicative, precative and one non-verbal clause, none of which have past reference in this function.

The concessive-conditional precative is then not merely a semantic notion but is rather definable as a distinct sub-paradigm having a clear value. As a pattern-related paradigm it is opposed to other pattern-related paradigms such as the sequenced precative pattern (§**4.4.4.0.2**) and the *-ma* conditional pattern when exhibiting a precative apodosis (**chapter 6**):

3.

clause I	connective	clause II	functions
liprus	*-ma* /→	*liprus*	precative sequence
liprus	***-ma*** **/→**	***iparras***	**(concessive-)conditional+apod.**
purus	*-ma* /→	*iparras*	precative+indicative (**4.4.4.2**)
iparras	*-ma* /→	*liprus*	conditional+precative apod.

The concessive-conditional precative acquires its value by the two basic axes, viz., paradigmatically, by the restricted set of possible forms in the protasis, and syntagmatically, by the pattern (which, in its turn, is paradigmatically opposed to the other related patterns). This syntactic distinctiveness is what enables us to consider the precative in this pattern a separate sub-paradigm, well defined and distinct from other occurrences of precative forms.

The concessive-conditional semantically resembles the interrogative sub-paradigm where we can find **absence of the injunctive feature**, which is present in the rest of the sub-paradigms. The token of this absence may be represented by the fact that the form *purus* (which generally keeps its injunctive feature throughout) **is excluded** as a main verbal form from the concessive-conditional sub-paradigm as well as from the interrogative sub-paradigm.

6

The *-ma* Conditional Pattern

6.0 Introduction

In discussing the sequenced precative in **§§4.4.4.0.2** and **4.4.4.2**, an abstract pattern of the type *liprus–ma liprus* was compared with other abstract patterns, representing the concessive-conditional pattern (*liprus–ma iparras*) and the *-ma* conditional pattern (*iparras–ma liprus*). Such an abstraction may create a wrong impression about the pattern; it may be much more diversified, since it is constructed of two co-occurring sets of possible forms which are interconnected via a connective. The present chapter is a description of the pattern of the *-ma* conditional pattern.

The paradigm which constitutes the protasis does not contain precative forms, but rather forms which, occurring in an ordinary declarative, independent clause, would regularly have indicative value. Yet, here, in this well-defined pattern, they are **conditionals** rather than indicatives.

The conditional protasis paradigm does not contain any precative forms, and unlike indicative paradigms, it is in both paradigmatic and syntagmatic interrelationships with sequenced precatives. In addition, as is hinted at in **§§4.4.4.0.2** and **4.4.4.2**, the conditional **pattern** does have a paradigmatic relationship with the sequenced precative **pattern**.

-ma conditionals in the AbB corpus are less frequent than *šumma* conditionals. They are often formed by two interconnected *iparras* forms (GAG §160b), but there are cases in which it is rather the *iprus* form which constitutes the first clause (GAG §173g). A typical example of such a conditional would be the following:

> **[6.1]** *urram rabiān u šībūt ālim* ***ul tubbalam–ma ul uballaṭka***
> Tomorrow, should you not bring me the city mayor and elders, I will not let you live. 1, 52:28–31

A superficial examination of such a conditional pattern may wrongly suggest that it could have a non-conditional interpretation as well. The conditional pattern under discussion, however, constitutes a distinct structural entity displaying various characteristic features, besides its usually uncontestable conditional value.

The *-ma* conditional pattern is an important member of the modal system in the corpus. The *iparras* form in *-ma* conditionals is morphologically identical to the present indicative form *iparras*. Nevertheless, these forms are syntactically and functionally different and each belongs in a distinct paradigm. The members of the conditional protasis paradigm have a **non-factual value** referring to a mere possibility (as opposed to *iparras* forms in declarative, independent clauses which, on the contrary, have a factual value reflecting reality).

6.1 Connected conditionals in general, and literature review

Conditionals are a special notion in the syntax of any language; one clause (the protasis) expresses possibility, on whose actualization the validity of the other clause (the apodosis) is dependent. That is just about all that can be assumed to be common to conditionals in general. Conditionals are a complex syntactic and semantic phenomenon which is signaled by various means in different languages. The *-ma* conditional pattern treated in this section is characterized first and foremost by the lack of a conditional particle and by an asymmetric coordination (see **§4.4.2** above) between the protasis and the apodosis. The following literature review attempts to examine similar or related structures in other languages.

Conditional patterns where the protasis and the apodosis are coordinated are treated much less in the linguistic literature than structures where the conditional protasis is part of the main clause, viz., a subordinate clause. Haiman 1983 treats the subject in various Papuan languages in which this type of conditional is effected via a coordination of two clauses, the first of which, however, does not exactly consist of a finite verb. A kind of **modal incongruence** which characterizes the connected conditionals in Hua (one of the Papuan languages treated in Haiman 1983:267) is reminiscent of the OB examples of the *-ma* conditional pattern.

The issue of connection between the protasis and the apodosis mostly comes up in treating coordinated conditionals, rather than subordinate ones (although such connection between a syndetic conditional and the apodosis is to be found as well, as in Arabic, via *fa*, e.g., Fischer 1987 §447). In English a few studies describe conditionals which are characterized by what is called in this literature "pseudo-imperatives" (Van der Awera 1986:206–11; Bolinger 1967:340–46; and Davies 1979), i.e., of the type ***make** one mistake **and** there'll be trouble* (Davies 1979:1039). Such conditionals rather resemble the conditional precative treated above (**chapter 5**).

French (and other Romance languages) show a variety of conditionals which are not introduced by a particle, but signaled mainly by subjunctive forms (analogous to the type *liprus–ma* /→ *iparras* treated in the previous chapter), but also by conditional, imperfect, and even by the present tense form:

> [6.2] *Le diable* ***entrerait*** *dans la maison, qu'on le laisserait faire*
> (If) the devil would enter the house, one should let him.

> [6.3] *On lui* ***parle****, elle ne répond pas*
> (If) they talk to her, she does not reply. de Boer 1947:323

These occurrences exhibit, once in a while, explicit connection (*et*) between protasis and apodosis (Sandfeld 1965:354).

The Semitic languages in general have a rich formation of conditional structures, both paratactic conditionals and conditionals introduced by a particle. As to the former type, which is our concern here, both Biblical Hebrew and Arabic have a structure containing two modal forms, imperative or jussive (Driver 1892:188–92; Reckendorf 1898:680–82):

> [6.4] *qālū kūnū hūdan ʾaw naṣārā tahtadū*
> They said: 'Become Jews or Christians, (and) ye will be guided aright'. Wright 1898 II:24a

> [6.5] *tāšɛṯ ḥōšɛḵ wīhī lāylā bō tirmōś kŏl ḥayṯō yāʿar*
> Should you cause darkness, and there should be night in which all the beast of the forest will creep. Ps. 104:20

This kind of conditional is more affiliated with the one treated in **chapter 5**. Other examples in Biblical Hebrew are more like the pattern examined here, containing forms otherwise used for the present tense:

> [6.6] *ʾattɛm timʿālū ʾănī ʾāp̄īṣ ʾɛṯḵɛm bāʿammīm*
> As for you, (if) you deceive, (and) I, for my part, will disperse you amongst the nations. Neh. 1:8

Hebrew has, in addition, a conditional effected by the juxtaposition of two *wəqāṭal* forms, pertaining either to the future or to the past (Driver 1892:185–87; Niccacci 1990:137–38; and Joüon 1996:627–28):

> [6.7] *lō yūḵal hannaʿar lāʿăzōḇ ʾɛṯ ʾāḇīw wəʿāzaḇ ʾɛṯ ʾāḇīw wāmēṯ*
> The lad cannot leave his father. Should he leave his father (and) he would die. Gen. 44:22

This example is closest to the OB examples with regard to the co-text of the conditional clause (see **§6.3.1** below).

As to OA, Hecker 1968 §135g treats both precative-conditionals and -*ma* conditionals under the same heading. In the present corpus these two are clearly two different structures carrying different values.

Von Soden describes both types of conditionals under the same heading

(GAG §160). *šumma* conditionals are described separately (§161).

Leong 1994 (:118–23; 218–24; 288–90; 333–37) treats the conditionals in the AbB corpus separately, each in a chapter devoted to a single verbal form (*iprus*, *paris*, etc.). *-ma* conditionals are discussed together with *šumma* conditionals. All the examples of *-ma* conditionals are classified under "real conditions". An important insight in Leong's work is that an injunctive form in the apodosis sets the conditional in the domain of real (as opposed to irrealis) conditionals (Leong 1994:289). This is important since *-ma* conditionals, like *šumma* conditionals, may have precative forms in the apodosis paradigm.

The values of the different verbal forms in the *šumma* protasis are treated by Leong in terms of past event (with respect to *iprus* forms) and in terms of current relevance (with respect to *iptaras* forms), assuming the same values for the different verbal forms in *-ma* conditionals as well. This is problematic, however, since the paradigmatic constitution of the protasis of the two kinds of conditionals is different — *iptaras*, for example, is unattested as the protasis of *-ma* conditionals. Different paradigms presuppose different values, even if the forms are morphologically identical. When we compare ***#lā iparras*** (# is a boundary marker, signaling here an independent clause) to *ammīnim* ***lā iparras*** we can see two identical syntagms which display different values: The first is a negative directive, while the second may be either a negative precative (that is, the negative counterpart of *liprus*) or a negative present indicative (that is, the negative counterpart of *iparras*). This difference is due to the syntagmatic possibilities conditioned by interrogatives.

6.2 The basic structure of *-ma* conditionals in the corpus

Von Soden notes that the forms used in *-ma* conditionals are quite often the present (*iparras*; GAG §160b), but adds that the preterite (*iprus*) is possible as well (GAG §173g). Leong 1994:289 adds that in the AbB corpus the predicative (*paris*) in this position occurs as well. The apodosis, besides the present (GAG §160b), may exhibit other forms as well, namely *paris*, a non-verbal clause and *liprus*. This means that the full pattern is more flexible than was previously assumed. (As a matter of fact, the apodosis is quite similar to the apodosis of a *šumma* clause; see Huehnergard 1997 §17.3.) The following sequences have been found to exist, all considered as belonging to the same pattern:

iparras**-ma* ***iparras

[**6.8**] *ina amtim u wardim ša bītiša ana bītika šūrubim* ***ukannūninni-ma*** *ana* GN *kalîš[u]* ***ummaqūninni***
Should they establish that I made a maid or a servant from her household enter your household, they will humiliate[1] me in all GN. 9, 49:9–13

iparras**-ma* ***non-verbal clause

[**6.9**] *anāku aššu[m] ṣētim adi inanna uḫḫir mušītam* ***arakkam–ma*** *šērtam–ma* ***ina pī nār*** DN ***anāku***[2]
As for me, I have been delayed until now because of the heat. If I travel by night, then *by morning* I will be at the mouth of the DN canal. 12, 11:16–19

iparras**-ma* ***paris

[**6.10**] *kâti̯* (MA-*ti-i*) *išūka–ma šaniam* ***eše''ī–ma ṭābkum***
Having you, should I look for someone else, would it please you? 9, 226:4–6

[**6.11**] *šumma bēlī atta* ***amât–ma ṭābkum***
If you are my lord, should I die, would it please you? 9, 232:21–22

iparras**-ma* ***liprus (any precative form, any person)

[**6.12**] 1 *pān suluppam ana bītiya̱ šūbilam* →[3] ***ul tanaddim–ma*** *ana awīlika* ***lā tašallanni***
Have 1 *pānum* (of) dates brought to my house; should you not give (it), do not ask me about your man. 6, 120:7–10

[**6.13**] *alkam–ma ... lūmur* → ***ul tallakam–ma lū tīde***[4] ***lū tīde***
Come so that I can see ... ; should you not come, be seriously warned.[5] 6, 207:13–19

---

1. See 9, 49, n. a to the translation.

2. The example is originally translated as purpose ("so that I ...").

3. For a discussion of the connection symbolized by "→" in this slot, see **§6.3.4.2** below.

4. *lū tīde* is interpreted as a member of the precative paradigm ("you better know") rather than a member of the asseverative paradigm ("you *do* know") for two reasons: First, as is apparent, directives occur in this syntactic slot, while there are no examples of asseveratives. Second, for such asseverative to occur, some kind of lexematic resumption, which does not occur here, would be expected. See example [**2.39**] in **§2.4.3.1** above.

5. The translation of this precative must contain a warning and yet keep its directive function.

iprus**–ma **iparras

[**6.14**] ... *alkam–ma* PN *apulli* (sic) → ***ul tallikam–ma*** *nāq mê ina bītika* ***ul izzibūni***
... Come and pay PN; if you have not come[6] they will not leave a water pourer in your house. 7, 67:13–18

[**6.15**] *aššum eqel šamaššammī ša* GN *mamman* ***ul taškum–ma*** *šamaššammū* ***immašša***ʾ (sic)
Regarding the sesame field of GN, if you have not appointed anyone, the sesame will be stolen. 11, 168:7–10

[**6.16**] ***ula taḫmuṭam–ma*** *šipātika* ***itabbalū***
If you have not hurried, they will take away your wool. 4, 145:34–35

***iprus**–ma* **non-verbal clause**

[**6.17**] ... *nāram šâti* ***ul tamḫur–ma*** (*ta-am-ku-ur-ma*) ***ul awātī***
... If you have not drawn off the canal, it will not be my affair. 11, 175:9–10

paris**–ma **liprus

[**6.18**] *ina* 4 *ūmī daltī* ***lū kamsat*** ... *ina* 4 *ūmī daltī* ***ul kamsa***[***t***]***–ma lū*** [***t***]***īdeā***
Let my door be completed within four days ... If my door is not completed within four days, be warned. 3, 34:19, 37–38

These combinations call for several preliminary remarks. First, the connective between the protasis and the apodosis is generally *-ma*. Yet, there are further examples below ([**6.23**] and [**6.33**]) showing the very same syntactic features (**§6.3**) and value of the conditional pattern, where no *-ma* occurs. This absence (rather than ø), which is interchangeable with *-ma* (but not with *u*), has been discussed above (**§§4.4.3** and **5.2**) and designated as "→". The following example is of the same essential structure as the examples adduced above, yet it displays *u* (rather than *-ma* / →) between protasis and apodosis:

[**6.19**] *umma anāku–ma kīma erēbika kaspam qāti awīlim usuḫ* // *kaspam qāti awīlim* ***ul tassuḫ u*** *kaspum ṣibtam* ***uṣṣab***
I (said) as follows: 'As soon as you come in, take the silver from the man'. You **did not take** the silver from the gentleman and the silver (now) bears interest. 12, 53:5–8

This, as is clearly reflected by the translation, is not a conditional. The example is followed by *dīn* DN *epēšum annûm ša tēpušu* ("This deed you did [deserves] a verdict of DN", ibid. 9) which means that the action

6. The translation of this *iprus* form attempts to reflect the idea of perfect or anteriority; see example [**6.20**] further below.

is regarded as already carried out, i.e., as factual.

The second point is the use of *iprus* in the protasis. Von Soden (GAG §173g) considered *iprus* and *iparras* to be the same in this context. It seems, however, that there is some difference after all. In most of these instances, where these *iprus* forms follow what looks like a directive (in fact it is a sequenced precative, see **§§6.3.4** and **6.3.4.2** below), past reference is out of the question. This is because the reference point, set by the sequenced precative, is necessarily from the point of utterance on. For instance, in example **[6.14]** (***alkam***–*ma* ... → *ul* ***tallikam***–*ma* ...) both the sequenced precative and the protasis belong to the same utterance, referring to the same action, which has not yet taken place. The solution is that *iprus* in this -*ma* conditional paradigm has to do with the linguistic notion of **perfect**. This notion is summarized in Comrie 1976:52: "The perfect indicates the continuing present relevance of a past situation". The same notion is found in OB as well (Maloney 1981:33) and it is generally expressed in OB via the *iptaras* form, mainly in temporal clauses (Leong 1994:159):

> **[6.20]** *[i]štu ū[r] našpakim ša gag[îm] u ša kīd[i]m* ***tessērā*** *ūrātikunu aḫ[i]ātim sērā*
> [A]s soon as **you have plastered** the storehouse ro[of] in the cloister and outside, (you may) plaster your other roofs. 12, 17:17–22

What makes it possible for *iprus* forms to express the notion of perfect is that according to the present method, the functions of verbal forms are not inherent to them. In different syntagms (i.e., different syntactic conditions) the set of interchangeable items in a given slot (in other words, the paradigm) may be different. When it is, the values of these paradigmatic items are different as well. This may be shown by *iparras* forms in *šumma* protases, which are assumed to denote modal or habitual connotations (GAG §161i, Huehnergard 1997 §17.3). This is mainly due to the fact that those *iparras* forms are modally neutralized in that syntagm (not being opposed to *liprus* forms, as they are in other syntagms) and are hence able to denote either indicative or modal notions (see examples **[4.19]**–**[4.21]** in **§4.2.2** above). The following example (cited in GAG §173g as well to show *iprus* form in the protasis) is instrumental in illustrating this value of the *iprus* form in the protasis paradigm:

> **[6.21]** *ištu inanna ana* 5 *ūmī ina maḫrīka wašbāku* ***adi allakam*** *ul* ***tukillaššu***–*ma* PN_1 *u* PN_2 *tappal*
> Within 5 days from now I will be with you. If you **have** not **prepared** him **by the time I come**, you will (have to) answer to PN_1 and PN_2. 6, 73:10–17

The temporal point of reference for the protasis is set by the clause *adi allakam,* which is to take place five days after the time of the utterance. The perfect, or anteriority, is here expressed by the *iprus* form, viz., that by the time the speaker arrives the addressee will be expected to **have already prepared** the slave, as opposed to just **prepare him** by that time.

The following **diagram 1** shows: **a.** The full paradigmatic formula for the *-ma* conditional pattern (both protasis and apodosis paradigms); and **b.** The possibilities and restrictions on the connections between the members of each paradigm.

1.

a.

iparras *paris* *iprus*	*-ma* /→	*iparras* *liprus* *paris* non-verbal clause

b.

	iparras	*liprus*	*paris*	NVC* (apodosis)
iparras	+	+	+	+
paris	+	+	–	–
iprus	+	–	–	+
(protasis)				

*non-verbal clause

To conclude, the structure of *-ma* conditionals is generally composed of two distinct paradigms interconnected by *-ma* /→. The protasis paradigm contains, in addition to the most often used *iparras, iprus* (to express the linguistic notion of perfect) and *paris* forms as well. The apodosis paradigm is identical, at least in principle, to the paradigm which constitutes the apodosis of *šumma* conditional clauses. The combinations which actually occur in this structure, as can be observed in **diagram 1b.**, are not infinite. A point already touched upon is the connection between the various members of the protasis paradigm and a precative, in view of the modal congruence in the corpus (**§4.4.4**). This is where the special syntagmatic relationship of the protasis paradigm with members of the precative paradigm comes in. The connection of *iprus* with these members is rare and not simple to interpret:

> **[6.22]** *kurummatam admiq–ma lā taḫašša*
> If I have succeeded with the food rations, do not be worried. 3, 39:18–19

This example is not very convincing and hence doubtful. Similar cases in the corpus are felt to be (scribal) errors (see **§4.4.4.2**) and for this reason they are sometimes emended to conform with the editor's *Sprachgefühl.*

6.3 Structural and semantic means to define the -*ma* conditionals

Semantics is not a sufficient criterion in order to distinguish sequences which are used as -*ma* conditionals from all other similar sequences. In order for a formal difference to be established, formal characterisitics of the present structure must be elaborated first. There are several typical peculiarities of the -*ma* conditional which make it distinct: 1. Polar lexical resumption; 2. The use of the opposite polarity to what is normal in certain expressions; 3. A special syntagmatic relationship with the precative paradigm; and 4. The use of *arḫiš* with negated verbal forms.

6.3.1 Polar lexical resumption

The term "polar lexical resumption" designates a phenomenon where in the co-text preceding the protasis there is a sequenced precative of the same (or a related) verbal lexeme as the one found in the protasis. The sequenced precative and the following protasis show opposite polarity (i.e., one is affirmative while the other is negative):[7]

> [6.23] ... ***šūriam*** ... → *awīlam šuāti* ***ul tušarriam*** → *ana abīka ašappar*
> ... Have (him) brought to me ... ; should you not have this man brought to me, I will write to your father. 6, 13:6, 10–13

As is made clear by the next example, the lexical resumption is flexible in nature:

> [6.24] *ana* PN_1 ***idnā***–*ma ana maḫrīya* ***liblam*** → *šīpātim*
> ***ul tušabbalānim***–*ma inūma ana* GN *tallakānim dabābam anniam maḫar* PN_2 *nidabbub*
> Give (it) to PN_1, and let him bring (it) to me; should you not have the wool sent to me, we will discuss this matter in the presence of PN_2 when you come to GN. 7, 168:5'–10'

The combination of *nadānum* and *wabālum* is quite close, semantically, to *šūbulum* in the protasis. This "approximate resumption" is found as well and is equivalent to the more usual, exact resumption.

A possible explanation of the effect created by the association of the co-textual sequenced precative and the seemingly indicative form is that a sequenced precative, much like a directive, generally presupposes future accomplishment or execution of the action in question. Therefore, there exists some basic logical incompatibility in the juxtaposition of these two forms in the same utterance, which can be settled only by an interpretation

7. This polarity is similar in nature to the one discussed at **§2.4.3.1** above. For comparison of the two types, see **§6.3.3** below.

of the structure as an unequivocal conditional. The protasis, containing the opposite polarity elements, creates the ground for discussing the possibility that the action in question may not take place as expected. The importance of this resumptive structure is paramount, as it highlights the possibility factor subsumed in the connected protasis. This possibility factor in fact introduces non-factuality, a feature to be found throughout the modal system in OB.

This resumption works in both directions, that is, the sequenced precative may be either affirmative or negative, as long as the protasis shows the opposite polarity:

<u>Affirmative–negative:</u>

[6.25] *âm bilassunu ana* G[N ***l*]*ikmis*[*ū*]*n*[*i*]*m*** → [...] [*ana* G]N ***ul ikammi*[*s*]*ūnim***–[*m*]*a aranšunu ana muḫḫik*[*a*] *iššakkan*
[Let] them bring the barley (of) their tax into G[N] ... ; should they not bring the barley of their tax ... their punishment will be upon yo[u]. 9, 192:10–17

[6.13] ***alkam***–*ma* ... *lūmur* → ***ul tallakam***–*ma lū tīde lū tīde*
Come so that I can see ... ; should you not come, be seriously warned. 6, 207:13–19

<u>Negative–affirmative:</u>

[6.26] 1 *uṭṭat kaspam* ... ***lā tušeṣṣe*** → 1 *uṭṭat kaspam* ***tušeṣṣē–ma*** *apāliya ul teleʾʾi*
Do not take out even one grain of silver; should you take out (as much as) one grain of silver, you will not be able to answer to me. 12, 53:17–20

[6.27] *rēqūssu* ***lā illakam*** → [*r*]*ēqūssu* ***illakam–ma*** [*b*]*ītī* *iṣabbat–ma ana bābim ušeṣṣeanni–ma*
He should not come empty-handed; should he come [em]pty-handed, he would seize my [hou]se and put me out the gate... 6, 140:20–23

The polar lexical resumption discussed heretofore is one of the most fundamental underlying principles of the *-ma* conditionals. In fact it is plausible to assume that this principle lies at the basis of each *-ma* conditional, whether explicitly, as in the examples presented above, or implicitly, as in the rest of them. Only in a very small number of cases is this possibility out of the question. The following section seems to corroborate this idea. The connection between the co-textual sequenced precative and the protasis has been designated by "→". This is possible in view of the examples adduced in **§6.4.3.2** further below, where this connection is effected via *-ma*, rendering it justifiable to regard this connection as *-ma* /→.

6.3.2 Verbal lexemes with opposite polarity to what is normal

The identification of *-ma* conditionals is especially incontestable when certain verbal expressions in the protasis seem to appear in opposite polarity to what is expected of them. The expressions which have been found to exhibit this behavior are *aḫam nadûm* (be negligent), *nīdi aḫim rašûm* (be negligent), *idam šuršûm* (raise objections) and *rēšam kullum* (be at the disposal of). The first three usually occur negated. The last one is generally in the affirmative.

aḫam nadûm:

As if to maintain the connection with the previous section, the first example exhibits, in addition, polar resumption:

> [6.28] *ana ša ašpurakkum* ***aḫka lā tanaddi*** → ***aḫka tanaddī****–ma di<ḫ>tika ašâ[l]*
> Do not be negligent regarding what I wrote you; should you be negligent, I will inqui[re] after you. 12, 64:31–33

nīdi aḫim rašûm:

In the following example the co-textual sequenced precative occurs **after** the apodosis:

> [6.29] *nidi aḫim* ***taraššê****–ma eqel kurummatim ... ul tukammasā ana êm kummusim* ***nīdi aḫ****[i]****m lā taraššiā***
> Should you be negligent, you will not (be able to) gather (the yield of my) subsistence field. Do not be negligent regarding gathering the barley. 1, 135, 8–12

In the rest of the cases this co-textual sequenced precative (*idam lā tušarša*, *rēška likillū*, etc.) does not occur, but the message is nevertheless clearly implied by the protasis:

> [6.30] *nīdi aḫim* ***taraššiāšim****–ma šumma eleppum šī imtūt ḫamuttam–ma ša kīma šâti nirtêb*
> Should you be negligent towards it, in case this boat does sink, will we be able to replace it *soon* with one just like it? 3, 35:26–28

idam šuršûm:

> [6.31] *ana ša ašpurakkum* ***idam tušaršā****–ma ina* GN *apāliya ul teleʾʾi*
> Should you object to what I wrote you, you will not be able to answer to me in GN. 7, 172:15–18

rēšam kullum:

[6.32] 8 *eḫzū rēška* ***ul ukallū–ma*** *lū tīde*
Should the 8 (copper) hatchets not be at your disposal, be warned.
6, 89:25–27

This preceding sequenced precative, even when missing, is implicitly present, triggering conditionality.

6.3.3 Polar lexical resumption: nexus focussing vs. *-ma* conditionals

A word should be said about the link to another, albeit similar, kind of resumption in the domain of modality. As is elaborated in **§2.4.3.1**, polar resumption is a very fundamental syntactic feature of nexus focussing as well. An example of nexus focussing phenomena would be the responsive utterance, e.g., to the question "why did you not send me the tablet?", which would be "(but) I ***did*** send you the tablet". The differences between the two kinds of resumption are tabulated in **diagram 2**:

2.

type / parameters	*-ma* conditional resumption	nexus focussing resumption
a. utterances:	1 only	1~2
b. co-text:	sequenced precative	unrestricted
c. polarity:	opposite	opposite ~ neutral
d. FSP effect:	not discussed	(nexus) focussing
e. semantic effect:	conditionality	insistence, oath, etc.

Remarks:

1. The conditional co-text exhibits a **sequenced precative** clause, whereas the nexus focussing co-text is **unrestricted**.
2. Both the co-textual sequenced precative and the following protasis belong in the **same utterance**, whereas nexus focussing is generally responsive to a **previous utterance**, possibly by **another interlocutor**.
3. The polarity in the first is strictly **opposite** (- → + or + → -), whereas in the second it may be **opposite** as well as **neutral** (that is, a contrast with some lingering doubt).
4. The FSP (functional sentence perspective, see **§2.4.1.1**) effect in the second is **nexus focussing**, whereas this effect is not discussed regarding the protasis. However, many linguists hold conditionals to be **topical** (Haiman 1978 is one prominent example). There are some reasons to accept this, particularly in this kind of conditionals, as the lexical resumption itself may be analysed as the **topic** (not the polar element, however). This issue certainly deserves a separate treatment.

5. The semantic effect in the first is **condition**, whereas in the second it is **insistence, oath**, or **rhetorical concession**.

One last important point which is related to polar resumption is the syntagmatic relationship with the precative paradigm. Lexical resumption is characterized by a **sequenced precative**, which belongs to the precative paradigm. This sequenced precative was suggested above to be, whether explicit or implicit, a fundamental feature of -*ma* conditionals. The next section further describes the syntagmatic relationship of the -*ma* conditional pattern with the precative paradigm.

6.3.4 The syntagmatic interrelationship with the precative paradigm

Exceptions to the modal congruence found in the language of the OB letters in the AbB series are comparatively rare. One specific case of such exceptions (i.e., the sequence *iparras–ma liprus*) ordinarily constitutes one of the sequences typical of -*ma* conditional clauses. Another case of such incongruence turns out to be when the co-textual sequenced precative is connected via -*ma* to the -*ma* conditional protasis (which is in fact the reason to regard it as a **sequenced precative**, rather than as a **directive**).

6.3.4.1 *iparras–ma liprus* and similar sequences

[6.33] *magallum* ***ippaṭṭar–ma liṣbatūni***
If a big boat is leaving, let them take (it for) me. 3, 14:5–6

[6.34] *pīḫātī apālam* ***u[l] e[l]eʾʾī–ma*** *ana mi[mm]ûya* (sic) *kīma ibaššû* ***lā teggî***
Should I no[t] be [a]ble to meet my obligations, do not be negligent towards my pro[per]ty, as much as there is. 6, 148:27–29

[6.35] *ša lā izzazzu mim<ma> ulileqqi* (sic) ... 7 *mana aklam išdudūnim* ***ulazzaz–ma*** (sic) *mannum* ***litēršu***
(Anyone) who does not serve may not take anything ... they provided me with seven minas of food; if I do not serve, who would pay it back? 11, 27:12–17

[6.36] *âm u šamnam nikkassak[i]* PN *liddinakki u* ***tarabbī–ma luš<al>limakki***[8]
Let *PN* give you barle[y] and oil, your balance, and in case you (have to) pay back,[9] let me pay (it) to you in full. 12, 110:14–17 (see 12, 117:19–21, same construction)

8. The emendation is due to the object -*ki* (*šalāmum* is generally an intransitive verb), and for semantic reasons as well.

9. *riābum*, see 12, 110, n. d to the translation.

[6.37] *kanikkam arḫiš* ***ul tušezzibšu–ma lū tīde***
Should you not have him make out a document quickly, be warned. 12, 25:19–20

The next group of examples has already been introduced; they are re-introduced in this context to reinforce the effect of quantity:

[6.32] 8 *eḫzū rēška* ***ul ukallū–ma lū tīde***
Should the eight (copper) hatchets not be at your disposal, be warned. 6, 89:25–27

[6.12] 1 *pān suluppam ana bītiya šūbilam* → ***ul tanaddim–ma*** *ana awīlika* ***lā tašallanni***
Have 1 *pānum* (of) dates brought to my house; should you not give (it), do not ask me about your man. 6, 120:7–10

[6.13] *alkam–ma ... lūmur* → ***ul tallakam–ma lū tīde lū tīde***
Come so that I can see ... ; should you not come, be seriously warned. 6, 207:13–19

The last example exhibits "→" between the protasis and the apodosis:

[6.38] *maškana ša* 5 *mana idîši–ma kilîši* → *amtum uznāša anni*[*š*]*–ma* ***iḫalliqki*** → *maškanu* ***libattiqši***
Put her in fetter(s) of 5 mina and detain her; the maid is intelligent — should she try to escape from you, let the fetter(s) hinder her. 1, 27:24–28

As is explained above (**§6.2** and see further references there), "→" is considered as the equivalent of the more frequent *-ma* (in this slot), constituting part of the same pattern. One finds both an approximate polar resumption between *maškana ... idîši-ma kilîši* and *iḫalliqki* and an incompatibility between chaining the maid and her escaping, which can be resolved only by interpreting *iḫalliqki* as a non-factual possibility.

paris–ma liprus

[6.18] *ina* 4 *ūmī daltī lū* ***kamsat*** ... *ina* 4 *ūmī daltī* ***ul kamsa***[***t***]***–ma lū*** [***t***]***īdiā***
Let my door be completed within 4 days ... If my door is not completed within 4 days, be warned. 3, 34:19, 37–38

[6.39] *u kallat* PN ***napiat–ma*** *ina nakkamtim* ***tu***<***še***>***ṣṣîši–ma*** *maḫrīki* ***lišib***
Furthermore, should the daughter-in-law of PN be distrained and you release her from the storehouse, let her stay with you. 9, 270:10–15

The sequence *iparras / paris–ma liprus* generally constitutes a conditional sequence in the AbB corpus. The close syntagmatic relationship (the token of which is the connection via *–ma* / →) between forms which are generally indicative in other environments (in declarative, independent clauses) and precative forms, is especially typical of the -*ma* conditional pattern.

6.3.4.2 *liprus–ma iparras–ma iparras* and similar sequences

The other case of such modal incongruence is when the conditional pattern is connected via -*ma* **to the co-textual sequenced precative (*liprus–ma* <u>*iparras–ma iparras*</u>)**:

> [**6.40**] *aššum muruṣ libbika ša taqbiam* ***luzziz–ma*** *dayyānūtam* ***lišāḫizū–ma*** *awīlam* ***tašaṭṭar**–ma* ... [*l*]*aqiašu mamman ul ileʾʾi*
> Concerning your bad feeling of which you told me, let me insist that they provide judicial procedure and should you register the gentleman, nobody will be able to take him ... 11, 137:12–19

The local implications of this connection via -*ma* between the co-textual sequenced precative and the protasis paradigm (which *never* contains precative forms, see **diagram 1a.** at the end of **§6.2**) are that it enables us to identify this non-marking of the connection, occurring in the same syntagmatic slot, as "→", a variant of -*ma*. As such it has the same values as does -*ma*. In the present case, i.e., when connecting clauses of opposite polarity (do → should you not do), "→" is rendered by ";", admittedly not representing the chaining factor. There are more examples of this type:

> [**6.41**] *ina nār* CN *nārta* ***muḫur–ma*** *eqlam ša* PN *mê* ***mullī–ma*** *ana errēšim* ***idin–ma*** *nāram šâti* ***ul tamḫur**–ma* (*ta-am-ku-ur-ma*) *ul awātī*
> Draw off a canal from the CN canal and fill PN's field with water and give (it) to the cultivator; if you have not drawn off the canal, it will be no affair of mine. 11, 175:5–10

> [**6.42**] PN_1 ... *ana ṣēr* PN_2 *tarū–ma atta–ma ṣirim–ma kaspam šuāti* [*š*]*uddim–ma ṣubātam ana pānīya* ***šām–ma*** *ana pānīya* ***ul tašâm*** → *mimma ul rāʾimī atta ittika ul adabbub*
> Bring PN_1 to PN_2 and *you* make the effort to collect the silver and buy a garment for me; should you not buy (it) for me, you do not love me at all, I will not speak to you. 8, 93:14–21

The three preceding examples testify to the tight syntagmatic connection between the protasis paradigm and the co-textual sequenced precative. Such tight connection means that the protasis paradigm is uniquely compatible syntagmatically with members of the precative paradigm on both its sides (both characterized by -*ma*/→). This is far from being typical with regard to the syntagmatic behavior of the forms *iprus*/*paris*/*iparras* **outside the protasis paradigm**. The next example is of the same basic structure (despite the fact that there is no polar lexical resumption, as in

[**6.40**] above, the special pattern is kept):

> [**6.43**] *ana dayyānī i nisniq* → *awâtini* ***līmurū–ma*** *šumma ša* PN *iqīšanniāšim mār[ū]šu leqûm kašid dayyānū* ***iqabbûniāšim***–*ma amtam nutār*
> We should go to the judges, let them look into our affairs and, if it is fitting for his sons to take what PN gave us as present, should the judges tell us, we will return the slave. 3, 2:18–23

This example, already containing one (*šumma*) conditional, is not interpreted as having in addition a -*ma* conditional in its translations in AbB 3 and in Huehnergard 1998:131. However, in view of the characteristics of these conditionals, it seems reasonable to assume that syntagms which exhibit the same structural characteristics would exhibit a similar value. This is one of the basic working hypotheses of the structural method.

There are **general implications** as well of the possibility of opposing the uncommon conditional sequence *līmurū–ma... iqabbûniāšim–ma ... nutār* to the unmarked and ubiquitous option of a precative sequence (of the type **līmurū–ma ... liqbûniāšim–ma ... i nutīr*). In view of the preceding examples and their implications concerning the nature of the connection between the co-textual sequenced precative and the conditional pattern, we can now oppose the **multi-clausal precative sequence**, discussed in **§4.4.4.0.2** above, to various conditional structures (i.e., including the co-textual sequenced precative and the conditional pattern). The opposition of conditional structures connected via -*ma* to the precative sequence is problematic since only one term is to be opposed, all other terms being equal:

3. *liprus-ma liprus-ma liprus-ma liprus* (**basic sequence**)
liprus-ma ***iparras****-ma* ***iparras*** [6.40]
liprus-ma liprus-ma ***iprus****-ma* ***non-verbal clause*** [6.41]

The difference between the sequences concerns two verbal forms, i.e., two variables, rather than just one. Yet, the conditional sequences which are connected by "→" constitute a convenient, one-term-only, opposition with a precative sequence, as is exemplified by the following scheme:

4. *liprus* → *iparras -ma liprus* [**6.12**]
liprus -ma liprus -ma liprus -ma liprus (**basic sequence**)
liprus -ma liprus → *iparras -ma liprus* [**6.13**]

The individual members of the multi-clausal precative sequence thus acquire their own value, whereas if it were not for the conditional structure, these members would have to be considered (and have a value) only as a sequence.

6.3.5 *arḫiš* as structural device

The adverb *arḫiš* ("quickly") exhibits a peculiar behavior when it is part of the protasis of the present pattern. The syntagm *arḫiš ... ul iparras* is normally to be found only in this kind of protasis. As such, it is yet another distinctive characteristic of *-ma* conditionals.

6.3.5.1 Dictionary meanings, syntagmatics and deviations therefrom

arḫiš is an adverb of manner. AHw:67b notes that it occurs mainly with injunctives, less often with *iparras* and seldom with *iprus*. To this we should add the fact that it joins infinitive constructions, mainly the modal infinitive syntagm (*ša parāsim*: *ša* ***arḫiš*** *bulluṭišu epuš* "see to it that he should quickly be healed", 8, 95:12–14) but also (rarely) the *ana / aššum parāsim* syntagms. This makes it special as it tends to be associated most readily with deontic modal forms and, more precisely, only with forms which are prospective, pointed toward the future from a given temporal point.

However, much more important in this connection is the fact that *arḫiš* is hardly ever associated with negation. Of the cases in which this happens in the AbB corpus, two are unique and convey a value of "not quickly", namely, "slowly":

> [6.44] ... *idnī–ma k*[*asp*]*um rēški likīl* ***arḫiš lā tanaddinī***
> Give ... but let the si[lve]r be at your disposal. Do not give it quickly (=give it slowly). 4, 161:24–26

> [6.45] *aššum ê* (še-e) ***arḫiš lā kamāsim*** *ša bēlī išpuram ...*
> Regarding the the slow collection of barley,[10] (of) which my lord wrote to me... 12, 31:3

This semantic outcome is quite expected; to illustrate this differently, the examples above are represented in the scheme as 1. [*ul arḫiš*] *V*. The other two interpretation possibilities for *arḫiš* are either 2. *arḫiš* [*ul V*] or 3. *ul* [*arḫiš V*]. The schemes do not attempt to reflect a syntactic reality, but rather the immediate constituent partition. This is because word order in the AbB corpus is quite fixed vis-à-vis negation and hence not very helpful in this case.

The first scheme ([*ul arḫiš*] *V*) is semantically equivalent to "slowly", as *ul* and *arḫiš* conjoin first (as is shown in the two examples above).

The second scheme (*arḫiš* [*ul V*]) theoretically reflects *arḫiš* when

10. The graphemic syntagm še-*e* is taken to denotes the genitive without mimation, functioning as an object of *kamāsim*. Interpreted as construct state, it would be rendered "regarding the barley (which is) to be collected slowly".

appended to a negated verbal form; as such it does not make sense, for *arḫiš* is an adverb requiring an action in the affirmative.[11]

The third scheme (*ul* [*arḫiš V*]) has to do with ***-ma*** **conditionals.**

6.3.5.2 Peculiar behavior in *-ma* conditionals

This third scheme represents a peculiar characteristic of these connected conditionals — the ability to contain both negation and *arḫiš*.

First it has to be established that these *arḫiš ul* conditionals conform with the type discussed above:

> [6.46] *ṣāb našpakātim* PN ***apul–ma*** *našpakātim ša qātišu līpuš* → ***arḫiš*** *ṣāb našpakātim* ***ul tappalšu***–*ma pīḫatum šī ana muḫḫika iššakkan*
> Supply PN with cargo boat workers so that he can build the cargo boats which are in his charge; should you not supply him quickly with cargo-boat workers, the responsibility will be yours. 2, 59:14–21

This long example is patterned *iparras–ma iparras*, the most common sequence for *-ma* conditionals, and it is characterized by polar lexical resumption with a co-textual sequenced precative. This should be enough to state that it is a characteristic *-ma* conditional.

The next example exhibits the link to the precative, being connected to it via *-ma*:

> [6.37] *kanikkam* ***arḫiš ul*** *tušezzibšu–ma lū tīde*
> Should you not have him make out a document quickly, be warned. 12, 25:19–20

The rest of the examples, containing *arḫiš ul*, are less well characterized as such, but they are nevertheless clearly conditionals:

> [6.47] *rakbī* ***arḫiš ul*** *tappalā–ma ... pānūkunu ul ibbabbalū*
> Should you not satisfy the(se) riders quickly, you will not be forgiven... 4, 11:29–33

> [6.48] [*aš*]*šumika wašbāku* **[a]*rḫiš ul*** *tallakam–ma* [*t*]*attal<la>kam* ... [x *man*]*a kaspam ušadd*[a]*nka*
> I am staying [for] your sake; should you not come [q]uickly and (instead) go away ... I will collect the [...] silver from you. 12, 194:14–18

The two cases left, although situated in a broken context, are felt to be

11. There is one example mentioned in CAD A2:256b under d: *apputtum arḫiš lā tuḫḫaram.* "Be slowly delayed" does not make good sense; "quickly do not be delayed" would be plausible only if we assume (as is originally translated ibid.) a pause between *arḫiš* and the verbal form, that is "please, quickly, do not be delayed".

-*ma* conditionals mainly because of *arḫiš ul*:

> [6.49] 5 *kur â[m]* ... ***[a]rḫiš u[l*** *t]uš[a]b[b]al[am-m]a x k[ur] âm aḫa[bbat]*
> Should [you] not se[nd] me quickly the 5 kor of barley ... I will (have to) bo[rrow] x k[or] of barley. 12, 68:22–24

> [6.50] ... ***[a]rḫiš ul*** *takall[a]* → *ûm iḫ[ḫašš]eḫ* [...] *ittīka ul [id]abbub*
> Should you not quickly withhold (it), barley will be n[eeded] [...] will not [s]peak to you. 12, 67:38

The adverb *arḫiš*, when coupled with *ul*, can thus be regarded as yet another characteristic of the -*ma* conditional pattern.

6.4 Conclusions

Several aims are attained by this chapter in describing the -*ma* conditional structure. First, the protasis of -*ma* conditionals is established as a distinct paradigm, which has a conditional value. A distinct conditional pattern is proven to exist by describing its structural characteristics. Second, a close syntagmatic relationship is shown to exist between the protasis paradigm and the sequenced precative paradigm, both in the apodosis and in the co-text. Third, establishing that what connects the co-textual sequenced precative with the protasis is the connective -*ma* / → makes it possible to compare conditional structures with precative sequences. In this way, the clauses in a multi-clausal precative sequence may be evaluated individually, rather than as an entire sequence. Fourth, this comparison (as illustrated in **diagram 4** above) shows that there are also paradigmatic relationships between the conditional protasis paradigm and sequenced precatives.

The -*ma* conditional protasis paradigm clearly demonstrates the decisive role played by syntax, where modality is signaled by various syntactic features.

7

The Nominalization of the Precative

7.0 Preliminaria

In the course of a description of the modal system of OB one must not fail to recognize the construction *ša parāsim*. Although it does not explicitly contain any of the members the precative paradigms (for which see **chapters 4** and **5**), it is nevertheless related to them. *ša parāsim*, of all other infinitive constructions (N *parāsim*, *ana parāsim*, *aššum parāsim*, etc.), has a constant and firm association with the precative paradigms, and more specifically, with the directive sub-paradigm.

The problem, as is well presented by Buccellati 1972, is that the members of the precative paradigms (Buccellati's "all moods of command") cannot be nominalized syntactically, at least not directly, as they do not occur in the position of syntactic attribute (the genitive-equivalent slot). In more mundane terms — they cannot be subordinated. Buccellati therefore suggests that it is (N) *ša parāsim* (along with N *parasim*), which in fact serves as the nominalization of the precative.

The term **nominalization** is defined as "the process by which any expression may be formed into a noun or into a construction assuming the function of a noun" whether by morphological or by syntactic means (Goldenberg 1983:170), or in other words, marking any syntagm as nominal. There is a formal functional equivalence between both options. The following pair of examples demonstrate nominalized clauses: The first is signaled by syntactic means, i.e., a *kīma* clause; the second by morphological means, i.e., the infinitive. Both equally occupy the slot of the object:

> [7.1] {***kīma*** *ālam lā* ***wašbāta***} *aqbi*
> I said {**that you** do not **dwell** in the city}. 7, 42:13–14

> [7.2] {***wašābšu*** *ina ālim* ...} *iqbûnim*
> They told me (of) {**his dwelling** in the city ...}. 9, 62:18–19.

The embedded sentence would have been "*ina ālim (ul) wašib*".

Every infinitive is a nominalization of an abstract embedded clause (*wašābšu~kīma uššabu*). Such nominalizations tend to neutralize some categories which are otherwise distinguished by verbal morphology, such as tense. This is exactly the reason that this treatment does not consider other infinitive constructions, such as N/*ana parāsim*, whose relation to the precative seems less persistent and is dependent upon external factors. Such infinitive constructions are dealt with here only when they have to do with the demarcation of *ša parāsim*.

The construction *ša parāsim* appears in all stages of Akkadian and has captured (along with another related construction — N *parāsim*) the attention of many scholars. It has been treated semantically in many grammars and separately in a chapter of a monograph (Aro 1961, chapter 2). It has also been given linguistic consideration in Buccellati 1972, where it is considered as the nominalization of the precative but almost without concrete signals to enable it to be regarded as the **formal** nominalization of the precative, or for that matter, that show that it has any formal relationship whatever with the precative.

Upon evidence found in both the AbB and the ARM corpora, it seems possible to establish this construction as having, in contrast with other infinitive constructions, a formal relationship with the directive sub-paradigm. Tools of the structural approach enable us to show a concrete relationship between the directive and *ša parāsim*. This formal relationship is one step forward in the attempt to prove that *ša parāsim* is indeed the formal nominalization of precative forms. In addition, an attempt is made to show that the modality of this construction is persistent throughout, in any syntactic environment in which it occurs.

7.1 Literature review, problematic issues and objectives

In a monograph which treats infinitive constructions in Akkadian, Aro 1961 devotes a chapter to such genitive constructions. He draws a line between N *parāsim*, *ša parāsim* and N *ša parāsim*, describing each separately. N *parāsim* is subdivided according to semantic classes of N. The negative form N *lā parāsim* is discussed separately. Both syntagms *ša parāsim* and N *ša parāsim* are said to have by and large the same values: 1. "das zum tun / für das tun" and 2. "das zu tun ist / was getan werden muß/soll/kann". The sections describing both syntagms are similarly organized, but the one about N *ša parāsim* contains a small section about apposition as well. Aro is concerned first about the structure of the construction and the meaning comes only second.

Buccellati 1972 explains all the above-mentioned constructions as nominalization of the precative. His arrangement is rather different than Aro's. Although nominalization has to do with either morphology or syntax, he chooses rather a semantic division according to the meaning. Three types of nominalization are distinguished: 1. nominalization of command, wish and potentiality; 2. nominalization of present-future action; and 3. nominalization of past action and of condition (including command, wish and potentiality in the past). The rest of his study is devoted to conclusions (the difference between constructions containing *ša* as opposed to *ana*) and the rationale for the existence of this nominalization in Akkadian. Buccellati mentions right at the outset (ibid. 4) that those semantic classes are notional rather than formal. He draws a correspondence between the notions of command, wish and potentiality in the precative and the ones felt to exist in the infinitive constructions he discusses.

Buccellati suggests that the constructions N *parāsim* and (N) *ša parāsim* should be regarded as nominalizations of generic present as well (Buccellati 1972:10). It seems, however, that this view is difficult to establish since this is not a formal distinction in Akkadian (*iparrasū* may serve as generic [=one decides] as well as specific [=they decide]) but rather a notional category. Moreover, most of the examples adduced in this connection are of the structure N *parāsim*, which is not regarded here as modal (being, much like the rest of the infinitive constructions, modally neutralized).

As to forms other than the precative, we know they are nominalized (or substantivized) since they are transparent. The form *iprus* is clearly recognizable inside *kīma* ***iprusu***. That this substantivized clause is (in this case) the equivalent of the infinitive is demonstrated by the fact that it is interchangeable with the infinitive, since both occupy the same syntactic slot (see examples **[7.1]** and **[7.2]** above). As far as the precative forms are concerned, nominalization is not evident because precative forms do not occur in nominalized or in substantivized clauses (i.e., *ša* and *kīma* clauses respectively). The closest we have, semantically, is a modally neutralized form[1] in a substantivized clause (*kīma iparrasu*), where the precative form does not occur. The infinitive equivalent of this syntactic substantivization is modally neutralized as well (for a detailed account see **§4.5** above). Therefore, it can be shown only indirectly that the precative and the syntagm *ša parāsim* (when taking the slot of a substantive or an adjective) are linked.

Another difficulty is that substantivized clauses or infinitives rarely occur as independent clauses as does the precative, which renders the task of legitimately comparing them quite impossible. As a matter of fact, it is impossible to compare items which do not belong in the same paradigm, for they never exist on the same syntactic level (as in the case of sequenced precatives and infinitive constructions, **§4.5**).

1. Such modal neutralization is discussed above in §§**4.2.2.2** and **4.4.4.0.3**.

Previously, to show the relationship between precatives and *ša parāsim*, one has had to rely upon semantics only. However, the situation here is different from other infinitive constructions, and one can rely upon a few cases where both *liprus* and *ša parāsim* occur in the same syntactic environment **as main clauses**. Various forms and syntagms (in fact almost any linguistic entity) may occur in the syntactic position of the **rheme** (that is, the logical predicate), but not as a clause. It is critical that two such forms, although radically different, commute: They belong to the same paradigm, and can thus be compared *ceteris paribus* on the same level, something which cannot be done with other infinitive constructions and finite verbal forms. As soon as we compare them at the same level, we can learn about them on other levels as well (for a nominal occurs as theme, object, adjective, rheme, etc.).

The object of this chapter is first the formal description of *ša parāsim* according to the various syntactic positions it occupies. Being able to compare the forms inside the paradigm when all other terms are being equal enables us to zoom in on the different semantic features of the construction.

The second aim is to show that *ša parāsim* has a consistent modal value,[2] which is one of its special features. The reason that only *ša parāsim* is treated here is because N *parāsim*, apart from being quite rare in the corpus and often limited to fixed expressions, is modally neutralized (very much like any other infinitive construction in the corpus).

The corpus is the same one which has served throughout this book (see definition of the corpus, **§1.2**), which means a narrower corpus than Aro's (whose examples served Buccellati as well) and hence possibly more specific results.

7.2 The syntactic role of *ša parāsim*

The following examples are intended to show the range of the inventory of the construction *ša parāsim*. In the course of this survey a few relationships will be examined anew: 1. between the directive and *ša parāsim*, 2. between N *parāsim* and (N) *ša parāsim*, and finally 3. between *ša parāsim* and the rest of the infinitive constructions, viz., *parāsam*, *aššum parāsim* and *ana parāsim*.

ša parāsim, like any *ša* clause or phrase, is a nominal syntagm. It can assume, by virtue of *ša* being its nucleus, the role of either a verbal adjective or a verbal substantive. Consequently, it acts as the functional

2. There are special cases such as *ša qabêm*, as well as cases of paradigmatic neutralization, which are treated below. These are, however, idiosyncratic cases rather than systematic traits.

equivalent of an (independent) attributive adjective, as a substantival appositive and as a substantive.

7.2.1 *ša parāsim* as rheme

The most significant cases by far as to the nature of *ša parāsim* are those in which the nominal syntagm *ša parāsim* is the rheme. In such cases the syntagm is semantically analogous to the directive in the same position:

> [**7.3**] *ṭēmum ša ana* RN *ašpuru* ***ša ḫamāṭim*** *kīma issanqūnikkum* ***lā ikkallû***
> The report which I sent to RN **is to be rushed**; when they (=the messengers) have reached you, **let them not be delayed**. ARM 28, 7:8–11

> [**7.4**] *ṭēmum annûm ana ṣēr aḫīka* ***liḫmuṭ***
> Let this report be rushed to your brother. 8, 12:15–17

ša ḫamāṭim in example [**7.3**] commutes with *liḫmuṭ* (example [**7.4**]) in the same syntagmatic conditions. However, for such commutation to be valid, certain conditions, which are commented upon below, have to be established first. In addition, there is a close semantic association between the urgency of the report (expressed by *ša ḫamāṭim*) and the idea that the messengers carrying this report should not be delayed (expressed by the negative directive *lā ikkallû*).

The next examples are both a comment on the results of water barrier repair works:

> [**7.5**] *mimma* ***ul ša naḫā[d]im***
> (There) **is nothing to worry about**. ARM 6, 1:28

> [**7.6**] *mimma bēlī* ***lā inaḫḫid***
> My lord **should not be worried** at all. ibid. 32–33

This pair of examples comes from the same letter. They exemplify the negative of *ša parāsim* and its paradigmatic relationship with a negative directive (*lā inaḫḫid*). An important point is that *ul ša naḫādim* constitutes a complete and independent nominal clause[3] (for *mimma* is neither the theme nor does it stand in apposition to it, but rather serves as an adverb). This capability of the syntagm to constitute a complete nominal clause (containing a nucleus, a verbal lexeme and the nexus, or a predicative link between them[4]) is crucial in allowing us to compare it with a finite verbal form. One cannot, for example, compare a predicative adverb and

3. This term is used, instead of the usual "non-verbal", only because the infinitive is not quite non-verbal, but it definitely is a nominal form.

4. For a discussion regarding the components of the verbal complex, see §**2.4.1.4** above.

a verbal form — the former would stand for the rheme only, whereas the latter represents all the rest of the sentential, or nexal, components as well (theme, nexus and rheme). The following example is similar in that the syntagm clearly constitutes, once more, a complete nominal clause:

[7.7] *aštalūka kalûš[unu n]awirū ina aš[talī š]unūti* ***ul ša šūṣê[m]***
Your singers are al[l s]plendid; no (one) **is to be excluded** from the[se sin]gers. ARM 1, 83:9–11

[7.8] *kaspam ina bītika* ***lā ušeṣṣû***
Let them not take out the silver out of your house. 3, 88:17–18

In example [7.7] the syntagm *ul ša šūṣêm* is a complete sentence as well, for it is not directly predicated about *ina aš[talī š]unūti*. It can therefore be formally compared with *lā ušeṣṣû* in [7.8].

These characteristics of *ul ša parāsim* are taken henceforth to hold in all its occurrences. As for the affirmative *ša parāsim* — example [7.14] below seems to contain a unique nexal occurrence thereof. Once the comparison of *ša parāsim* with its corresponding directives has been established as valid, the value of *ša parāsim* can be determined exactly by means of such comparison.

The difference between a directive and its corresponding *ša parāsim* is not immediately apparent; such is the case between *ul ša naḫādim* and *lā inaḫḫid* (examples [7.5] and [7.6] respectively). There are but a few cases where there is an opposition[5] between *ša parāsim* and the corresponding directive occurring in linear succession, pertaining exactly to the same action:

[7.9] *erištam itti aḫīya ēriš umma anāku–ma immerī aḫī lipqidanni u kêm taqbi umma atta–ma kūṣum ina kīma inanna immerū* ***ul ša nadānim*** *i[n]a dīšim anaddinakkim annītam tašpuram inanna anumma dīšum immerū* ***ša nadānim*** *aḫī* ***liddinam***
I asked a request from my brother, saying: 'Let my brother hand sheep over to me'. And so you said: 'It is winter just now (and) the sheep **are not to be given** (but) I will give (them) to you in the spring'. Thus you wrote me. Now it is spring, the sheep **may be given**, (so) **let my brother give** (them) to me. Dossin 1939, 124:5–17

A few issues come up in example [7.9]. One issue is the co-occurrence of *ul ša nadānim* and of *ša nadānim*, both predicated about the sheep. This co-occurrence formalizes the relationship between the negative and the affirmative forms of the syntagm (which is not self-evident based upon the external form only). The other issue is the opposition between

5. **Contrast** is kept for **syntagmatic relationships** (see **§§2.4–2.5**) whereas **opposition** is used pertaining to the comparison of items belonging **in the same paradigm** (which is exactly the case here). See **§1.1** in the introduction.

the predicative syntagm *ša nadānim* (conveying the new state of being of the sheep) and the directive *liddinam*. This opposition emphasizes and clarifies the differences of value between them. The syntagm *ša nadānim* is less specific as to the source for the permission (here; it could denote volition, obligation or potential as well, see Buccellati 1972:1–9) to give the sheep, as opposed to *liddinam*. In other words, unlike the directive, the syntagm does not necessarily have to do with volition or obligation stemming from the speaker, but it could reflect some external constraint just as well. Another point is that *ša nadānim* does not quite have injunctive force, whereas *liddinam*, being a directive, is used to instigate action. *liddinam* is still a directive (albeit a polite one), although the appeal here is made to a king.

The next case exhibits a close association between *ul ša parāsim* and a directive as well:

> [7.10] *šanītam aššum* PN_1 *ša tašpuram awīlum šū barātim mali ... awīlam šâti aṣbat-ma aššum kaspišu lā ḫalāqim ... ana qāt* PN_2 *apqissu umma anāku-ma [aw]īlum šū* ***lū [b]aliṭ*** *adi maḫar bēliya ... uštaka[n]nū inanna ... awīlum šū* ***ul ša balāṭ[im*** *bēlī]* ***l[iš]ālšu***
> Secondly, as to PN_1 about whom you wrote me, the man is rebellious ... I caught the man and entrusted him to PN_2 in order for his silver not to get lost ... So I (said): '**Let the [m]an [l]ive** until they have (him) testify ... in front of my lord'. Now ... the man **is not to live; let [my lord k]ill** him. ARM 28, 105:21'–31'

The example exhibits a complex opposition, first between the directive *lū baliṭ* (uttered prior to the point of writing) and *ul ša balāṭim* (expressed at the point of writing), both predicated about *awīlum šū*, regarding the same issue, i.e., his life. They are quite literally the opposites of one another in that *lū baliṭ* is called off by *ul ša balāṭim*. The differences become clear upon scrutiny of the opposition between *ul ša balāṭim* and *lišālšu* (having the Mari value "to kill"). The former describes a modal state of being, i.e., that the man is such as not to live anymore, or more exactly, that it is permitted now to kill him. The directive on the other hand instigates action (again, politely, since it is addressed to a king). The source of modality in *ul ša balāṭim* is indeed the speaker but it is not the form that tells us that, but rather the context. In directives, the source of volition or obligation, as a rule, is the speaker (see **§4.3.1**).

Another feature of the syntagm *ša parāsim* becomes evident in comparing the following pair of examples:

> [7.11] *eqlum šū* ***ul ša nandîm***
> This field **is not to be neglected**. 10, 15:22

[7.12] *eqlī* ***lā innandi***
Let my field **not be neglected**. 1, 23:15

Example [**7.11**] features a formally passive infinitive. This infinitive allows symmetry of diathesis with the corresponding verbal construction (*eqlī lā innandi* in [**7.12**]). In all of the other examples, the construction, when involving a transitive verb, seems to be indifferent to diathesis, forcing a passive translation of an externally active infinitive. Formally it is neutralized as to diathesis, which explains why *ul ša* ***nadānim*** is translatable only as (*they*) *are not* ***to be given*** (example [7.9]) rather than (*they*) *are not* ***to give***. This is a result of the fact that in most of the *ša parāsim* syntagms containing a transitive verb, the nucleus represents the recipient, rather than the agent of the action. Example [**7.11**] is an exception to this tendency. In the syntagms containing an intransitive verb the nucleus represents the agent. The agent may optionally be represented by a genitive pronominal suffix:

[7.13] *zērum kûm–ma šamaššammû ša leqê****ki***
The seed is *yours* and you may take (the) sesame (lit."it is of your taking"). 4, 141:13–14

In the following example, however, the genitive pronominal suffix does not represent the agent, but rather the recipient (see also example [**7.27**] *ša duppuriya* "that they should remove me"). The subsequent pair of examples exhibits the syntagm *lā ša parāsim*, which is predicative as well:

[7.14] *ana arḫim šuāti* ***ša kalîša ū lā ša kalîša ša rašê šī*** *adi šinīšu ašpurakkum–ma*
As to this cow, **is it to be kept or is it not to be kept? Is it to be acquired?** I wrote to you twice... 9, 174:9–12

There are three different variations of *ša parāsim* in this example. The first is *ša kalîša*. It seems to be a complete nominal clause because the cow is not marked as formal subject in nominative but rather as topic in extraposition.[6] The translation here is different from the edition's ("whether to keep her..."), which does not reflect a nexus. *lā ša kalîša* is the symmetrical opposite of the former, for it serves the same function (compare the very same structure in example [**7.15**] and the ensuing discussion). The use of *lā* for *ul* is accounted for as some kind of contamination between the independent nexal use of the syntagm (*ul ša parāsim*) and its use as appositional content of a substantive such as *ṭēmum* (example [**7.34**] *ša waššurišunu ū lā waššurišunu*). The third variation, *ša rašê šī*,

6. Such topicalization, just like any casus pendens, requires a complete clause which serves as its rheme.

which is a basic (albeit rare, see Huehnergard 1986:235) type of a nominal clause, helps corroborate that the whole series is nexal. *ša rašê šī* (as opposed to *ša kalîša*, which by itself would not tell us whether it is predicative or not) is no doubt a full nominal clause. This series of *ša parāsim* seems to denote a deliberative question ("should it be held?", etc.). This is not surprising in view of the conclusions arrived at by the end of **§4.3.3.2**, that a precative form in general does not occur in deliberative nexus questions, and that this slot is rather taken by modally neutralized *iparras* forms. For other occurrences of a deliberative *ša parāsim* and its relation with the precative interrogative sub-paradigm see examples **[7.36a]**, **[7.36b]**, and **[7.37]** below.

One finds the syntagm *lā ša parāsim* functioning as a full clause in the following example as well:

> **[7.15]** *kīma ēpiš ṣibûtim* ***lā ša šuta''îm*** *šū–ma ul tīde*
> ***lā tušta''āšum***
> Don't you know that *he* (rather than anyone else) performs a duty (and) **is not to be trifled with? Do not trifle with** him! 4, 53:15–17

Example **[7.15]** is a little more complicated but the underlying principle is the same as before: *lā ša šuta''îm* is a nominal clause within a *kīma* object clause and *lā tušta''āšum* is the corresponding 2nd pers. directive. The construction is complicated by *šū*, the syntactic theme in that kind of non-verbal pattern (Huehnergard 1986:224–25), whose function is overruled by *-ma*, which marks it as focus or as rheme (for the difference see **§2.4.1.1** above).

An important detail is that *lā ša šuta''îm* is of the same essential structure as *ul ša balāṭim* (example **[7.10]**), and both function similarly as well: Both may serve as nominal clauses, as opposed to *ša lā balāṭiya* (example **[7.25]**) which does **not** serve as such but rather as an infinitive equivalent. *lā* is accounted for by the occurrence of the syntagm in a *kīma* clause. The construction is not interchangeable here with a precative form because it is a genitive equivalent clause, an environment from which precative forms are as a rule excluded. This is an important point — the *ša parāsim* construction, being a nominal syntagm, is much more flexible syntactically than precative forms, which are rather restricted in this respect. This means that precative forms and *ša parāsim* are not interchangeable everywhere, but only in a very specific environment, viz., in independent clauses. Yet, the semantic content of the nominal syntagm, when compared to the directive, seems to be consistently the same everywhere else as well. Here, although it is in a subordinate environment, the semantic opposition between *lā ša šuta''îm* and *lā tušta''āšum* is analogous to the results obtained above — the former denotes a reported obligation whose source is unspecified; the latter is a directive, instigating an action willed by the speaker.

Such comparison as is carried out above helps to zoom in on the differences, besides the striking similarity, between the directive and *ša parāsim*. The resulting differences are as follows:

1. **Person category**: As opposed to a directive, where person-marking is obligatory, in the *ša parāsim* construction person-marking is optional as well as marking the recipient (or for that matter, differentiating between agent and recipient).

2. **Temporal frame**: The directive, although not inflected for tense, is consistently fixed to the point of utterance (see **§4.3.1**), occurring in dialogue rather than in reporting past events. The nexal *ša parāsim* described heretofore is atemporal, like any nominal clause. As will be seen below, in constituting a part of another sentence, it adopts the temporal frame of the main clause. As such it is not confined to dialogue and can be a part of reporting as well.

3. **Modal frame**: Both the directive and *ša parāsim* are deontic, having to do with will or obligation. However, the directive is intended to bring about a change in reality while *ša parāsim*, although carrying almost the same semantic value that something should/may/must be done, is **not** a directive. The source of this obligation is the speaker in directives but remains unspecified in *ša parāsim*.

4. **Marking predication**: The ability to constitute a nominal clause is formally shown only in negation — the sentential (or nexal) **negative particle** + ***ša*** *parāsim* as opposed to the non-nexal ***ša*** + **negative particle** + *parāsim*. That is to show that *ša parāsim*, as opposed to directives, may or may not constitute a clause.

In addition to *ša parāsim* in the present category, one rarely finds *ana parāsim*:

> [**7.16**] [*š*]*umma ekallum–ma lā iqbi ṣuḫāru šū* ***ana wuššurim*** *mīnu ṣuḫāra šâtu lā tuwaššaraššu inanna šitāl–ma ṣuḫāra šâtu* ***wuššeraššu***
> If the palace itself did not order (otherwise), this servant **is to be released**. Why don't/won't you release the servant? Now think (this) over and **release** this servant. 1, 74:23–28

Here *ana wuššurim* functions just like a rhematic *ša parāsim*. It is not at all certain, mainly due to the scarcity of similar examples, whether it could stand for a complete nominal clause.[7] For this reason one cannot

7. Cf., at the end of a letter, *ana šemê bēliya* "For your information! (lit. in order for my lord to hear)" (6, 147:21). However, it is quite certain that this

state whether it is in paradigmatic relationship with *wuššer*. Otherwise it shows a remarkable semantic similarity to *ša parāsim*.

7.2.2 *ša parāsim* as part of the sentence

The subsequent sections describe *ša parāsim* when it occurs as **part of a sentence,** namely, as attribute, as theme, as object or as object appositive. In all these instances, *ša parāsim* is **not interchangeable with any precative forms**. Despite this fact, it seems that *ša parāsim* keeps its value (determined and described above in opposition to directives) in other syntagmatic environments as well. This value, however, can be formally arrived at now only by opposing it to other infinitive constructions.

In contrast to finite verbal forms, which are liable to have considerably different values in different paradigms, *ša parāsim* resembles a verbal adjective (as, e.g., in Hebrew) in being apt to function either as the sentence or as part of it, and seems to keep its basic value throughout.

7.2.2.1 *ša parāsim* in the role of an appositive attribute

The following cases show the nominal syntagm under discussion as attribute of the object, which happens rather frequently:

> [**7.17**] *ṣeḫram* ***ša šapārim*** *tīšu*
> You have a child **who may be sent** (or: whom you may send). 4, 145:17–18

The two options of translation originate in the fact that no person marker occurs in this case. Example [**7.18**], representing a very typical use of *ša parāsim* which has the same verbal lexeme as does the finite verb, does show a personal marker:

> [**7.18**] *u adi atta tariqqu mamman* ***ša šakānika*** *šukun-ma*
> And as long as you are free, appoint **anybody you want to appoint**... 9, 217:17–20

mamman is the entity to which *ša šakānika* is appositive.

7.2.2.2 *ša parāsim* in the role of object

In contradistinction to the two preceding cases, where *ša parāsim* is an appositive attribute to the object, example [**7.19**] contains the syntagm *ša leqêm* itself as its object. Like any *ša* syntagm, *ša parāsim* is capable of being independent of any concrete substantival referent. This use of *ša*

---

example has no theme, unlike the *ul ša parāsim* examples examined above.

parāsim having the same verbal lexeme as does the main verb seems to be quite frequent as well:

[**7.19**] *wuddi* [***š***]***a leqêm*** *ana wardī telteqe*
You surely have already taken as slaves (those) **[wh]o needed to be taken**. ARM 1, 29:17–18

ša parāsim occurs as object in constructions such as the one with *epēšum*. *ša parāsim* represents the modal content of *epēšum* ("to see to it that .../to do what is necessary to ..."). *šā parāsim*, as conceptual nominalization of the precative, is essential for a verb to have an unequivocal deontic complement, since directly embedding a directive is impossible. It should be noted that the only possible object of *epēšum* in such examples is *ša parāsim*, which is not interchangeable with anything else:

[**7.20**] *assurre–ma mūšam ... nakrum šū ana mātišu uramma*[*m–ma*] *ina qāt bēliya uṣṣi* (IṢ-*ṣi*) *bēl*[*ī ina lib*]*biš*[*u*] *lištāl–ma* ***ša*** *nakrum* [*šū ina*] *qāt bēliya* ***lā waṣêm*** *bēlī l*[*īpu*]*š*
It is to be feared[8] lest this enemy will set out for his country at ... night [and] escape from my lord. Let [my] lord think it over and let my lord a[ct] in such a way **that** [this] enemy **should not escape** [fr]om my lord. ARM 26, 419:9–13

Example [**7.20**] contains both the problem that the enemy might escape and the solution offered, preventing the enemy from escaping.

The next example, besides exhibiting again *ša parāsim epēšum*, brings out the difference between *ša parāsim* and *aššum parāsim*. *aššum* is used mainly to signal the topic:

[**7.21**] ***aššum alāk*** PN *ana ṣēriya awâtim šunniḫ dububšum–ma* ***ša alākišu*** *ana ṣēriya epuš*
As to PN's **coming** to me, change (or repeat) the words, entreat him and see to it **that he should come** to me. ARM 26, 438:34'–35'

The topic here is marked by *aššum*. The content thereof is indifferent to modality (see §**4.5.3**). Modal value, whenever present in *aššum* clauses, is not inherent in the preposition itself. It has to do with the whole construction, depending on the nature of the governing verb and the context.[9] The complement of *epuš*, however, being *ša parāsim*, is modal. This modal value has nothing to do with the finite form of *epēšum* being a directive, nor is it triggered by it; it may be any other form of *epēšum* just as well (*ša epēšim* ***ippeš***, ARM 1, 22:30–31). Methodologically, modality

8. I follow the formulation offered in Wasserman 1994.

9. For example, the verbal lexeme *qabûm*, which many times has a complement exhibiting modal notion, definitely does not have such a complement in [**7.1**] (*wašābšu ... iqbûnim*), as the context tells us (see §**4.5.1**, n. 38).

here is difficult to establish because nothing else can fit as the object clause of *epēšum* save our construction.[10] This seems somewhat similar to what Marouzeau terms "mode grammatical"[11]: In the Romance languages one finds many slots where the use of the subjunctive is obligatory, and since it has no alternative in that very slot it has no modal value. Yet, *ša parāsim* in this slot is not deprived of its modal value. This value can be circumscribed in other verbal lexemes where there is choice:

[7.22] ***ša napāṣi*** *amrī*
See to it **that** it (=sesame) **should be crushed**. 4, 141:20

[7.23] *âm* ***šarāq***[***šunu***] *nīmu*[*r*]
We sa[w their] **stealing** the barley. 3, 70:19–20

Here, with the verbal lexeme *amārum*, there is a choice between two infinitive constructions. So when opposed to *parāsam* in this slot, *ša parāsim* does have a modal value. The same idea is to be found in the next set of examples:

[7.24] ***ša lā balāṭika*** *ina šaptī awīlim ittanaškan*
It is repeatedly uttered by the man that **you are not to live**. 9, 155:12–13

ša lā balāṭika in [**7.24**] is difficult to evaluate for lack of opposition. A quite similar construction, containing the same verbal lexeme, is found in [**7.25**]. With *dabābum* as main verb, the construction is used as a nominalization of what had presumably been said directly, using a precative form:

[7.25] [*i*]*na pānītim* ***ša lā balāṭiya*** [*awī*]*lum id*[*b*]*ub–ma*
The [m]an said [b]efore **that I should not live**... ARM 5, 4:9–10

This is the way to report indirectly a deontic utterance, i.e., either directives or members of the wish sub-paradigm, both containing an element of will. The various precative forms are part of the dialogue and cannot (unless directly quoted) be part of a reporting texteme (a syntactic unit larger than the clause). *ša parāsim* as the nominalization thereof can both be part of reporting and report the deontic value of the precative form. The deontic modal value of *ša balāṭiya* may be arrived at by

10. Aro 1961:72 remarks that the only other infinitival complement *epēšum* may have is *alākam* meaning (together) "set out (on, for)".

11. "Il arrive que la valeur propre du mode soit altérée ou supprimée par le jeu du mécanisme syntaxique, et que le mode aboutisse à n'être plus qu'une forme grammaticale dépourvue de sens propre..." ("It happens that the very value of the mood is changed or suppressed by the syntactic mechanism, and the mood ends up being but a grammatical form which is deprived of its own meaning..." Marouzeau 1951:147).

comparison with *dâkam* in the following example, both infinitives are similar in constituting the object of *dabābum*:

[**7.26**] *kakkī u* ***dâk*** *nakrim–ma libbi wardī bēliya idabbub*
The heart of my lord's servants speaks only of weapons and of **beating** the enemy. ARM 2, 118:21–22

The deontic value of *ša lā balāṭiya* in example [**7.25**] becomes immediately apparent once compared with *dâk nakrim* in [**7.26**].

Finet 1956 §86e considers the *ša parāsim* cases to be irregular constructions ("tournures abérrantes"), failing to appreciate that there is a difference in form which corresponds to different values: One construction denotes modality, whereas the other is modally indifferent (and actually neutralized as well, see §**4.5.1** above).

The following is similar but slightly more complicated; it has the construction *ša duppuriya* in focus:

[**7.27**] *ištu awīlum šū illikam pī ālim kalîšu elīya ušbalkit u* ***ša duppuriya–ma*** *ina ḫa<za>nnūtim kalûm–ma idabbub*
Since this man came he turned the whole city against me and (what practically) *everybody* says (is) ***that I should be removed*** from the position of mayor. ARM 2, 137:33–35

The ability to be marked as the focus of the utterance is another feature of *ša parāsim*,[12] whereas that is not possible for a verbal complex such as *liprus* in its entirety. It is only possible for each of the verbal components in itself (see §**2.4.1.4**) or for various nominalizations of the verb, of which *ša parāsim* is one case.

In order to demonstrate the structural and semantic difference between *ša parāsim* and *parāsam* (the latter corresponding to *kīma iprusu / iparrasu*), Buccellati 1972:13 uses the following pair:

[**7.28**] *annītam lā annītam bēlī lišpuram* ***ša qabê*** *bēliya lūpuš* ARM 2, 29:3'–4'

[**7.29**] *annītam lā annītam bēlī lišpuram–ma* ***ša bēlī iqabbû*** *lūpuš* ARM 2, 29:6'–7'

These two examples are translated "...what(ever) my lord **might** decide, I will do" and "what my lord **will** say, I will do" respectively. It is indeed tempting to understand it this way, but there is a problem: If we were to perceive *ša qabêm* as the equivalent of any other *ša parāsim* we would have to interpret it with the value "anything he can/should/must say" — which does **not** fit here. The epistemic value of the modal verb "might"

12. It should be noted that this sentence contains two focal elements — *ša duppuriya* and *kalûm* — but not on the same level. See §**2.4.3.3**.

is generally not part of the construction's value. The solution is at hand — *ša qabêm* is an idiom, in which this distinction does not work. As a matter of fact Aro 1961:57 treats *ša qabêm* separately as a special case and translates it "was X sagt od[er] befielt". The next example shows this peculiarity of *ša qabêm*:

> **[7.30]** *ša pīka u qabêka līp[ušū]*
> Let the[m d]o what you say and order. ARM 1, 73:57

The nominalizing converter *ša* is in construct state with both *pûm* and *qabûm*. It is obvious that the first is not a verb, and by analogy neither is *qabûm*. It is a substantive (rather than an infinitive, which is a verbal substantive), and the addition of *ša* has the value *ša* usually does with a substantive — "something that has to do with...".

7.2.2.3 *ša parāsim* as object appositive

The examples in the present section are analogous to the examples adduced in **§7.2.2.1** above (example **[7.17]**: *ṣeḫram ša šapārim tīšu*) but semantically they are different, representing **the content of the object**:

[7.31]	*pâkunu ešmē–ma*	I heard your word and I will be [r]eady for you in GN_2
28	*qadum rēdî šarrim* *u un<ne>dukkat šarrim*	with soldier(s) of the king and a sealed document of the king
30	***ša** adi* G[N]$_1$*–ma* *mamma ana p[ā]nīkunu* ***lā parākim*** *ina āl* GN_2 *r[ē]šk[u]nu* *ukāl ištu ina[nn]a*	(saying) that all the way[13] up to G[N]$_1$ nobody (is) **to hinder you.** 5 days from n[o]w
35	5 *ūmī pānīkunu lūmur* ... ... *aḫum aḫ[am ...]* ***lā ipa[rrik]***	let me see you. ... ... **One should** **not hin[der]** the oth[er].
40	*ištēniš k[i]l[allūkunu]* *atta u* P[N] *arḫiš pānīk[unu lūmur]* 9, 112:27–42	You and P[N], b[oth of you] together, [let me see yo]u quickly.

In example **[7.31]**, *unnedukkat šarrim* (which is a substantive representing some verbal message) is followed by ***ša** adi* GN–*ma mamma ana*

13. This is an attempt to translate the focus marking of *adi* GN.

pānīkunu ***lā parākim***, which, besides being appositive like any attributive *ša* clause, contains the verbal message. The formal difference is to be found in paradigmatic relationships of each of these two types: The attributive *ša* clause is the equivalent of an adjective whereas the appositive content is theoretically exchangeable for an infinitive. As this kind of appositive content is always marked in Akkadian by *ša*, it is impossible to follow this line of proof. There is, however, one difference — that appositive content may be represented by direct speech preceded by *ša* (GAG § 155c):[14]

> [7.32] *ṭuppi awīlim ša* ***adi allakam ina*** **GN-*ma lū wašbāti*** *illikam*
> The gentleman's tablet, which (says) 'Stay *in GN* until I come', came here. 9, 117:7–9

Another, more tangible trait of these clauses, is the alternative expressed by the structure *ša parāsim ū lā parāsim*:

> [7.33] ***ṭēm*** *êm šâti* ***ša turri ū lā turrim*** *ammī[nim l]ā tašpurīm*
> Wh[y] did you [n]ot send me **instruction(s)** regarding this barley, **whether** (it is) **to be returned or not to be returned?** 4, 156:7–9

Both the preceding and the next example show the substantive *ṭēmum* when appositive to an indirect question of a **deontic** nature (namely, such that requires a **directive** for an answer):

> [7.34] *bēlī* ***ṭēm*** *awīlê [š]unūti* ***ša waššurišunu ū lā waššurišunu*** *lišpuram*
> Let my lord write me an **order** concerning [t]hese people (namely) **whether** (they are) **to be released or not to be released.** Dossin 1939:994 (cited in Finet 1956 §23g)

ša parāsim occurs with substantives such as *ṭēmum* when the putative original content of the latter would have to do with a directive. Another option, N *parāsim*, being modally neutralized, may be used to represent either a factual[15] or modal content. The next instance, containing such an N *parāsim*, is adduced in order to show the difference:

> [7.35] ***ṭēm alākišu ū lā alākišu*** ... PN *ana ṣēr bēliya ubbalam*
> PN will bring the report, (saying) **whether he comes** (or: **came**) **or not**, to my lord. ARM 26, 411:60–61

14. There are very few cases where the substantive, whose verbal content is introduced by *ša*, is to be inferred: *u ana* PN *rēʾīm ša* ***arḫam šuāti amurši itaplas-ma ṭēmka terram*** "Moreover, as for PN the herdsman, who (was told) 'look that cow over, examine (her) and send me your report'" (9,174:15–18). It is quite clear here that this *ša* clause does not describe the man directly.

15. For example *ūm alākišunu* "the day they go/went", which clearly shows a non-modal notion. See the following note.

The syntagm *ṭēm alākišu ū lā alākišu* is taken to represent an indirect **factual** question, "whether he **comes** (or came)", as opposed to "whether they **should be released**" in example [**7.34**]. N *parāsim* may occasionally have a modal notion, depending upon its context or paradigmatic factors, but by no means as a rule.[16]

The structure of the next example is very much like [**7.34**]:

> [**7.36a**] ***pu[r]u[ssâm*** *ša] ṣāb bēliya* ***ša wašābišu ū lā w[ašābišu]*** *itti bēliya ul [elq]iam*
> I did not [rece]ive from my lord the **de[cision** concerning] the army of my lord, **whether** it (is) **to stay put or not t[o stay put]**. ARM 26, 390:5''–7''

The context a few lines later expresses the same contents by other means, referring to the very same decision:

> [**7.36b**] *in[a]nna šumma ṣābum* (sic) *awīl* GN_1 *ana* GN_2 *ūlū–ma ana* GN_3 *issaniq ṣāb bēliya ina libbi ālim* ***uṣṣêm-ma̱ ittallakam*** *ūlū–ma ina li[bbi] ālim* ***ikkalla*** *bēlī puru[ssâm ša] ṣābišu annītam lā annītam li[špuram]*
> Now, if the army, the king of GN_1[17] has proceeded against GN_2 or GN_3, **should the army** of my lord **exit** the city and **go away** or **should it be retained** in[sid]e the city? Let my lord [write] me his deci[sion concerning] his army, either this or that. ARM 26, 390:12''–17''

The content of the decision in [**7.36a**] (*ša wašābišu ū lā wašābišu*) is very similar to that of [**7.36b**] (*uṣṣêm–ma̱ ittallakam ūlū–ma ... ikkalla*): *ša wašābišu* (an indirect nexus question: "whether it (is) to stay put") corresponds *ikkalla* (a direct nexus question: "should it be retained?") while (*ša ...*) *lā wašābišu* corresponds *uṣṣêm–ma̱ ittallakam* ("should it leave and go away?"). The difference is mainly syntactic: The first is an appositive nominal syntagm representing an **indirect** deontic question while the second is a **direct** deontic nexus question. Such deontic nexus questions are described in **§4.3.3.2** and the conclusion arrived at is that they are more readily expressed by a modally neutralized *iparras* forms (such as we encounter in [**7.36b**]) than by precative forms.

---

16. Some substantives naturally call for a modal content. An example for such a substantive is *ṣimdatum* "royal decree": ***kīma ṣimdat*** *iššiakkim* ***duppurim*** *baʾlat ul ṯīde* "Don't you know that the royal decree that the land agent **must go away** prevails?" (6, 75:6'–7').

17. The expression is ^{lú}èš-nun-na, pertaining to the king of Ešnunna. It seems plausible syntactically, at least in this context, to read *ša ešnunna*.

7.2.2.4 *ša parāsim* in the role of theme

ša parāsim is rather rare in the role of theme. Example [**7.37**] only seems to be of essentially the same structure as the predicative examples (example [**7.3**] *ṭēmum ... ša ḫamāṭim*), but it is not so functionally. It is cleft-like both structurally and functionally:[18]

> [**7.37**] *umma atta–ma ammīni unnedu[k]kaka lā illikam anāku* ***ša unnedukkim šūbulim***
> Thus you (said): 'Why has your tablet not arrived here?' '(Am) *I* the one who should send the tablet?' or '(Was) *I* to send the tablet?' 1, 23:7–11

An analysis shows that *ša ... šūbulim* here is **not** the rheme of the sentence, but rather an independent adjectival syntagm functioning as **theme**, whereas *anāku* is the **rheme** (or even the **focus**). Huehnergard 1986:225, n. 34 noticed and formulated the fact that in non-verbal clauses, when the personal pronoun occurs first, it is **emphasized or contrasted**.

The reason that *ša parāsim*, rather than an interrogative precative, is used here is similar to what is briefly mentioned in the remarks to example [**7.36b**] above. Deliberative nexus questions tend to be expressed not by precative forms but by alternative forms, one of which is *ša parāsim*. In example [**7.14**] above, *ša rašê šī* is part of a deontic nexus question, but the order of elements is different — the pronoun *šī* is the theme while *ša rašê* is the rheme.

Another example where *ša parāsim* functions as theme seems not to belong with the rest of the examples:

> [**7.38**] *šumma awīlum iššallil–ma ina bītišu* ***ša akālim*** *lā ibašši...*
> If a man is taken captive and there is not anything to eat in his house...
> CH XXIX (=rs. VI):37–41 (=§134)

ša akālim is much like *ša qabêm*, which has been discussed above (pertaining to examples [**7.28**]–[**7.30**] in §**7.2.2.2**) and shown to be an idiosyncratic case. *ša akālim*, like *ša qabêm*, has the value of *ša* N, viz., "anything that has to do with N" or, in this case "anything to eat", rather than "what must/may/should be eaten".

18. Buccellati 1972:6, 22 refers to the following *ṭēmum šū ša ḫamāṭim* ("This message is to be hurried", ARM 6, 53:7) as cleft ("Constructions of this type are mostly used for emphasis in cleft sentences..." ibid. 22). It does resemble a cleft structure in Biblical Hebrew (*ʾănī hū ʾăšer ḥāṭātī* "It is I who have sinned" 1 Chr. 21:17), in Syriac or in western European languages, in containing a resumptive pronoun (*šū*). There are two reasons why this analysis is incorrect: 1. In OB clefts such resumptive pronoun is not required as it is in Hebrew or in Syriac (see §**2.4.1.3**), and 2. For it to be cleft, we would expect to see the nominalized part functioning rather as **theme** and not, as happens here, as rheme.

7.2.2.5 *ša parāsim* as genitive attribute

The syntactic position of genitive attribute, which is reserved for substantives or their syntactic equivalents, is quite rare with *ša parāsim*. In the following example, *lāma* and *ša parāsim* form a prepositional syntagm, the syntactic equivalent of an adverb:

> [**7.39**] [*ina l*]*ibbi qemîm šâtu* [*l*]*āma* ***ša akālim*** [*ī*]*kulū*
> They (impersonal) ate [from] this flour [b]efore **it should** (have) **be**(en) **eaten**. ARM 3, 27:10–12

The precative in general is incapable of referring to any other temporal point other than to the point of utterance and is part of the dialogue. *ša parāsim* fills these gaps left by the syntactic and semantic constraints of the precative in being able to pertain to the past and to be integrated in a reporting chain. Buccellati 1972:16 mentions that only such a formulation with the infinitive allows such a notion as "negative command in the past". This is not a command in the strict sense, for a command (what is termed here *directives*) cannot be issued in the past. *ša parāsim* here is a reported command.

7.3 Conclusions

This treatment of the syntagm *ša parāsim* is based first and foremost upon its structure and function. This syntagm's value is determined through comparison with other members co-occurring in the same paradigm — first with directives and then with other infinitive constructions. The relationship between *ša parāsim* and the directive paradigm is thus formalized, in addition to the already acknowledged semantic relationship between them. Working with a smaller and better defined corpus (OB letters) than in Aro 1961 and Buccellati 1972 (which covered all periods of Akkadian) facilitates the task of getting conclusions as precise as possible.

7.3.1 Results

A few points are cleared up with regard to the relationship of *ša parāsim* to other infinitive constructions. N *parāsim* and *aššum parāsim* or *parāsam* are different from *ša parāsim* mainly in that, although perfectly capable of reflecting modal notions, they show no consistent relationship with precative forms or modality. None of them commutes with precative forms. As to *ana parāsim* (see example [**7.16**] and **§4.5.2**), although it is notionally closer to *ša parāsim* than the rest vis-à-vis modality, it has some non-modal functions as well. In addition it is semantically related to the sequenced precative, whereas *ša parāsim* is formally related to the directive. The syntactic and semantic relationship between *ša parāsim* and directives is encapsulated in the following table:

***ša parāsim* vs. directives**

form	directive	*ša parāsim*
type of form	verbal	verbo-nominal
value:		
- general	let X do, X should/must do (3rd pers.)	(X) which should/must/may be done
- specific	directive, wish	embedded report of directive and deliberative questions
agent marking	obligatory	optional
diathesis	marked	generally neutralized
temporal frame	not marked for tense consistently referential to the point of utterance	atemporal, adopts the temporal frame of matrix clause (when not predicative)
modality:		
- kind	directive - active demand for action	reported deontic state or action
- source	speaker	general or obscure
syntactic constraints	only alone in independent position	may function as a full sentence or as part of it
	appears only in dialogue	may occur anywhere

The construction *ša parāsim* is somewhat more diversified than the use of an infinitive-for-an-imperative use in modern European languages. When used either appended to some theme or as an independent clause, it is very similar to a directive, except for the instigative element demanding that the order should be fullfilled. Occurring as part of another sentence, it is capable of reporting or representing a directive where the latter cannot figure.

7.3.2 The place of *ša parāsim* in the modal system of OB

The modal system of OB may be divided in three: 1. asseverative modality; 2. epistemic modality; and 3. deontic modality.

The first has to do with the various asseverative forms (*lū* V/*lā* V-*u*) and also with alternative mechanisms which compensate for the syntactic incompatibilities of the asseverative paradigm (see **chapter 2**).

The second has to do with levels of certainty or commitment of the speaker toward what is said. It includes condition (see **chapter 6** for *-ma* conditionals) as well as modal particles such as *midde, tuša, pīqat* and so on (which are outside the scope of this book).

The third is about expressing volition or obligation. Directives, wishes, and deontic nexus questions can only be found in independent environments (including a quotation which is brought unchanged). ***ša parāsim* is the exponent of these values when indirectly reported or embedded.**

ša parāsim is a member of the deontic group in the OB modal system, yet it is not as restricted as the various precative forms and is therefore most versatile syntactically. The syntagm keeps a constant deontic value throughout as opposed to the other infinitive constructions, in addition to the paradigmatic relationship it is shown to have with the directive.

8

General Conclusions

Givón 1995 begins the fourth chapter of his account of functionalist theory, which is devoted to modality, as follows:

> A strictly structure-guided typological account of modality turns out sour ... a synchronic typology of modality is opaque without access to the relevant diachrony. (ibid. 111)

Givón refers mainly to a typological treatment of modality, which is a comparison of various synchronic facts belonging to different languages. The foregoing structure-guided, synchronic account of modality in OB is neither sour nor opaque: The information regarding a synchronic state is found in the corpus, and must be recovered and arranged. This last chapter is a synopsis of the array of the various modal categories of epistolary Mesopotamian OB and their respective place in the modal system.

This work has attempted to achieve two interrelated aims:

1. To identify various formal features which consistently correspond to certain modal values. These formal features are described in terms of syntagmatic and paradigmatic relationships, which are very similar to topographical coordinates of a specific geographic location; each such (sub-)paradigm has a distinct semantic domain, or category.

2. To formulate, as precisely as possible, the interrelationships between the various (sub-)paradigms, as they all belong to one system.

These two original aims have proved fruitful. Some of the groups described were found to be involved in more than one system (e.g., the asseverative group, having to do with modality, functional sentence perspective, and discourse functions). Other groups were found to be more pattern-related than others, that is, allegedly identical forms seem to function differently in different syntactic patterns.

The first group described is **the asseverative paradigm**, which is an isolated group with regard to all the other modal paradigms. The abstract formula for the asseverative forms is as follows:

1. **affirmative** **negative**

lū V (or øV-*u*)	*lā* V-*u*	(V=verbal forms, including the stative)
lū N	*lā* N	(N=nominal rheme)

Despite the morphological similarity of some forms of the asseverative paradigm with the analytic forms belonging to the precative paradigms, this group is distinct both co-textually and functionally. These forms prove to have both a distinct modal value (acknowledged for a long time) and a syntactic function, namely, **nexus focussing**. To establish the case for this function, various **focus phenomena** in OB have been described and it has been shown, based upon Goldenberg 1985, that focus may have any component of the predicative relationship (embodied in the verbal form) in its scope — including the **nexus**. Among the properties typical of the asseverative paradigm is a resumption of the co-textual verbal lexeme, either exhibiting polar contrast with the co-text or in contrast with a lingering doubt or other types of incompatibility, whether in the following co-text (as in the case of concessive), or possibly altogether outside the text (as often happens in oaths). The OB asseverative serves in three traditional notions, viz., in insistence, in an oath and as concessive. The relationship between these notions is explained on the basis of these common co-textual properties.

The link to modality, although almost obvious in Edzard 1973, is not evident, for nexus focussing (or, in semantic terms, *emphatic assertion* and *counterpresuppositional assertion,* which are the terms used in the linguistic literature to refer semantically to these phenomena) is mostly not mentioned in modal contexts. Nevertheless, the value of this paradigm reflects both **non-factuality** (in that it does not make a straightforward statement about reality) and **subjectivity**. Classifying this type of modality according to the two major types of modality, i.e., deontic and epistemic, is judged impossible at this point.

The group comprising the various **precative paradigms** turns out to be a complex of different (sub-)paradigms whose common denominator is that they all contain precative forms in different paradigmatic constitutions, having diverse values: One group thereof contains the **directive**, the **wish**, and the **interrogative (sub-)paradigms**. Another group is composed of two more precative sub-paradigms which are pattern-related: The **sequenced precative** and the **concessive-conditional precative**.

The **directive sub-paradigm** is the main representative of deontic modality in the corpus and indeed the most common function of precative forms. Directives express the will of the speaker with the intention of bringing about a change of reality in the (immediate) future beginning at the moment of utterance. Directives exhibit three notional scales which are not formally marked: Between order and supplication, between order and permission and between immediate and postponed orders. There are discernible value distinctions between analytic and synthetic directive forms: The former are generally used for willing a situation, rather than action, in the affirmative only. In the negative, since the formation *lā paris* is quite rare, *lā iparras* neutralizes the stative and fientive value distinction.

All persons of the directives are considered as belonging to one paradigm, despite certain idiosyncrasies of each grammatical person, for they co-occur in the same syntagmatic conditions. These idiosyncrasies are deemed inherent to the respective persons. The 3rd pers. directive conveys an indirect order directed at a third party, whereas the 2nd pers. directive conveys a direct order. The injunctive feature of the 1st pers. is actualized as exhortation. The 1st pers. plural directive serves as a unifying factor of the various idiosyncrasies communicated by each grammmatical person: Rather than being the exact plural of the singular it may represent
1. the speaker(s) and the addressee(s) (=inclusive), thereby being similar to the 2nd pers. directive in being aimed (additionally) at the addressee;
2. the speaker(s) and a third party (=exclusive), thereby being similar to the 3rd pers. directive in containing an indirect order;
3. just the speakers (=exclusive), resembling the 1st pers. singular directive.
These nuances, however, are notional in that they are not consistently and formally distinguished and the 1st pers. plural form may equally express each possibility. Their importance is that they show that these idiosyncrasies may cohabit the same *signifié*.

Table 2 represents the directive sub-paradigm:

2.

	affirmative	negative
1 sg.	*luprus* / *lū parsāku*	*lā aparras*
2	*purus* / *pursī, lū parsāta* / *i*	*lā taparras* / *ī*
3	*liprus, lū paris* / *parsat*	*lā iparras* (*lā paris* / *parsat*)
1 pl.	*i niprus*	*lā niparras*
	etc.	

The distinctive characteristics of the directive sub-paradigm are the combination of *purus* form, the negative form *lā iparras* and the absence of neutralization with indicative forms. Note that each (sub-)paradigm markedly differs, as regards its peculiar paradigmatic constitution, from the other (sub-)paradigms.

The **wish paradigm** usually has the same syntagmatic restrictions as directives. However, since this group by and large occurs at the beginning of the letter, in its own territory so to speak, it can hardly ever co-occur with members of other (sub-)paradigms. Moreover, the paradigmatic constitution (and hence value) is clearly different from the directives. These two reasons are enough to accord this group the status of a distinct paradigm:

3.

	affirmative	negative
1	*lū šalmāku* (?)	—
2	*lū šalmāta* (/*ti*/*tunu*)	—
3	*lū šalim* / *likīl* (/*likillū*)	*ayyirši* / *ayyīg*(ʾ)*û*(ʾ)

The 1st pers. may well not exist at all; the 2nd pers. is made up exclusively of analytic forms. The 3rd person seems to be the fullest, containing both negative and affirmative forms: The former are vetitive forms, while the latter may be of either analytic or synthetic formation and exhibit some productivity in the choice of verbal lexeme. This group clearly exhibits optative value, containing an element of will, but is used for blessing rather than for the purpose of instigating an action.

The **interrogative precative sub-paradigm** refers to precative forms in a pronominal question (the asterisk marks non-attested, but possible forms, which are mentioned in GAG §153g):

4.

		affirmative		negative
		modal	non-modal	modal/non-modal
(*mīnam*)	1	***luprus***	***aparras***	**lā aparras*
(*mīnam*)	2	*taparras*		*lā taparras*
(*mīnam*)	3	***liprus***	***iparras***	**lā iparras*

Both paradigmatic constitution and value are different from the directive group: The 2nd pers. and the negative forms show neutralization of modality, which is otherwise distinguished. The value of the precative forms is different here in that an element of will is not necessarily present; when it is, it applies to the **addressee**, to whom the appeal is made, rather than to the speaker.

Precative forms in **nexus questions** are rare; the notion assumed for them, **deliberative**, is found to exist within modally neutralized *iparras* forms. **Modally neutralized** forms (either due to lack of formal distinction or due to absence of opposition, as we find in *šumma* protases and in genitive equivalent position) are considered neither indicative nor modal and may therefore denote both extremes.

The **sequenced precatives** constitute a separate paradigm: The syntagmatic conditions are clearly different from the directive's (which is not a part of a sequence), the different paradigmatic constitution (which is similar but not identical to the directive's) and as a result different sets of oppositions, leading (sometimes) to different values. The most prominent feature of precative sequences is **modal congruence**, a strong tendency of precative forms to connect to other precative forms by means of *-ma* (or "→", symbolizing its by-form). The relatively few cases where this congruence is not observed seem to be pertinent, that is, they are in opposition with the precative sequence, constitute different patterns and have distinctive values. The sequenced precative paradigms acquire their value only by opposition with different paradigms in other **patterns** such as the **concessive-conditional precative pattern** and the ***-ma* conditional pattern.** Both the present pattern and its oppositions with paradigms in other patterns are illustrated in the following table:

5.	clause I	connective	clause II	combined function
(1)	*iparras* *iprus* etc.	*-ma*/→	*liprus*	conditional+precative
(2)	***liprus*** ***purus*** ***luprus*** **etc.**	***-ma*/→**	***liprus*** ***purus*** ***luprus*** **etc.**	**precative sequence**
(3)	*liprus*	*-ma*/→	*iparras*	concessive+indicative

Pattern **(2)** represents the ubiquitous precative sequence. The paradigms in this sequence acquire their value by opposition with paradigms in other sequences; this can be seen in the vertical rectangles — first upward, with pattern **(1)**, and then downward, with pattern **(3)**. The second clause of the precative sequence pattern neutralizes the notions of indirect command, purpose, a sequence of actions (which is characteristic of any *-ma* sequence), etc.

The relatively rare **concessive-conditional pattern** is represented by pattern **(3)** in the table above. The first clause of this pattern has either a **conditional** or a **concessive-conditional** value. The **concessive-conditional protasis paradigm** is not easy to formulate, for it depends on the pattern for its complete characterization. The following table shows the paradigmatic constitution of both protases and apodoses of concessive and conditional precative clauses:

6a. Conditional pattern

protasis	connective	apodosis/consequent
liprus *ē taprus*	***-ma*** / →	*lū aparras* / *lā aparrasu* *iparras* non-verbal clause

6b. Concessive-conditional pattern

liprus *luprus* *lū paris* *lū* N-*ma*	***-ma*** / →	(*ul*) *iparras* (*ul*) *paris* *lā iparras* non-verbal clause

The connective is not a paradigm but rather a free variation of *-ma*/→. The form *ē taprus* in the conditional protasis is irregular for the entire OB letter corpora; it does, however, have similar functions in OA. This vetitive form is the reason for the establishment of two distinct protasis paradigms. These forms and their function illustrate the (dis)similarities between concessives, concessive-conditionals and conditionals in general. Both this pattern and the following one (the ***-ma* conditional pattern**) are examples of an exponent of modality which is pattern-dependent. Special attention is paid to the differentiation between morphologically identical occurrences of concessives belonging to this paradigm and those belonging to the asseverative paradigm.

The third pattern (the first in the multi-pattern table **5** above) belongs to the ***-ma* conditional pattern**, where one may find *iparras*, *iprus*, and *paris* forms at the same slot in which the precative is found in the other patterns. It is for this reason that the protasis paradigm is not a part of the precative paradigms, yet it is interrelated to them both syntagmatically and paradigmatically. These forms do not have an indicative value in such constructions but rather **conditional value**:

7. The *-ma* conditional pattern

protasis	connective	apodosis
iparras *paris* *iprus*	*-ma* / →	*iparras* *liprus* *non-verbal* *paris*

This pattern is characterized by various syntagmatic and other features which make it quite distinct with respect to indicative patterns. One of these features is the typical occurrence of a sequenced precative preceding the protasis, with which it shares the verbal lexeme, but it is marked for the opposite polarity. This sequenced precative is connected to the protasis by *-ma* /→. This fact has a general implication: The sequences thus created are instrumental in that they are opposable with the **multi-clausal precative sequence:**

8. The oppositions of the multi-clausal precative sequence

a.	*liprus* →	*liprus*	*-ma*	*liprus*		**(cond. sequence)**
b.	*liprus -ma*	*iparras*	*-ma*	*iparras*	*-ma liprus*	**(prec. sequence)**
c.	*liprus -ma liprus*		→	*liprus*	*-ma liprus*	**(cond. sequence)**

The individual members of the multi-clausal precative sequence (represented by **8b**) acquire their own value through this possibility for opposition *ceteris paribus*, i.e., when all other terms are equal. If not for the conditional structure (represented by sequences **8a** and **8c**) these members would have to be considered (and have a value) only as a sequence.

The last section has been devoted to the description of the **modal infinitive construction, *ša parāsim***. The idea that it serves as nominalization of precative forms is partially corroborated. It has been insisted upon throughout that this syntagm is invariably modal, as opposed to the other infinitive constructions which are modally neutralized. Formal grounds for the relationship between the precative and *ša parāsim* are provided by the fact that the latter may constitute an independent nexus and is therefore commutable (and hence comparable) with the directive. Such a paradigmatic relationship enables the determination of the value of *ša parāsim* where it occurs with the precative when both refer to the same action. The value of *ša parāsim,* when it is not commutable with the precative, is determined by opposing it to other infinitive constructions.

This study contributes to the linguistic knowledge of OB in being a syntactic description of the modal system of OB. This system is composed of an array of paradigms, some of which have not been characterized syntactically before: The syntactic behavior and features of the asseverative forms; the classification of precative forms into (sub-)paradigms which feature disparate functions based upon syntactic environments and paradigmatic constitution, e.g., the concessive-conditional precative and the sequenced precative; the characterization of the *-ma* conditional pattern.

The contribution to general linguistics lies mainly in that this study is an application of the European structural method, describing a linguistic system in terms of formal features, rather than by semantic criteria. In addition, the various functions of nexus focussing and its connection with modality are discussed linguistically, and finally, syntactic patterns are shown to be an important signal of modality.

Bibliography

Anbar, M.

1975 Textes de l'époque babylonienne ancienne. *Revue d'Assyriologie* 69:109–36.

Aro, J.

1961 *Die akkadischen Infinitivkonstruktionen.* Studia Orientalia 26. Helsinki: Societas Orientalis Fennica.

Birot, M.

1993 *Correspondance des gouverneurs de Qaṭṭunân.* Paris: Éditions Recherche sur les Civilisations (ARM 27).

Boer, C. de

1947 *Syntaxe du français moderne.* Leiden: Universitaire Pers Leiden.

Bolinger, D.

1967 The Imperative in English. Pp. 335–61 in M. Halle, ed., *To Honor Roman Jakobson* 1. The Hague: Mouton.

1983 Affirmation and Default. *Folia Linguistica* 18:99–116.

1986 *Intonation and Its Parts.* Stanford, California: Stanford University Press.

Bottéro, J. and Finet, A.

1954 *Répertoire analytique des tomes I-V.* Paris: Imprimerie nationale (ARM 15).

Boyer, G.

1958 *Textes juridiques.* Paris : Imprimerie nationale (ARM 8).

Bravmann, M.

1953 *Studies in Arabic and General Syntax.* Cairo: Institut Français d'Archéologie Orientale.

Buccellati, G.

1968 An Interpretation of the Akkadian Stative as a Nominal Sentence. *Journal of Near Eastern Studies* 27:1–12.

1972 On the Use of Akkadian Infinitive after 'ša' or Construct State. *Journal of Semitic Studies* 17:1–29.

1996 *A Structural Grammar of Babylonian.* Wiesbaden: Harrassowitz.

Bybee, J.
1985 *Morphology: A Study of the Relation between Meaning and Form.* Amsterdam: Benjamins.

Bybee, J. et al.
1994 *The Evolution of Grammar – Tense, Aspect and Modality in the Languages of the World.* Chicago: The University of Chicago Press.

Cagni, L.
1980 *Briefe aus dem Iraq Museum.* Leiden: Brill (AbB 8).

Cavineaux, A.
1989 Le nom akkadien du grain. *Nouvelles assyriologiques brèves et utilitaires* 3 no. 52.

Charpin, D.
1988 *Archives épistolaires de Mari* I/2. Paris: Éditions Recherche sur les Civilisations (ARM 26).

Cohen, E.
2004 Paronomastic Infinitive in Old-Babylonian. *Jaarbericht Ex Oriente Lux* 38:105–12.

Comrie, B.
1976 *Aspect.* Cambridge: Cambridge University Press.

Damourette, J. and Pichon, E.
1911–52 *Des mots à la pensée. Essai de grammaire de la langue française.* 7 vols. Paris: Éditions d'Artrey.

Davies, E. E.
1979 Some Restrictions on Conditional Imperatives. *Linguistics* 17:1039–54.

Delitzsch, F.
1889 *Assyrische Grammatik.* Berlin: Reuther.

Deutscher, G.
2000 *Syntactic Change in Akkadian: The Evolution of Sentential Complementation.* Oxford: Oxford University Press.

Dik, S. C.
1997 *The Theory of Functional Grammar*². 2 vols. Berlin: de Gruyter.

Dik, S. et al.
1980 On the Typology of Focus Phenomena. Pp. 41–74 in T. Hoekstra et al., eds., *Perspectives on Functional Grammar.* Dordrecht: Foris.

Di Meola, C.
1997 *Der Ausdruck der Konzessivität in der deutschen Gegenwartssprache.* Tübingen: Niemeyer.

Dossin, G.
1938 Les archives épistolaires du palais de Mari. *Syria* 19:105–26.
1939 Benjaminites dans les textes de Mari. Pp. 981–96 in *Mélanges Syriens offerts à M. R. Dussaud par ses amis et ses élèves* II. Paris: Geuthner.

1946 *Correspondance de Šamši-addu et de ses fils*. Paris: Imprimerie nationale (ARM 1).

1951 *Correspondance de Šamši-addu et de ses fils* (suite). Paris: Imprimerie nationale (ARM 4).

1952 *Correspondance de Iasmaḫ-addu*. Paris: Imprimerie nationale (ARM 5).

Driver, S. R.

1892 *A Treatise on the Use of the Tenses in Hebrew*[3]. Oxford: Clarendon.

Durand, J-M.

1988 *Archives épistolaires de Mari* I/1. Paris: Éditions Recherche sur les Civilisations (ARM 26).

1997–2000 *Documents épistolaires de Mari*. 3 vols. Littératures anciennes du proche-orient 16-18. Paris: Cerf.

Edzard, D. O.

1973 Die Modi beim älteren akkadischen Verbum. Pp. 121–41 in G. Buccellati, ed., *A Volume of Studies Offered to Ignace Jay Gelb* (*Orientalia* 42 1/2). Rome: Pontifical Biblical Institute.

Eilers, W.

1968 Der sogenannte Subjunktiv des Akkadischen. Pp. 241–46 in *Gedenkschrift W. Brandenstein*. Innsbrucker Beiträge zur Kulturwissenschaft 14. Innsbruck: Innsbruck University Press.

Falkenstein, A.

1963 Brief König Anams an Sînmuballiṭ von Babylon. *Baghdader Mitteilungen* 2:56–71, Taf. 10–11.

Finet, A.

1956 *L'accadien des lettres de Mari*. Brussels: Palais des Académies.

Fischer, W.

1987 *Grammatik des klassischen Arabisch*[2]. Wiesbaden: Harrassowitz.

Frankena, R.

1966 *Briefe aus dem British Museum*. Leiden: Brill (AbB 2).

1968 *Briefe aus der Leidener Sammlung*. Leiden: Brill (AbB 3).

1974 *Briefe aus dem Berliner Museum*. Leiden: Brill (AbB 6).

1978 *Kommentar zu den altbabylonischen Briefen aus Lagaba und anderen Orten*. Leiden: Nederlands Instituut voor het Nabije Oosten.

Fraser, B.

1971 An Analysis of 'Even' in English. Pp. 150–78 in Ch. J. Fillmore and D. T. Langendoen, eds., *Studies in Linguistic Semantics*. New York: Holt, Rinehart and Winston.

Frayne, D. R.

1990 *Old Babylonian Period (2003–1595 BC)*. The Royal Inscriptions of Mesopotamia. Early Periods 4. Toronto: University of Toronto Press (RIME 4).

Frei, H.
1968 Syntaxe et méthode en linguistique synchronique. Pp. 39–63 in H. Schnelle, ed., *Methoden der Sprachwissenschaft*. Enzyklopädie der Geisteswissenschaftlichen Arbeitsmethoden, 4. Lieferung. München: R. Oldenbourg.

Gelb, I. J.
1961 *Old Akkadian Writing and Grammar*². Chicago: University of Chicago Press.

Gelb, I. J. and Kienast, B.
1990 *Die altakkadischen Königsinschriften des dritten Jahrtausends v. Chr.* Freiburger altorientalische Studien 17. Stuttgart : Steiner.

George, A. R.
2003 *The Babylonian Gilgamesh Epic*. 2 vols. Oxford: Oxford University Press.

Givón, T.
1994 Irrealis and the Subjunctive. *Studies in Language* 18:265–337.
1995 *Functionalism and Grammar*. Amsterdam: Benjamins.

Goetze, A.
1936 The t-form of the Old Babylonian Verb. *Journal of the American Oriental Society* 56:297–334.

Goldenberg, G.
1971 Tautological Infinitive. *Israel Oriental Studies* 1:36–85 (=Goldenberg 1998:66–115).
1983 Nominalization in Amharic and Harari: Adjectivization. Pp. 170–93 in S. Segert and A. J. E. Bodrogligeti, eds., *Ethiopian Studies Dedicated to Wolf Leslau on the Occasion of His Seventy-fifth Birthday*. Wiesbaden: Harrassowitz (=Goldenberg 1998:343–66).
1985 On Verbal Structure and the Hebrew verb. Pp. 295–348 in M. Bar-Asher, ed., *Language Studies* 1. Jerusalem: Magnes (in Hebrew; English translation in Goldenberg 1998:148–96).
1998 *Studies in Semitic Linguistics*. Jerusalem: Magnes.

Grayson, A. K.
1987 *Assyrian Rulers of the Third and Second Millennia BC*. The Royal Inscriptions of Mesopotamia. Assyrian Periods 1. Toronto: University of Toronto Press (RIMA 1).

Grevisse, M.
1980 *Le bon usage*¹¹. Paris: Duculot.

Haiman, J.
1978 Conditionals are Topics. *Language* 54:564–89.
1983 Paratactic If-clauses. *Journal of Pragmatics* 7:263–81.

Hajičova, E.
1994 Topic/Focus and Related Research. Pp. 245–75 in P. A. Luelsdorff, ed., *The Prague School of Structural and Functional Linguistics – A Short Introduction.* Amsterdam: Benjamins.

Halliday, M. A. K.
1967 Notes on Transitivity and Theme in English (part 2). *Journal of Linguistics* 3:199–274.

Hecker, K.
1968 *Grammatik der Kültepe Texte.* Analecta Orientalia 44. Rome: Pontifical Biblical Institute.

Heller, Joseph.
1965 *Catch 22.* London: Corgy.

Hjelmslev, L.
1961 *Prolegomena to a Theory of Language.* Translated from Danish by F. R. Whitfield. Wisconsin: University of Wisconsin Press.

Huehnergard, J.
1983 Asseverative *la and hypothetical *lu/law in Semitic. *Journal of the American Oriental Society* 103:569–93.
1986 On Verbless Clauses in Akkadian. *Zeitschrift für Assyriologie* 76:218–49.
1987 'Stative', Predicative Form, Pseudo-verb. *Journal of Near Eastern Studies* 47:215–32.
1997 *A Grammar of Akkadian.* Harvard Semitic Studies 45. Atlanta: Scholars Press.
1998 *Key to a Grammar of Akkadian.* Harvard Semitic Studies 46. Atlanta: Scholars Press.

Illingsworth, N. J. J.
1990 *Studies in the Syntax of Old Babylonian Letters.* Ph.D. diss. University of Birmingham, Birmingham.

Irving, John.
1979 *The World According to Garp.* New York: Pocket Books.

Izre'el, Sh.
1998 *Canaano-Akkadian.* München: Lincom Europa.

Jacobsen, T.
1960 *ittallak niāti. Journal of Near Eastern Studies* 19:101–16.

Janssen, C.
1991 Samsu-iluna and the Hungry Naditums. *Northern Akkad Project Reports* 5:3–39.

Jean, Ch. F.
1950 *Lettres diverses.* Paris: Imprimerie nationale (ARM 2).

Jespersen, O.
1924 *The Philosophy of Grammar.* London: Allen and Unwin

1933 *Essentials of English Grammar.* London: Allen and Unwin

1961 *A Modern English Grammar on Historical Principles.* 7 vols. London: Allen and Unwin.

Joly, A. and O'Kelly, D.

1987 DO dit 'emphatique' en anglais contemporain. *Modèles Linguistiques* 9:93–111.

Joüon, P. A.

1996 *A Grammar of Biblical Hebrew.* Translated and revised by T. Muraoka. 2 vols. Rome: Pontifical Biblical Institute.

Kiefer, F.

1987 On Defining Modality. *Folia Linguistica* 21:67–94.

1994 Modality. Vol. 5 pp. 2515–20 in R. E. Asher and J. M. Y. Simpson, eds., *The Encyclopedia of Language and Linguistics.* Oxford: Pergamon.

Kienast, B.

1960 Das Punktualthema **japrus* und seine Modi. *Orientalia* 29:151–67

Kjellmer, G.

1989 Even If and Even Though. *English Studies* 70:256–69.

König, E.

1986 Conditionals, Concessive Conditionals and Concessives: Areas of Contrast, Overlap and Neutralization. Pp. 229–46 in E. C. Traugott et al., eds., *On Conditionals.* Cambridge: Cambridge University Press.

1988 Concessive Connectives and Concessive Sentences: Cross-Linguistic Regularities and Pragmatic Principles. Pp. 145–66 in J. A. Hawkins, ed., *Explaining Language Universals.* Oxford: Blackwell.

1994 Concessive Clauses. Vol. 2 pp. 679–81 in R. E. Asher and J. M. Y. Simpson, eds., *The Encyclopedia of Language and Linguistics.* Oxford: Pergamon.

Kouwenberg, N. J. C.

2000 Nouns as Verbs: The Verbal Nature of the Akkadian Stative. *Orientalia* 69:21–71.

Kraus, F. R.

1964 *Briefe aus dem British Museum.* Leiden: Brill (AbB 1).

1970 *Briefe aus dem Archive des Šamaš-Ḫāzir in Paris und Oxford.* Leiden: Brill (AbB 4).

1972 *Briefe aus dem Istanbuler Museum.* Leiden: Brill (AbB 5).

1973a *Vom mesopotamischen Menschen der altbabylonischen Zeit und seiner Welt.* Amsterdam: North-Holland Publishing Co.

1973b Ein altbabylonischer '*i* Modus'? Pp. 253–65 in M. A. Beek et al., eds., *Symbolae biblicae et mesopotamicae Francisco Mario Theodoro de Liagre Böhl dedicatae.* Leiden: Brill.

1977 *Briefe aus dem British Museum.* Leiden: Brill (AbB 7).

1984 Nominalsätze in altbabylonische Briefen und der Stativ. *Mededelingen der Koninglijke Nederlandse Akademie van Wetenschappen*. Afd. Letterkunde, Nieuwe Reeks, deel 47/2 Amsterdam: North-Holland Co.

1985 *Briefe aus kleineren westeuropäischen Sammlungen*. Leiden: Brill (AbB 10).

Krebernik, M. and Streck, M. P.

2001 *šumman lā qabiʾāt ana balāṭim* ... Wärst du nicht zum Leben berufen ... Der Irrealis im Altbabylonischen. Pp. 51–78 in R. Bartelmus and N. Nebes, eds., *Sachverhalt und Zeitbezug: Semitistische und alttestamentliche Studien, Adolf Denz zum 65. Geburtstag*. Jenaer Beiträge zum Vorderen Orient 4. Wiesbaden: Harrassowitz

Kuhr, E.

1968 *Die Ausdrucksmittel der konjunktionslosen Hypotaxe in der aeltesten Hebraeischen Prosa*. Hildesheim: Georg Olms (reprint of the Leipzig 1929 edition).

Kupper, J. R.

1950 *Correspondance de Kibri-dagan gouverneur de Terqa*. Paris: Imprimerie nationale (ARM 3).

1954 *Correspondance de Baḫdi-lim préfet du palais de Mari*. Paris: Imprimerie nationale (ARM 6).

1998 *Lettres royales du temps de Zimri-lim*. Paris: Editions Recherche sur les Civilisations (ARM 28).

Lakoff, R.

1971 If's, And's and But's about Conjunctions. Pp. 114–49 in Ch. J. Fillmore and D. T. Langendoen, eds., *Studies in Linguistic Semantics*. New York: Holt, Rinehart and Winston.

Lambert, W. G.

1967 The Language of Mari. Pp. 29–38 in *La civilisation de Mari: 15e Rencontre Assyriologique Internationale*. Paris: Les Belles Lettres.

Lambrecht, K.

1994 *Information Structure and Sentence Form*. Cambridge: Cambridge University Press.

Leong, T. F.

1994 *Tense, Mood and Aspect in Old Babylonian*. Ph.D. diss. University of California, Los Angeles.

Livingstone, A.

1997 The Akkadian Word for Barley. *Journal of Semitic Studies* 42:1–5.

Lyons, J.

1977 *Semantics*. 2 vols. Cambridge: Cambridge University Press.

Maloney, J. F.

1981 *The T-perfect in the Akkadian of Old Babylonian Letters, with a Supplement on Verbal Usage in the Code of Ḫammurapi and the Laws of Ešnunna*. Ph.D. diss. Harvard University .

Marouzeau, J.
1951 *Lexique de la terminologie linguistique.* Paris: Geuthner.

Martinet, A.
1960 *Éléments de linguistique générale.* Paris: A. Colin.

Moran, W. L.
1960 Early Canaanite *yaqtula*. *Orientalia* 29:1–19.

Morel, M. A.
1996 *La concession en français.* Paris: Ophrys.

Niccacci, A.
1990 *The Syntax of the Verb in Classical Hebrew Prose.* Sheffield: Sheffield Academic Press.

Orlinsky, H. M.
1940–42 On the Cohortative and Jussive after an Imperative or Interjection in Biblical Hebrew. *Jewish Quarterly Review* 31 (1940–41):371–82; 32 (1941–42):191–205, 273–77.

Palmer, F. R.
1965 *A Linguistic Study of the English Verb.* London: Longman
1986 *Mood and Modality.* Cambridge: Cambridge University Press.
1994 Mood and Modality. Vol. 5 pp. 2535–40 in R. E. Asher and J. M. Y. Simpson, eds., *The Encyclopedia of Language and Linguistics.* Oxford: Pergamon.
2001 *Mood and Modality*^{2}. Cambridge: Cambridge University Press.

Patterson, D. A.
1971 *Old Babylonian Parataxis as Exhibited in the Royal Letters of the Middle Old Babylonian Period and in the Code of Ḫammurapi.* Ph.D. diss. University of California, Los Angeles.

Pientka, R.
1998 *Die spätaltbabylonische Zeit.* 2 vols. Münster: Rhema.

Polotsky, H. J.
1944 *Études de syntaxe Copte.* Cairo: Publications de la Société d'Archéologie Copte.

Rainey, A. F.
1976 Enclitic *-ma* and the Logical Predicate in Old Babylonian. *Israel Oriental Studies* 6:51–58.
1992 Topic and Comment in Byblos Akkadian. *Bibliotheca Orientalis* 49:329–57.
1999 Topic and Comment in the Amarna Texts from Canaan. Pp. 63–87 in R. Chazan et al., eds., *Ki Baruch Hu: Ancient Near Eastern, Biblical, and Judaic Studies in Honor of Baruch A. Levine.* Winona Lake, Indiana: Eisenbrauns.

Reckendorf, H.
1895–98 *Die syntaktischen Verhältnisse des Arabischen.* Leiden: Brill.

Reiner, E.
1966 *A Linguistic Analysis of Akkadian.* The Hague: Mouton.

Salonen, E.
1967 *Die Gruss- und Höflichkeitsformeln in babylonisch-assyrischen Briefen.* Studia Orientalia 38. Helsinki: Societas Orientalis Fennica.

Sallaberger, W.
1999 *'Wenn du mein Bruder bist, ..': Interaktion und Textgestaltung in altbabylonischen Alltagsbriefen.* Groningen: Styx.

Sandfeld, K.
1965 *Syntaxe du français contemporain: Les propositions subordonnées*². Genève: Droz.

Saussure, F. de.
1972 *Cours de linguistique générale.* Édition critique preparée par Tullio de Mauro. Paris: Payot.

Schorr, M.
1913 *Urkunden des altbabylonischen Zivil- und Prozessrechts.* Vorderasiatische Bibliothek 5. Leipzig: Hinrichs (VAB 5).

Sgall, P.
1987 Prague Functionalism and Topic vs. Focus. Pp. 169–89 in R. Dirven and V. Fried, eds., *Functionalism in Linguistics.* Amsterdam: Benjamins.

Shisha-Halevy, A.
1986 *Coptic Grammatical Categories: Structural Studies in the Syntax of Shenoutean Sahidic.* Analecta Orientalia 53. Rome: Pontifical Biblical Institute.
1995 Structural Sketches of Middle Welsh Syntax. *Studia Celtica* 29:127–223.
1998 *Structural Studies in Welsh Syntax.* Münster: Nodus.

Siertsema, B.
1965 *A Study of Glossematics: Critical Survey of Its Fundamental Concepts.* The Hague: M. Nijhoff.

Smith, Betty.
1985 *A Tree Grows in Brooklyn.* London: Pan.

Soden, W. von
1961 Akkadisch. Pp. 33–57 in G. della Vida, ed., *Linguistica semitica: presente e futuro.* Studi Semitici 4. Roma: Istituto di Studi del Vicino Oriente, Università.
1965–81 *Akkadisches Handwörterbuch.* 3 vols. Wiesbaden: Harrassowitz
1995 *Grundriß der akkadischen Grammatik*³. Analecta Orientalia 33. Rome: Pontifical Biblical Institute.

Soldt, W. H. Van
1990 *Letters in the British Museum.* Leiden: Brill (AbB 12).

1994 *Letters in the British Museum, Part 2*. Leiden: Brill (AbB 13).

Steele, S. et al.
1981 *An Encyclopedia of AUX: A Study in Cross-linguistic Equivalence*. Cambridge, Mass. : MIT Press.

Steiner, G.
1985 Umstandssätze im Akkadischen. Pp. 86–102 in W. Röllig, ed., XII. Deutscher Orientalistentag, ausgewählte Vorträge. *Zeitschrift der deutschen morgenländischen Gesellschaft*, Supplement 6. Wiesbaden.

Stol, M.
1981 *Letters from Yale*. Leiden: Brill (AbB 9).
1986 *Letters from Collections in Philadelphia, Chicago and Berkeley*. Leiden: Brill (AbB 11).

Sweetser, E.
1990 *From Etymology to Pragmatics*. Cambridge: Cambridge University Press.

Tobler, A.
1902 *que* Sätze anknüpfend an adverbiale Ausdrücke der Versicherung, Beschwörung, Vermütung, Bejahung, Verneinung an Interjektionen. Pp. 57–66 in *Vermischte Beiträge zur französischen Grammatik, erste Reihe*[2]. Leipzig: S. Hirzel.

Ungnad, A.
1914 *Babylonische Briefe aus der Zeit der Ḫammurapi-Dynastie*. Vorderasiatische Bibliothek 6. Leipzig: Hinrichs (VAB 6).

Van der Awera, J.
1986 Conditionals and Speech Acts. Pp. 197–214 in E.C. Traugott et al., eds., *On Conditionals*. Cambridge: Cambridge University Press.

Wasserman, N.
1994 The Particle *assurre / ē* in the Mari Letters. Pp. 319–35 in D. Charpin and J-M. Durand, eds, *Florilegium marianum 2, Recueil d'études à la mémoire de M. Birot*. Mémoires de NABU 3. Paris: Sepoa.

Wierzbicka, A.
1987 The Semantics of Modality. *Folia Linguistica* 21:25–43.

Whiting, R. M. Jr.
1987 *Old Babylonian Letters from Tell Asmar*. Assyriological Studies 22. Chicago: The Oriental Institute of the University of Chicago.

Wright, W.
1891 *A Grammar of the Arabic Language*[3]. Revised by W. Robertson Smith and M. J. de Goeje. Cambridge: Cambridge University Press.

Yaron, R.
1988 *The Laws of Eshnunna*[2]. Jerusalem: Magnes (LE).

Subject Index

(Italicized page numbers refer to definitions)

asseverative *17*
— forms 19, 23–25
— paradigm 25–26
— tense distinctions 26
traditional values of — 26–29
(*see also* nexus focussing)
auxiliary stress 40–45
(*see also* nexus focussing)

boundaries
.... *see* interclausal connection

category 3–5
cleft construction 35
(*see also* focus)
commutation *3*
concessive *59, 145–46*
— conditional 149–52
— conditional in OB 152–57
rhetorical — 60–61
rhetorical — in OB 61–65
(*see also* nexus focussing)
conditional *162*
— and polar lexical resumption
.... 169–73
— and sequenced precative
.... 169–70, 173–76
— apodosis 168
— patterns
.... 147–49, 151–52, 161–79
arḫiš and — 177–79
paratactic — 162–64
(*see also* concessive)

contrast *3*
— and focus 30, 33–35
polar — *42*
corpus 6–8
co-text *4*
co-textual sequenced precative
.... *see* sequenced precatives

deliberative questions
.... see interrogatives
deontic modality *11*
— and directives 89
— and nexus questions 108–12
— and *ša parāsim* 189, 191–93
directives 89–100
— and indicatives 92–94
— and sequenced precatives
.... 115–16
— and *ša parāsim* 184–90
— value 89–94
different persons of — 95–100

emendation 136–37
emphatic affirmation, assertion and negation .... *see* nexus focussing

focus *29–30*
— in OB 31–36
— of verbal components 36–38
— of the nexus 38–45
(*see also* nexus focussing)
multi-focality 54–56

(focus continued)
types of — 30–31
(*see also* cleft construction)
Functional Sentence Perspective
(FSP) *29*
rheme *19, 30*
theme....................*29*
(*see also* topic, focus)

genitive attribute 5

indicative 92–94
(*see also* modality, subjunctive)
infinitive constructions....................
....................137–42, 180–200
ana parāsim 139–42, 189–90
aššum parāsim....................142
parāsam 138–39
paronomastic —....................37–38, 52
ša parāsim....................180–200
insistence .... *see* nexus focussing
interclausal connection...........118–22
→....................120–21
//....................122
— via *-ma* 119
— via *-ma/→*....................120–21
— via *u* 119–20
asymmetric — 115
non-marked —....................120–22
interrogative
— elements....................36
— context and modality 105–12
— sub-paradigm....................105–8
(*see also* nexus question)

juncture
.... *see* interclausal connection

lexical resumption
polar — 48–51, 169–70
types of —.................... 172–73

-ma .... *see* focus
and interclausal connection
-ma/→.... *see* interclausal connection
method 1–6

modal attraction 124
modal congruence...........123, 132–37
exceptions of — 132–37
modal neutralization
......75, 84–87, 107, 110–112, 137–42
(*see also* subjunctive)
modal values and notions
indirect command 129–30
non-factuality.................... *10*
permission....................91–92
purpose 128–29
subjectivity *10*
supplication.................... 91
uncertainty 105
will of the speaker.........89–91, 106
(*see also* directives, wishes, interrogative, *and* sequenced precatives)
modality....................9–12
(*see also* deontic modality)
— of non-verbal clauses 82
asseverative —.................... 67
(*see also* nexus focussing)
epistemic —....................*11*, 65–67
speaker-oriented —....................*89*
mood 11

nexus 37
nexus focussing 38
— and modality....................65–67
— in OB....................45–54
values of —....................56–65
(*see also* oath *and* concessive)
nexus question *84*
deontic —.................... 108–12, 196
nominalization.................... 180–81
— and cleft 35–36
— and directives.................... 184–89
— and focus....................33–34
— and nexus questions.......196–97
— and sequenced precatives
....................127–28
— as complement....................117
— of direct speech....................93
notion 3, 5

oath..27, 56–59
assertory/promissory —............26
(*see also* nexus focussing)
opposition...................... *3*, 5, 185–186
order of elements............. *see* pattern

paradigm 3–5
paradigmatic..................................2, 4
paradigmatic constitution............3–4
paronomastic infinitive 37–38, 52
pattern
cleft — 35
concessive-conditional —...144–60
focal —....................................34–35
-*ma* conditional —..............161–79
perfect
functions of — forms
....................................53–54, 71, 167
linguistic — 167–68
pertinence......................................2, 5
precative
— complementation..........117, 137
— forms 78–79
— functions 87–89
— in nexus questions......... 108–12
— in pronominal questions 105–8
— paradigms.........................73, 87
— sequence............124–27, 175–76
— syntax................................79–87
analytic vs. synthetic — 94
(*see also* directives, wishes, interrogative, *and* sequenced precatives)
pronominal question...... *84*, 105–108
(*see also* interrogative)

questions
............*see* interrogative, precative

reportative sequence.......................50
responsive function........................ 39
(*see also* nexus focussing)
rheme *19*, *30*
(*see also* functional sentence perspective)

sequenced precatives 112–32
— and conditional protasis
(co-textual —).........169–70, 173–76
— and nominalized clauses
....127–28
connectives and — 118–22
notions of —....................... 128–32
(*see also* modal congruence, precative)
structural analysis.........................1–6
subjunctive
— and modal neutralization 85–86
— and mood...........................12–13
sub-paradigm...................................89
syntagmatic *2*, 4

ša parāsim 181
— and directives......... 184–89, 199
— and nexus questions.......196–97
— vs. other infinitive constructions......................................191–96

theme... *29*
topic... *29*
(*see also* functional sentence perspective)
transcription 15

value 3, 5
verbal lexeme............................ *16*, 37
verbal root 16

wishes.....................................101–104

Index of Texts

AbB

1, 1:4–18 111
1, 10:17–21 .... 33, 37
1, 14:27–29 141
1, 15:10–11 141
1, 23:7–11 .... 112, 197
1, 23:15 187
1, 27:24–28 174
1, 28:35–36 131
1, 29:17–18 129
1, 30:18–19 15
1, 30:19–21 110
1, 33:40–43 112
1, 35:18–20 .... 84, 109
1, 50:20–23 109
1, 51:34–36 112
1, 52:7 102
1, 52:28–31 161
1, 65:7–10 135
1, 74:23–28 .... 90, 107, 140, 189
1, 105:4–5 102
1, 106:29 103
1, 117:10–12 141
1, 123:11–13 140
1, 133:17–19 33
1, 135, 8–12 171

2, 33:14–16 91
2, 47:6–15 .... 50, 62
2, 58:17–18 94
2, 59:14–21 178
2, 78:12–14 98
2, 81:29 117
2, 83:17, 37 116
2, 88:34' 98
2, 96:20–21 98
2, 100:14–16, 17–19, 22–23 85
2, 108:10–12 102
2, 115:6–16 .... 27, 49, 54, 61
2, 119:14–16 .... 97, 130
2, 128:6'–7' 139
2, 129:4–5 27
2, 142:6–11 115

3, 2:29–30 120
3, 2:41–42 .... 84, 117
3, 2:43–45 135
3, 2:45 .... 86, 127, 135
3, 13:13–15 120
3, 14:5–6 173
3, 15:24–28 91
3, 21:26–29 120
3, 22:4–5 103
3, 22:6–7 .... 84, 106
3, 22:36–38 120
3, 23:16–17 141
3, 25:10–12 136
3, 27:5–12 64
3, 34:19, 37–38 .... 166, 174
3, 34:28–29 .... 81, 94
3, 35:13–14 120
3, 35:26–28 171
3, 38:31–32 148
3, 39:18–19 168
3, 40:6–7 102
3, 47:7 102

3, 50:5–6....104
3, 52:24–26....82
3, 52:6....103
3, 60:10–11....104
3, 60:12–15....103
3, 61:8–9....102
3, 70:8–10....139
3, 70:19–20....138, 192
3, 74:26–33....139
3, 76:4–9....34
3, 83:6–11....117
3, 85:4–10....116
3, 85:5–10....81, 129
3, 88:9–12....136, 157
3, 88:17–18....185
3, 90:24–28....135

4, 11:29–33....178
4, 37:21–24....132
4, 53:15–17....188
4, 80:4–17....80
4, 111:11–14....94
4, 141:13–14....187
4, 141:20....139, 192
4, 145:17–18....190
4, 145:34–35....166
4, 154:30–31....129
4, 156:7–9....195
4, 161:24–26....177

6, 1:13–16....62
6, 4:12–15....150
6, 7:12–13....83
6, 10:16....114
6, 13:6, 10–13....169
6, 18:14–18....91, 93
6, 19:7–16....140
6, 38:9–12....86, 134
6, 39:7–8....94, 121
6, 64:7....102
6, 64:15–17....33
6, 73:10–17....167
6, 75:6'–7'....198
6, 88:22–23....136
6, 89:25–27....172, 174
6, 91:9....102
6, 92:12–16....130
6, 120:7–10....126, 165, 174
6, 126:20–22....122
6, 133:9–12....135
6, 140:20–23....170
6, 147:21....189
6, 148:27–29....173
6, 178:18–19....132
6, 179:25–28....127
6, 181:8'–13'....26, 63
6, 181:13'....15
6, 207:13–19....165, 170 ,174

7, 1:7–9....140
7, 4:27–28....129
7, 5:17–18....103
7, 17:11–15....86, 128
7, 17:17–18....128
7, 21:29–31....136
7, 36:5–7....110
7, 42:13–14....180
7, 44:9....121
7, 55:18....97
7, 67:13–18....166
7, 68:12–16....121
7, 84:6'–8'....155
7, 86:30....36
7, 90:3'–6'....135
7, 97:19–20....121
7, 112:23....140
7, 118:5–6....103
7, 122:14–17....137
7, 123:25–29....80
7, 132:12–13....141
7, 132:14–17....130
7, 141:8'–13'....110
7, 152:7....107
7, 154:17–20....133
7, 155:1–6....146
7, 168:5'–10'....169
7, 171:16–17....132
7, 172:15–18....171

8, 12:15–17....184
8, 23:21–22....106
8, 24:4–7....51, 103

8, 24:23–24....136
8, 93:14–21....175
8, 95:12–14....177
8, 109:6–8....49, 55
8, 109:26–28....137
8, 134:10–14....93
8, 139:14'–16'....107
8, 148:5–7....104

9, 1:25–26....126, 134
9, 12:6–8....33
9, 15:7–11....28
9, 14:6–7....84
9, 37:18–22....136
9, 39:15–21....58–59
9, 49:9–13....165
9, 49:36–39....109
9, 51:17–22....34
9, 62:13–15....139
9, 62:18–19....139, 180
9, 86:15–19....134
9, 92:20–22....126, 136, 149
9, 112:27–42....194
9, 115:4–9....128
9, 117:7–9....195
9, 119:6'–7'....132
9, 130:10–13....135
9, 132:10–12....91
9, 137:9–14....35
9, 139:5–11....124
9, 140:5–21....92
9, 141:5–7....92, 105
9, 146:21–22....98
9, 149:4–15....79, 96
9, 155:12–13....192
9, 174:9–12....187
9, 174:15–18....195
9, 174:16–18....85
9, 181:17–18....155
9, 192:10–17....170
9, 226:4–6....165
9, 228:16–20....156
9, 232:21–22....165
9, 238:4–9....80
9, 250:4–9....137
9, 260:10–15....153
9, 264:4–8....153
9, 270:10–15....174

10, 15:22....186
10, 23:18–19....155
10, 32:30–32....133
10, 198:17....15

11, 14:21–22....130
11, 16:17–20....134
11, 27:12–17....173
11, 27:16–17....105
11, 34:5–6....52
11, 36:7'–11'....80
11, 40:9–21....154
11, 40:14–16....28
11, 49:14–20....97
11, 49:19–20....83
11, 61:2'....102
11, 90:29....106
11, 90:33–35....131
11, 94:7–9....51, 62, 156
11, 105:11–12....102
11, 105:15....104
11, 105:7....102
11, 106: 26'–29'....118, 129
11, 106: 30'–33'....111
11, 106:5'–7'....102
11, 107:19'–25'....93
11, 115:3–10....140
11, 119:27–30....103
11, 135:22–24....131
11, 137:12–19....175
11, 139:10–13, 27–28....82
11, 154:15–18....157
11, 158:24'–26'....117
11, 160:23–28....111
11, 167:16–17....155
11, 168:7–10....166
11, 175:5–10....175
11, 175:9–10....166
11, 189:20–22....138
11, 193:13–23....123
11, 194....87–88

12, 2:6–8....122

12, 11:16–19 165
12, 13:6–18 142
12, 13:12–13, 17–18 138
12, 17:5–9 90
12, 17:17–22 167
12, 18:7–26 53
12, 23:6–15 130
12, 25:19–20 .... 174, 178
12, 30:13–14 97
12, 31:3 177
12, 37:6–8 129
12, 38:8 102
12, 44:13–18 122
12, 50:23–28 .... 79, 96
12, 53:4–5 36
12, 53:4–9 122
12, 53:5–8 166
12, 53:17–20 170
12, 64:31–33 171
12, 67:38 179
12, 68:22–24 179
12, 70:5'–8' 92
12, 99:14–17 91
12, 110:14–17 173
12, 117:19–21 173
12, 125:20–22 91
12, 169:15–26 58
12, 169:20–26 .... 28, 148
12, 175:14 82
12, 178:3'–6' 121
12, 180:11–13 119
12, 190:2'–3' 137
12, 194:14–18 178

13, 3:9–18 121
13, 4:18' 106
13, 18:4–12, 22–28 52
13, 21:13 39
13, 60:45–46 146
13, 104:5'–6' 94
13, 109:7–10 35
13, 110:10–15 107
13, 119:6'–8' 126, 130
13, 131, 4–10 122

Anbar 1975:121 .... 25, 147

ARM

1, 22:30–31 191
1, 22:34–38 108
1, 29:17–18 191
1, 31:30–32 50
1, 73:57 194
1, 83:9–11 185

2, 29:3'–4', 6'–7' 193
2, 118:21–22 193
2, 137:33–35 193

3, 27:10–12 198

4, 68:14–16 151

5, 4:9–10 192

6, 1:28, 32–33 184
6, 53:7 197

8, 1:21 152

26, 21:5–10 51
26, 145:6 14
26, 207:15–17 .... 134, 156
26, 214:9–14 .... 28, 146
26, 232:9–11 33
26, 306:33–34 36
26, 310:14–15 48
26, 310:24 47
26, 326:10'–11' 36
26, 384:3"–6" 38
26, 390:5"–7" 196
26, 390:12"-17" 110, 196
26, 391:28–30, 35–39 .... 48–49, 55
26, 404:17–31 47
26, 411:60–61 195
26, 419:9–13 191
26, 438:34'–35' 191
26, 449:25–27 37

27, 151:94–95 25

28, 7:8–11 184
28, 52:4–7 52

28, 95:5–6, 22–24 58
28, 95:10–12.................................50
28, 105:21'–31'.............................186

CH XXIX:37–41 (=§134) 197

Dossin 1938, 124:5–17....................185

Dossin 1939:994 195

Falkenstein 1963:58, III:11–15 64
Falkenstein 1963:59, IV:7–14 ....47, 54–55

Gilg Ishchali:15' 134, 148

LE
A ii:15–18 57
A ii:33–34 151
B i:8–9...147
B i:13–15.....................................147

MARI 6, 263–64:4–8........................ 54

RIMA
1, 64 col. II':1–11...........................70
1, 64-65 col. III':1–13 70

RIME
4, 348:22.. 71
4, 381:16–24...................................70
4, 382:55–61...................................70
4, 654–55:12–22............................ 70
4, 656:29–36...................................70
4, 671–72:12–21............................ 70
4, 673:10–23...................................70
4, 673:22.. 71
4, 673:36–47...................................70
4, 673–74:48–57............................ 70

VAB
5, 8:9–12.......................................152
5, 9:7–9...152
5, 156:1'–3" 28, 131, 152
5, 287:18–22.............................25, 59

6, 186:22–25................................109
6, 218:12–15..................................27

Whiting 1987, 9:8–16.....................149

www.ingramcontent.com/pod-product-compliance
Lightning Source LLC
Chambersburg PA
CBHW021402290426
44108CB00010B/356
9781575069210